NOT TO BE TAKEN FROM THE LIBRARY
THE COLLEGE OF NEW JERSEY LIBRARY
2000 PENNINGTON ROAD
EWING, NJ 08628

Women and Political Participation

Political Participation in America
Raymond A. Smith, Series Editor

African Americans and Political Participation,
Minion K.C. Morrison, Editor

Conservative Christians and Political Participation,
Glenn H. Utter and James L. True

East Asian Americans and Political Participation,
Tsung Chi

Gay and Lesbian Americans and Political Participation,
Raymond A. Smith and Donald P. Haider-Markel

Jewish Americans and Political Participation,
Rafael Medoff

Latino/a Americans and Political Participation,
Sharon A. Navarro and Armando X. Mejia, Editors

Native Americans and Political Participation,
Jerry D. Stubben and Gary A. Sokolow

Women and Political Participation,
Barbara Burrell

Women and Political Participation

A Reference Handbook

Barbara Burrell

A B C ≋ C L I O

Santa Barbara, California • Denver, Colorado • Oxford, England

Copyright © 2004 by Barbara Burrell

All rights reserved. No part of this publication may be reproduced, stored in a retrieval system, or transmitted, in any form or by any means, electronic, mechanical, photocopying, recording, or otherwise, except for the inclusion of brief quotations in a review, without prior permission in writing from the publishers.

Library of Congress Cataloging-in-Publication Data
Burrell, Barbara C., 1947–
  Women and political participation : a reference handbook / Barbara Burrell.
      p.   cm. — (Political participation in America)
  Includes bibliographical references.
  ISBN 1-85109-592-6 (hardback : alk. paper)
  ISBN 1-85109-597-7 (eBook)
1.Women in politics—United States.   2. Women in politics—United States—Handbooks, manuals, etc.   I. Title.   II. Series.

HQ1236.5.U6B875 2004
305.42'0973--dc22

07 06 05 04   10 9 8 7 6 5 4 3 2 1

This book is also available on the World Wide Web as an e-book.
Visit abc-clio.com for details.

ABC-CLIO, Inc.
130 Cremona Drive, P.O. Box 1911
Santa Barbara, California 93116-1911

This book is printed on acid-free paper.
Manufactured in the United States of America

Contents

Series Foreword, Raymond A. Smith — ix
Foreword, Carol Moseley-Braun — xi
Preface — xiii
Acknowledgments — xv

1 Overview — 1

The First Wave of Feminism, 4
The Second Wave of Feminism, 9
Contemporary Feminism, 11
The Impact of Feminism on Public Opinion, 13
Women's Current Status, 15
Controversial Current Issues, 20
References, 26

2 Protest Politics — 29

Suffrage Protests, 29
Second-Wave Protests, 32
Case Study: The Clarence Thomas Hearings, 34
Case Study: Marches for Women's Lives, 36
   Peace Activism, 41
Case Study: Women Strike for Peace, 42
Case Study: The Million Mom March, 44
Case Study: CODEPINK, 46
References, 47

3 Women's Movements and Organizations — 49

Suffrage and the National Woman's Party, 50
The League of Women Voters, 52
The Women's Bureau, 53
The Second Wave: Equal Rights under the Law, 54
The Equal Pay Movement, 59

Title VII of the Civil Rights Act (1964), 60
The National Organization for Women (1966), 62
Hispanic Women's Movements, 65
The National Women's Political Caucus, 67
Women of Color Organizations, 68
The National Black Feminist Organization, 69
The Combahee River Collective, 70
The National Women's Conference (1977), 71
The Campaign for the Equal Rights Amendment (1970s to 1980s), 73
Concerned Women for America, 78
The National Political Congress of Black Women, 78
The Fund for a Feminist Majority, 79
The Independent Women's Forum, 80
The Rise of Feminist Interest Groups, 82
Case Study: NARAL Pro-Choice America and Feminists for Life, 84
References, 85

4 Participation in Electoral Politics 89

The Impact of Suffrage, 91
The Gender Gap, 96
Political Involvement beyond Voting, 98
Women and Political Parties, 102
Feminist Issues at the Polls, 106
The Effect of Gender on Elections, 112
Case Study: Soccer Moms, 117
Case Study: "W Stands for Women," 118
Case Study: NASCAR Dads, 122
Case Study: Women's Voices, Women Vote, 124
References, 124

5 Women in Public Office 129

Women in Congress, 130
Case Study: The Sanchez Sisters, 133
Women State Officials, 135
Women Governors, 136
The United States in Comparative Perspective, 137
The Political Parties and Women Elected Officials, 140
Campaigning for Public Office, 143
A Woman for President? 145

Case Study: Geraldine Ferraro, Vice Presidential Nominee, 146
Case Study: EMILY's List and the WISH List, 147
Women in Legislative Leadership Positions, 150
Case Study: Nancy Pelosi, House Minority Leader, 152
Women's Leadership in State Legislatures, 153
Do Women in Public Office Make a Difference? 154
Case Study: The Congressional Caucus for Women's Issues, 155
Presidential Appointments and Presidential Staff, 158
Women in the Judiciary, 161
Conclusion, 162
Appendix: Women Elected and Appointed to Public Office, 164
References, 178

Documents	181
Key People, Laws, and Terms	195
Resources	207
Chronology	233
Annotated Bibliography	247
Index	259
About the Author	277

Series Foreword

Participation in the political process is a cornerstone of both the theory and the practice of democracy; indeed, the word "democracy" itself means rule by the people. Since the formation of the New Deal coalition in 1932, the study of U.S. politics has largely been organized around the concept that there exist distinct "blocs" of citizens, such as African Americans, women, Catholics, and Latinos. This trend was reinforced during the 1960s when the expansion of the media and the decline of traditional sources of authority promoted direct citizen mobilization. And more recently, the emphasis on "identity politics" has reinforced the notion of distinct groups organized along lines of shared personal characteristics rather than common economic interests.

Although political participation is a mainstream, even canonical, subject in the study of U.S. politics, there are few midrange reference materials available on this subject. Indeed, the available reference materials do not include works that provide both a systematic empirical base *and* explanatory and contextualizing material. Likewise, because of the fragmentation of the reference material on this subject, it is difficult for readers to draw comparisons across groups, even though this is one of the most meaningful ways of understanding the phenomenon of political participation. The Political Participation in America series is designed to fill this gap in the reference literature on this subject by providing key points of background (e.g., demographics, political history, major contemporary issues) and then systematically addressing different types of political participation, providing both substance and context for readers. In addition, each chapter includes case studies that either illuminate larger issues or highlight some particular subpopulation within the larger group.

Each volume of the ABC-CLIO Political Participation in America series focuses on one of the major subgroups that make up the electorate in the United States. Each volume includes the following components:

- Introduction to the group, comprising a demographic, historical, and political portrait of the group, including political opinions and issues of key importance to members of the group
- Participation in protest politics, including marches, rallies, demonstrations, and direct actions
- Participation in social movements and interest groups, including involvement of members of the group in and through a wide variety of organizations and associations
- Participation in electoral politics, including a profile of involvement with political parties and voting patterns
- Participation in political office-holding, including elected, appointed, and "unofficial" offices from the local to national levels

The end of each book also includes an A–Z glossary featuring brief entries on important individuals and events; a chronology of political events salient to the group; a resource guide of organizations, newsletters, Web sites, and other important contact information, all briefly annotated; an annotated bibliography of key primary and secondary documents, including books and journal articles; excerpts from major primary documents, with introductions; and a comprehensive index to the volume.

Raymond A. Smith
Series Editor

Foreword

Our country was founded on the principle that individual rights to freedom and fairness is God given, because every person is a reflection of the divine. But when Thomas Jefferson, on behalf of the framers of the Constitution, wrote, "We hold these truths to be self evident, that all men are created equal, that they are endowed by their creator with certain unalienable rights, that among these are life, liberty and the pursuit of happiness," he wasn't telling the truth, or at least the truth he was telling was not self evident. Women and poor people could not vote, and blacks were counted as three-fifths of a person for purposes of the census. The vast majority of the population could not participate in this noble experiment in democracy.

But the compelling strength of the core concept of our republic drew the country in the direction of those truths, and the whole of American history has been written by the progress we have made in the direction of that ideal. The liberation of the human spirit so that all humankind, of whatever color or race, religion or gender, can enjoy life, liberty, and the pursuit of happiness has been the driving force behind the movements to make America live up to its promise and the noble calling of its creation.

Not all of the women who stand for office consider themselves feminists, but the truth is that by their example they are helping to remove barriers to the full and equal participation of women in civil society. These women are no more and no less than the patriots who demanded the removal of social structures and restrictions that make women less human, less equal, less free than any other American. By taking up electoral politics, these are women who were prepared to challenge conventional thinking and the convenience of familiar inequalities to make certain that our nation continued to progress in the direction of its vision.

Political participation, particularly as elected officials, is one of the frontiers of the emancipation of women and is a bell weather of society's progress. The product of the participation of women in electoral politics is revealed every time a girl gets a chance to compete in the Olympics, or receives an equal salary in the workforce, or has the law intervene to stop violence against her in the home.

The women who engage in electoral politics give life to the notion that women are equal in capacity and citizenship and they have a contribution to make that this country cannot afford to waste. Their stories need to be told, and their contributions celebrated if we are, as a nation, to enjoy the great potential women hold for America and for the world. Their voices help make our republic more democratic, and our democracy can help the world.

Thank you for inviting my comments to this volume on womens' political participation. It is essential that the scholarship be undertaken to document and analyze this important subject.

Ambassador Carol Moseley-Braun

Preface

Although women have been involved in the politics and political struggles of the country from the earliest days of nation building, they were not able to exercise their citizenship fully during much of U.S. history. The history of women's efforts to become equal political actors with men and expand their involvement in the political life of the nation is an intriguing study. Women had to develop a consciousness that they indeed should and could be participants in the political process as women and that women as a group could make political demands. Even in the twenty-first century, women have not achieved consensus that they have equal responsibilities and rights regarding the governing of the nation. This volume is about the many ways in which women have sought to have their voices included in the political process. It shows the ways women have affected the very definition of what is politics and what the public domain should be about.

Women are a diverse group. Not all women view governmental action as the way to achieve equality. Not all women have the same view of equality. Class, race, and ethnicity affect the meaning of politics for women. Political ideologies, such as liberalism or conservatism, have influenced women's perspectives and political participation. Women have sought political leadership while expressing a variety of ideologies, just as men have. Women have expanded the range of issues considered in the political domain and how issues are addressed.

Chapter 1 provides an overview of women's relationship to the public life of the nation. From a historical perspective, it describes the development of a political consciousness on the part of women in the United States and shows how changes in women's lives more generally have influenced their political participation. There have been waves of feminism and political activism on the part of women for women as a group.

Women have not always politely asked for a greater role in the public life of the nation. They have demanded it. Chapter 2 describes the use women have made of protest politics to achieve their goals. It shows the multiplicity of public-policy concerns that have motivated women to march, to demonstrate, and to challenge the political establishment throughout the course of American history.

Chapter 3 addresses the development of a group consciousness on the part of women and their formation of social movements to promote political equality. It describes the various organizations women have established to work to affect public-policy making that addresses issues of particular concern to women. It looks at the organizations minority women as well as middle-class white women have created to promote their interests in the political process.

Chapter 4 explores women's participation in the electoral process and describes how U.S. political parties have responded to women's claims for a greater voice within them. It describes the development and character of the gender gap, the differences between men and women in their political perspectives, which became a political phenomenon in the last quarter of the twentieth century and has been at the center of electoral politics since then.

Chapter 5 provides an account of women becoming political leaders in the United States. It chronicles their ascent into elective and appointive office at the state and national level. It looks at the organizational efforts women have undertaken to promote the candidacy and election of women to public office and describes what we know about the difference women in public office make with respect to which issues get on the public agenda and how those issues are addressed in public debate.

The reference chapters of the volume include a glossary of key people, U.S. Supreme Court cases on women's rights, and legislation regarding issues of particular concern to women; a chronology of women's political participation; a resource guide to organizations of women engaged in the political process, and an annotated bibliography.

Barbara Burrell

Acknowledgments

I would particularly like to thank two graduate students in the Political Science Department at Northern Illinois University for helping to put together this volume. Misty Sampson updated the research on court cases regarding women as citizens and wrote several of the profiles included in the volume. Misty and fellow graduate student Andy Schott reviewed the text for clarity and coherence. Katie Wildenradt of the Public Opinion Laboratory assisted in organizing the material.

1
Overview

Try to imagine a country in which women could not vote, serve on juries, attend institutions of higher learning, speak in public, and upon marriage were considered to be economic nonentities. Although women have been citizens of the United States since its founding, they have never shared equally with men in the rights and obligations of democratic citizenship. At one time women were barred from becoming doctors, lawyers, or other professionals. These are all activities women in the United States had to fight to be able to perform. Women are the majority of the population, yet they have had to organize many movements over two centuries for equal status in the political, social, and economic domains of U.S. society.

Since prerevolutionary days, women have been involved in the public life of the country. In the revolutionary era in America, the quest for independence energized women, and they were active in the resistance to British rule. Women organized public demonstrations to protest the high cost of food and household goods. They boycotted English tea to protest high taxes. The economic boycott that American leaders used against Great Britain mandated the involvement of women because it "could succeed only if white housewives and their daughters refused to purchase imported goods and simultaneously increased their production of homespun" (Norton 1980, 165). The boycotts politicized women's daily activities. Women formed organizations such as the Daughters of Liberty and Anti-Tea Leagues to promote revolutionary activities. Women wrote patriotic poems and political tracts, signed public petitions, raised money for the cause, and demonstrated (Evans 1989). By the 1780s, women were "reading widely in political literature, publishing their own sentiments, engaging in heated debates over public policy, and avidly supporting the war effort in a variety of ways" (Norton 1980, 156).

During the Revolutionary and Civil Wars, women participated both on the battlefield and in more traditional tasks consistent with their gender roles, such as nursing, cooking, and sewing clothes for soldiers. Some women, Molly Pitcher, for example, who received a pension from Pennsylvania, were recognized for their contributions to the Revolutionary War effort. Deborah Sampson twice joined the American army disguised as a man and was honorably discharged in 1783. Afterward, she went on the lecture circuit to tell of her exploits as a soldier. A group of women from Groton, Massachusetts, became famous for dressing as men and taking several British soldiers captive during the fighting at Lexington and Concord (O'Connor 1999).

But as the new nation sought to construct a government, women were excluded from formal political participation, so they lobbied those closest to them for early political recognition. Abigail Adams issued the now famous plea to her husband, future president John Adams, that in writing the new constitution, he "remember the ladies and be more generous and favorable to them than your ancestors. . . . If particular care and attention is not paid to the ladies, we are determined to foment a rebellion, and will not hold ourselves bound by any laws in which we have no voice or representation." Her plea was ignored.

As a result of their war effort, women conceived of a more political role for themselves. But the ideology of the American Revolution offered them no positive role in political life. Instead, the idea of the "Republican Mother" emerged. The Republican Mother integrated political values into women's domestic life. In this role, which was still within a private domain, women would not only provide physical sustenance to those engaged in the public life of the community, but they would also undertake the duty of developing political character in potential leaders and citizens. "The Republican Mother was to encourage in her sons civic interest and participation. She was to educate her children and guide them in the paths of morality and virtue" (Kerber 1980, 283). Thus, women could claim a significant political role, although it was to be played in the home.

Until the mid-1800s, common law, known as *coverture,* defined married couples as one entity, which the husband represented in civil society. This system contributed to women's lack of power in the public sphere. Wives were indivisible from their husbands; therefore, they could not vote or control property. They could not sign contracts and had no title to their earnings or even to their children in cases of legal separation. They were considered to be "civilly dead" (Flexner 1974, 7). For many decades after the founding of the republic, women's voices were legally and systematically excluded from the public process of democratic debate. "The political domain was virtually entirely male" (Junn 1997, 389). Women had to fight for their economic and political rights.

In order to gain a greater political role for themselves, women first sought to become educated. The idea of the Republican Mother helped make education for women of some importance. Then they began to enter the public sphere through their participation in the temperance and abolition movements and through charitable work. Even before they obtained the vote, women were active partisans participating in party and community events. Alexis de Tocqueville, noting in *Democracy in America* that Americans were particularly preoccupied with politics, wrote that "even the women often go to public meetings and forget household cares while they listen to political speeches" (2004, 279). Black women were leaders in fighting slavery.

Women have a rich history of political participation in the United States and have waged a long campaign to achieve equality in political leadership positions and equity in public policy. Their political history involves efforts both to become active and engaged in the political process as individuals and to achieve collective equality for women as a group. Working-class as well as professional women have challenged power relations; and women of color have sought to make connections between sex, race, and class in advocating for change in the political system. Women have employed the full repertoire of political tools, strategies, and tactics to gain their rights. They have marched, protested, and demonstrated. They have petitioned and lobbied public officials. They have lectured and written political tracts. Feminist organizations have worked for change in the law, the courts, universities, health-care systems, and corporations. Grassroots organizing and the empowerment of women in their communities have been a focus of groups of women. They have sought political leadership positions for themselves and organized to elect more women to public office. Among other organized efforts at the beginning of the twenty-first century is the White House Project, aimed at electing a woman to the presidency of the United States.

The First Wave of Feminism

There have been waves of feminism, the belief that women are a group that has not been treated equally in society and that women must work together to alter their roles and achieve equity. Feminism rejects traditional roles for women and favors equality with men. It calls for a broad-based agenda of changes in the fundamental arrangement of home and work, and for women's participation in the public domain. Not all feminists have agreed about the roots of the problem or how society must be changed to achieve equity. Those whose goal is that women be treated as individuals, as men are, are usually referred to as liberal feminists, whereas others, often known as radical feminists, have sought a broader change in society. Liberal feminists tend to work within the existing political system and structures. Contemporary liberal feminists seek to reform the legal and political system so that women will have access to opportunities and resources that should produce a state of equality between men and women. Liberal feminists target laws that distinguish between men and women based on sex. They see women as autonomous individuals achieving in society based on their own merits and efforts (Ford 2002). Radical feminists do not believe that "reforming" the system would produce equality for women. Radical feminists believe it is the "sex-gender" system itself that is the source of women's oppression. They are concerned with women's liberation from the limitations imposed by this system, so they have advocated a total revolution (Ford 2002).

The first wave of feminism, beginning in the 1850s, was centered on obtaining the vote. The second wave of feminism, which emerged in the 1960s, attacked inequalities from a wide range of perspectives and sought to alter women's position in society. Women's rights groups have expanded the definition of the political. "The personal is political" became a rallying cry of the second wave of feminism. Feminists asserted a direct relationship between politics and everyday life and between the individual's everyday needs and social change, which broadened the political agenda substantially. Issues previously considered as women's individual or private problems—abortion and reproductive rights, violence against women, sexual harassment, child care, and housework, for example—became hotly contested in national political discussions and debates (Bookman and Morgen 1988). In the 1980s and 1990s, some saw a third wave of feminism emerging, and others argued that feminism was dead. But in the twentieth-first century, women are more active than ever, both as individuals engaged in political activities and seeking political leadership positions, and as groups working to affect the political process for women specifically and for other societal goals such as peace.

Historically, women first campaigned to win the right to vote. But even among those women who initially sought to improve the position of women at Seneca Falls during the first women's rights convention in 1848, the vote was controversial. Gaining rights to their personhood, their earnings, and their property and the right to be educated were of more immediate concern. But suffrage—voting—soon became the central focus of their efforts. Suffragists used a variety of arguments to win the right to vote. In the early years of the suffrage campaign the principal argument was one of justice, that is, that women were equal to men and therefore should have equal rights in the public sphere. These early suffragists based their arguments on the same ones men had used several generations previously to form their own government. If all men were created equal and had the inalienable right to consent to the laws by which they were governed, women were created equal to men and had the same inalienable right to political liberty. In asserting that natural right applied also to women, the suffragists stressed the ways in which men and women were identical. They emphasized the sameness of men and women. At the heart of this suffragist argument was the common humanity of men and women (Kraditor 1965). They claimed women had the same intellectual and spiritual endowment as man, that women were human beings equal with men and thus deserved equal or the same opportunities men had to advance and develop themselves (Cott 1987).

Elizabeth Cady Stanton, one of the foremost advocates of women's rights in the nineteenth century and a leader of the suffrage movement, addressed a congressional hearing in 1876 in which she laid out perhaps most strongly the natural rights argument as it related to women. This address was titled "The Solitude of Self."

Stanton reasoned:

> In discussing the rights of woman, we are to consider, first, what belongs to her as an individual, in a world of her own, the arbiter of her own destiny, an imaginary Robinson Crusoe, with her woman Friday

on a solitary island. Her rights under such circumstances are to use all her faculties for her own safety and happiness.

Secondly, if we consider her as a citizen, as a member of a great nation, she must have the same rights as all other members, according to the fundamental principles of our government.

Thirdly, viewed as a woman, an equal factor in civilization, her rights and duties are still the same, individual happiness and development.

Fourthly, it is only the incidental relations of life, such as mother, wife, sister, daughter, that may involve some special duties and training. (1896)

Later in the campaign for the vote, the suffragists switched the emphasis of their claim for suffrage from one based on basic rights and equality to one that emphasized the benefits that woman suffrage would bring to society because women had something different to offer and that they needed the vote to protect themselves. Equality and natural rights arguments lessened somewhat in importance in the political debates regarding woman suffrage. Women needed the vote, suffragists began to argue, to protect themselves from the actions of men who spent their wages on liquor rather than supporting their families and who beat their wives after consuming large amounts of liquor. Light sentences were meted out to rapists because legislators did not understand the seriousness of sexual crimes. Furthermore, women working in factories needed the vote to protect themselves against the special hazards to health and morals they faced there.

The suffragists also began to argue that women were different from men and would bring a unique perspective to public-policy making and therefore should have the vote on that account. Their votes would also help with progressive reforms. Political life increasingly influenced the maintenance of the home, as governments passed laws concerning food, water, the production of clothing, and education. Government became more active in providing for the public welfare and legislating in areas that traditionally fell in women's domain. Thus, the statement that the home was the woman's sphere was not an argument against woman suffrage but emerged as an argument in favor of it, for government was now engaged in "enlarged housekeeping" and required the experience and knowledge of the nation's homemakers. It was in women's interest to see that sound laws were passed and implemented in these areas so that they could be good housekeepers. These housekeepers assumed that their training as cooks, seamstresses, housecleaners, and mothers qualified them to assist in developing legislation concerned with food inspection, sweatshop sanitation, street cleaning, and public schools (Kraditor 1965). Women were qualified for lawmaking because government was now involved in large-scale housekeeping or "social housekeeping."

Suffragists also accepted racial arguments to obtain the vote. In the years immediately preceding the passage of the Nineteenth Amendment, colored women's suffragist organizations were discouraged from becoming part of the National American Woman Suffrage Association (NAWSA). Some argued that white women's votes were needed to offset the votes of Black men and uneducated immigrants to protect society. In 1903, NAWSA adopted the principle of "states' rights" as a basis of the relationship of state suffrage organizations to one another and to NAWSA. This principle meant that southern members were free to express racist views from NAWSA convention platforms and that northern members could announce that the southerners possessed the right to do so (Kraditor 1965). NAWSA leaders acted expediently on this issue because they needed votes from at least some southern members of Congress to get a national amendment adopted in that body.

Women won the right to vote nationally in 1920 after a seventy-year campaign. The NAWSA, which had led the campaign for woman suffrage, transformed itself into the nonpartisan League of Women Voters (LWV) in 1920, dedicated to educating women for their new citizenship responsibilities and advocating a broad range of reforms. Joining the league was the National Federation of Business and Professional Women's Clubs (BPW), which had grown out of war work carried out by business and professional women. The federation also supported a range of goals designed to appeal to the newly enfranchised electorate. These two large groups joined with eight other women's organizations to establish the Women's Joint Congressional Committee (WJCC) in 1920, which would serve as a clearinghouse for lobbying on such issues as independent citizenship for women, maternity legislation, and a child labor amendment. Women also worked to gain influence within the political parties and engage in electoral activity. A few women were elected to public office.

The decades after suffrage was won until the 1960s have been called the "doldrums" or the "bleak and lonely years" as far as activism to achieve equal rights for women is concerned (Rupp and Taylor 1987). Women did not turn out to vote in large numbers, nor did many women seek political leadership positions. Women's role in the workforce was debated, and those who believed in equality had different visions. But feminism remained alive among some groups of women, and social reformers worked to improve the lives of women.

Not all women have agreed that they were or are a disadvantaged group, and the women who have organized to improve women's status have not been of the same mind as to what equality would look like or how to obtain it. Female activists after 1920 divided into two groups, those who wished to remove a specific inequality and those who aimed to transform the attitude of the entire society toward women. Social feminists, for example, viewed suffrage as a lever for social-welfare reforms. "Hard-core" feminists, in contrast, perceived the vote as only an intermediate step on the road to full sexual equality. In the years between 1920, when women won the vote, and the 1960s, when the second women's rights movement emerged, activists were divided between advocating for protective legislation for women in the workforce, on the one hand, and the passage of an equal rights amendment, on the other, which suggested that rather than protection, women needed equal rights.

Women were recruited into the workforce in unprecedented numbers during World War II because they were needed to replace the men who joined the armed forces. But after the war, the government instituted a campaign called "return to normalcy" to convince women to leave the workforce and return to their responsibilities at home. By that time, however, most of the social prohibitions against married women working had fallen by the wayside, a direct result of women's wartime experiences. Women had learned to accommodate the dual burdens of work and family. They were provided with an alternative environment in which to learn. They gained new information and new skills. According to the Rosie the Riveter Historic Trust, a nonprofit organization, an estimated 18 million women worked in World War II defense industries and support services, including steel mills, foundries, lumber mills, aircraft factories, offices, hospitals, and day-care centers. The 1942 song "Rosie the Riveter" popularized the image of women outfitted in overalls and wielding industrial tools. The song provided a nickname for all women who worked in wartime industries.

The post–World War II period was a time of contradictions for women regarding their roles in society. They were encouraged to return to the home and find satisfaction in being wives and mothers. But many continued to work and further their education. Women's participation in the labor force, which never returned to its low prewar levels, continued to climb. The second women's rights movement, which emerged in the 1960s, and women's increasing involvement in the political process since then have been affected by changes in women's lives, most notably in their educational and economic status and in their participation in the workforce.

The Second Wave of Feminism

Second-wave feminism is an ideology that argues women should have political, economic, and social rights equal to those of men. Eleanor Smeal, one of the foremost leaders of this movement, former president of the National Organization for Women (NOW) and president of the Fund for a Feminist Majority, describes feminism as a "multi-issue movement committed to extremely long-term goals: the ending of a patriarchy [the rule of fathers and a system in which men exercise control over social, economic, and political resources], the achievement of economic, political, and social equality for all women; and the creation of a world free from sexism, racism, homophobia, classism, ageism, ableism, violence, and environmental exploitation" (Smeal 2003).

Historian Nancy Cott (1987) found that the term *feminism* entered the English language about 1895 and then meant a complete social revolution in the roles of women. The main tenet of feminism is that women should be the equal of men. No gender is superior. Women's roles and status are a product of the social structure and thus changeable. Women are self-identified as a social group; thus they are positioned to act as a group to change their status.

But within this general ideology there are a number of approaches or perspectives about similarities and differences between men and women and the best way to achieve equality. Liberal feminists in the contemporary women's rights movement have sought equality with men in the workforce and focused on individual rights, whereas more-radical feminists have argued that only a broader change in society would lead to equality for women. They advocate more of a "revolution" and argue that women have been oppressed. Whether difference or similarity characterizes males and females has been a source of contention within the feminist movement, and women of color have challenged the feminist movement to focus on the intersection between race and gender and class.

Black women who participated in the Black liberation movement and the women's movement were often discriminated against sexually and racially. The inability of Black men and white women to acknowledge and denounce their oppression of Black women and to meet the needs of Black women prompted the formation of the Black Feminist Movement. Although the movement had been gathering momentum for some time, the founding of the National Black Feminist Organization in New York in 1973 marked its formal beginning.

What most clearly distinguishes Black feminism from the politics of mainstream American feminism is its focus upon the multiplicity of oppressions that affect Black and other women of color, especially racism, sexism, class oppression, and homophobia. Issues of particular concern to Black women, such as lynching or sterilization abuse, cannot be solely attributed to gender discrimination, these feminists have argued. Issues that affect all women, for example, battering, are simultaneously shaped by racial identity, class status, and sexual orientation as well as by gender.

Three areas of oppression in particular intersect to make women of color second-class citizens: pervasive poverty and the lack of economic opportunity, political disenfranchisement, and a cultural ideology that presents degrading images and beliefs about them as women. Black feminists in particular who trace their resistance to the dominant political, social, and economic culture back to the nineteenth century have responded to these multiple sources of oppression through strategies of workplace resistance, traditional and nontraditional political organizing, and the replacement of negative stereotypes with positive images of strength and beauty. Black feminists have often challenged white feminists, charging the latter with not understanding the "multiple jeopardy" that Black women daily face. Sexism, they have asserted, cannot be separated from racism or classism or any of the other "isms" with which women have to deal. Thus, feminists of color have called on white women's rights groups to address the experiences of women of color and poor women of all races when issuing theoretical positions and prescriptions for change. They resist isolating different sources of oppression, rejecting the argument that gender is a more definitive source of oppression than race. They have noted, for example, that feminist platforms focusing on making careers more accessible to women ignore the historical reality of the labor-force participation of African American women, who have always been employed outside the home in larger percentages than white women and usually at lower levels of pay, thus challenging the idea that paid work is necessarily liberating for women. Similarly, issues regarding childbirth have had different meanings for various groups of women. Although some feminists have struggled to secure women's access to birth control and abortion, feminists of color have pointed out that poor African American, Native American, and Hispanic women have been subjected to social policies that have restricted their ability to bear children, including involuntary sterilization.

In an effort to meet the needs of Black women who felt they were being racially oppressed in the women's movement and sexually oppressed in the Black liberation movement, the Black Feminist Movement was formed. All too often, "Black" was equated with Black men and "women" was equated with white women. As a result, Black women were an invisible group whose existence and needs were ignored. The purpose of the movement was to develop a political philosophy that could adequately address the way race, gender, and class were interconnected in their lives and to take action to stop racist, sexist, and classist discrimination (see Jull, Scott and Smith 1982).

Contemporary Feminism

Contemporary, or third-wave, feminism characterizes the feminist beliefs and perspectives of the generation of women who came of age in the 1980s and 1990s. These younger feminists express more-individualist attitudes toward their activism, as opposed to the more-collectivist drive that defined the feminist movement during its second wave. Leaders describe feminism as emerging from a movement focused on a small number of issues into a movement that pervades all aspects of society. Although feminists in the second wave were generally focused on fighting for gender equality in the workplace, abortion rights, and economic parity, current activists say they are looking at a wider range of topics through the feminist lens. Because of their greater freedom, younger women have the liberty to offer their unique perspectives on everything from arts and culture to prison reform.

Third-wave feminism is marked by the idea that a person is whoever she is but has a political consciousness. The primary organization of third-wave feminism is the Third Wave Foundation, located in New York. The Third Wave Foundation provides grants and scholarships to young women activists and the organizations they lead, to implement their "cutting-edge strategies to get the resources needed to help change our communities." The foundation engages in public education campaigns to highlight issues that concern young women and bring them to the attention of policy makers; it also undertakes what it calls relationship-building programs to create opportunities and resources for young women to expand their knowledge and skills to make their work more effective, lasting, and vibrant in their communities. Its inaugural project was Freedom Summer '92 in which 120 people went to twenty-three poor and urban locales considered not political centers to register voters and educate them on how and why they should vote (see Baumgardner and Richards 2000, and the Third Wave Foundation Web site, www.thirdwavefoundation.org).

In the 1990s questions emerged about the continuing relevance of feminism and the women's movement. Some saw a postfeminist generation emerging, one whose members believed that fighting for women's rights was no longer necessary. These observers of American culture saw young women who enjoyed the fruits of the women's movement, such as better access to employment and equal education, being taken more seriously and believed the battle had been won. Some commentators declared feminism dead as an ideology. For example, in 1992, journalist Sally Quinn in a syndicated column asked: "Is it possible that feminism as we have known it is dead? I think so. Like communism in the former Soviet empire, the movement in its present form has outlasted its usefulness.... What's happening in this country now is that more and more women are falling away from feminism because it doesn't represent, or more importantly, they feel it doesn't represent, them or their problems." In response Patricia Ireland (1992), then president of the National Organization for Women, the leading women's rights organization, cited a number of public opinion polls showing women's growing support for the women's movement. According to Ireland, "A December 1991 poll by the Times Mirror Center for the People and the Press found that support for the women's movement has continued to grow, not decline. Seventy-one percent of the adults polled have a favorable view of the women's movement, up from 53 percent in 1985. A 1989 Time Magazine/CNN Poll found an overwhelming consensus among women that the movement has helped women become more independent (94 percent), has given women more control over their lives (86 percent) and is still improving the lives of women (82 percent)."

The Impact of Feminism on Public Opinion

A survey the American Association of University Women (AAUW) conducted in 1970 with some of the most highly educated men and women in the nation showed that 60 percent of the men and 43 percent of the women believed that a woman's major role should be as a wife or mother. Less than half of U.S. women were full-time homemakers in 1970 (48.4 percent), however, and perspectives were changing among the general public.

In 1971 and 1972, Louis Harris and Associates undertook the Virginia Slims American Women's Opinion polls to survey women's political involvement and opinions on efforts to achieve equality and the feminist movement. The 1971 poll found that 42 percent of women "favor efforts to strengthen and change women's status in society," and 43 percent opposed those efforts. Among Black women, the poll showed 62 percent approved and only 20 percent opposed. A year later, overall women's approval had climbed to 48 percent, and 36 percent remained opposed.

Public opinion surveys since then have chronicled women's rising support for a more equal role in politics. Several survey questions provide a picture of women's perspectives on their roles during the contemporary feminist era. Figure 1.1 shows that the percentage of women who believe that men are better suited emotionally for politics than women declined from 40 percent in 1974 to 20 percent in 2002. Presented in the American National Election Study with the comparative statements "some people feel that women should have an equal role with men in running business, industry, and government; others feel that women's place is in the home," and asked to place themselves on a 7-point scale regarding their reaction to these statements, the percentage of women placing themselves at the most egalitarian end of the scale increased from 31 percent in 1972 to 61 percent in 2000. Figure 1.2 shows the rise and then leveling of positive ratings of the women's movement on a thermometer scale from the National Election Studies (NES) at the University of Michigan. On a 100-point thermometer scale the mean score in women's feelings toward the women's movement has been well in the "warm" range since 1986.

According to a 1992 Gallup Organization poll of a national sample of women, 33 percent said they considered themselves to be a feminist, while 61 percent said they did not. Women asked in a 2001 survey whether they agreed or disagreed with the idea that the United States continued to need a strong women's movement to push for

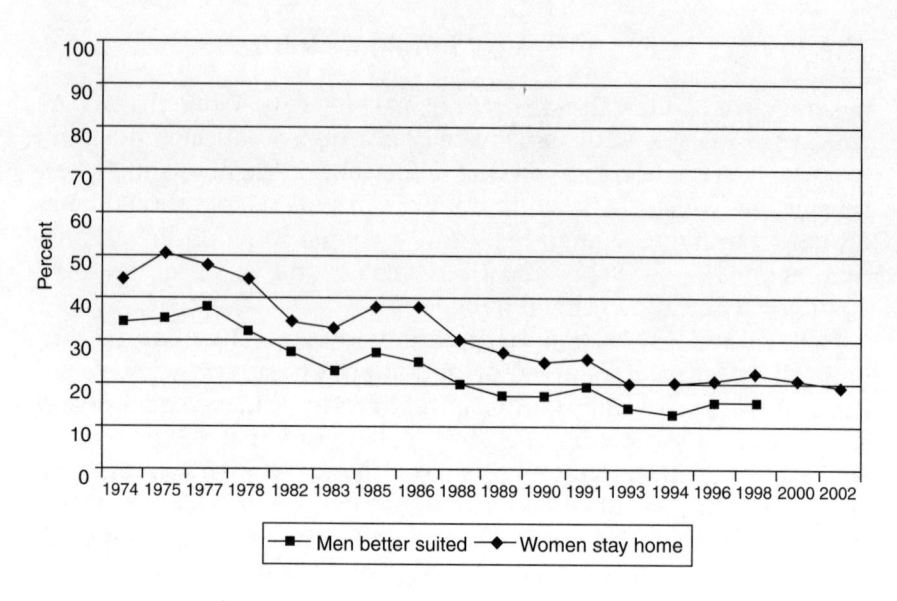

FIGURE 1.1 Percent of women who agree with the General Social Survey question: "Most men are better suited emotionally for politics than women."

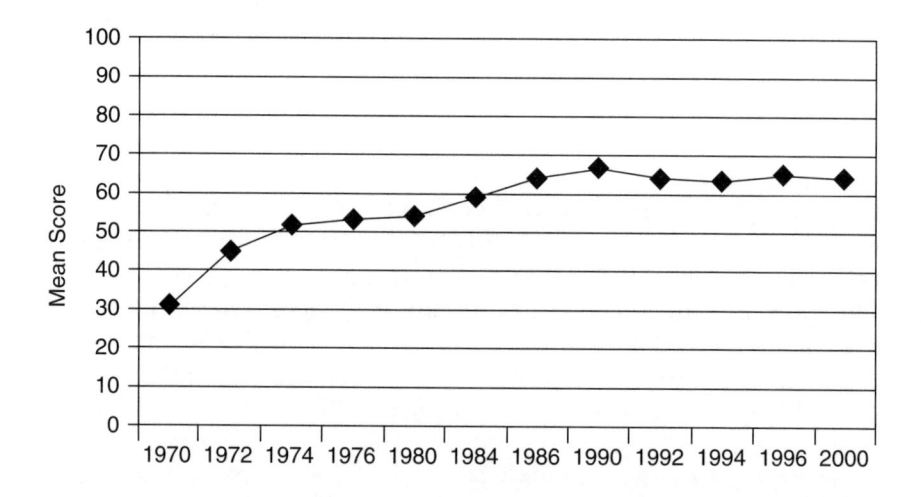

FIGURE 1.2 Mean Score on Rating of Women's Movement Thermometer
Source: National Election Studies

changes that benefit women, 68 percent agreed either strongly (47 percent) or not strongly (21 percent). And in 2004, asked how satisfied they were with the position of women in the United States, 67 percent of women said they were either very or somewhat satisfied (Mason 2004).

Women's Current Status

Educational Attainment

The women's movement targeted inequalities in the educational system that had had the effect of hurting women's job and earnings' opportunities. In 1972, Title IX of the Education Amendments prohibited sex discrimination in elementary and secondary schools as well as in postsecondary institutions that received federal monetary assistance. Modeled on the equal protection aspects of Title VI of the Civil Rights Act of 1964, Title IX states, "No person in the United States shall, on the basis of sex be excluded from participation in, be denied the benefits of, or be subjected to discrimination under any education program or activity receiving federal financial assistance." The 1974 Women's Educational Equity Act provided funds for research and development to support women's efforts toward gaining equality in education. These acts broadly affected the educational opportunities of women. Other laws addressed more specific areas of sex discrimination, such as the Comprehensive Health Manpower Training Act, which prohibited sex discrimination in medical and dental schools receiving special grants. The 1975 Department of Defense Appropriations Act permitted the appointment and admission of women to the United States Military, Naval, and Air Force Academies.

Women have been going to college in ever-increasing numbers. In 1983, the Bureau of the Census reported that women were expanding their enrollment lead over men; 108 women for every 100 men in 1981 were enrolled in college. Between 1960 and 1998, national education statistics show that college-enrollment rates of female high-school graduates increased from 38 percent to over 69 percent. At the same time, men had increased their college-enrollment rates from 54 percent to 62 percent. Women with college degrees have increased from approximately 5 percent of women twenty-five and older in 1940 to nearly 25 percent in 2000. At the beginning of the twenty-first century, women between the ages of twenty-five and thirty-five, whether white, Black, or Hispanic, are more likely to be college graduates than their male counterparts in the same age group. But at the same time, Hispanic women lag behind their white and Black female counterparts in educational attainment.

In the twenty-first century more women than men are earning college degrees. In the age groups under thirty-five, a larger proportion of women than of men are college graduates. Increasing numbers of women are also earning doctoral or professional degrees. Over the last quarter of the twentieth century, women overtook men in earning associate, bachelor's, and master's degrees and significantly narrowed men's lead in earning doctoral and first professional degrees. As recently as 1970, women received less than 10 percent of law and medical degrees. In the past thirty years women have made major advances and at the turn of the millennium were earning more than 41 percent of the degrees in medicine and 44 percent of the degrees in law. If women advance through the first decade of the twenty-first century as much as they did during the 1990s, they will achieve parity by 2010.

Labor-Force Participation

Women's rights activists have achieved a number of national legislative successes during the contemporary era regarding discrimination on the basis of sex. Discrimination in employment on the basis of sex was banned in the Civil Rights Act of 1964, and equal pay for equal work was mandated with the passage of the Equal Pay Act of 1963. In the 1970s legislation concerning federally funded employment programs began to prohibit discrimination on the basis of sex. Examples of such legislation include the Comprehensive Employment and Training Act (CETA), passed in 1973, which along with amendments in 1978 required that programs work toward eliminating sex stereotyping by giving opportunities to "women, single parents, and displaced homemakers," among others.

Women can no longer be discriminated against in employment on the basis of being pregnant. Two pieces of national legislation related to discrimination against pregnant workers were passed during the late 1970s. Before these statutes were enacted, pregnant workers often were required to take leave without pay or unemployment compensation before and after childbirth, were denied coverage under employer-sponsored health and disability insurance plans, lost seniority during maternity leave, and were subject to dismissal due to their condition. Amendments enacted in 1976 to the federal unemployment compensation program that had been established in the

1930s prohibited denial of benefits solely on the basis of pregnancy or termination of pregnancy. The Pregnancy Discrimination Act, passed in 1978, amended Title VII of the Civil Rights Act of 1964 to prohibit discrimination on the basis of pregnancy in employer-related fringe benefit programs, such as health or disability plans. The act also protected a woman's job seniority during absence due to pregnancy or pregnancy-related causes (Gladstone 2001).

Thus, the second half of the twentieth century saw a steady increase in women's labor-force participation, that is, the number of women employed as a percentage of the number of women eligible for employment. Their presence in professional employment expanded and was accompanied by an increase in their earnings relative to men's. But during this same time period, the feminization of poverty, meaning that women and their children disproportionately composed the ranks of the poor, also came to characterize the economic life of the nation.

In 1948, women's labor-force participation rate was 32.7 percent. By the late 1960s, when the second women's rights movement emerged on a national scale, nearly 40 percent of all women were employed outside the home. By 2000 that figure had climbed to 60.2 percent (see Table 1.1). The majority of women now work full-time, year-round, and close to two-thirds of mothers who have children under six are in the workforce. Traditionally, Black women have been more likely than white women to be in the paid workforce.

Women's share of employment in occupations typified by high earnings has grown. In 2002, 47.5 percent of full-time wage and salary workers in executive, administrative, and managerial occupations were women, up from 34.2 percent in 1983, the first year for which comparable data are available. Over the same period, women's share of full-time employment in professional specialty occupations rose from 46.8 percent to 53.1 percent (U.S. Department of Labor, 2003).

Women's earnings have experienced an upward trend over time while men's earnings have declined, yet women still earn less than men on average. In 1979, the first year of comparable earnings data, women earned 63 percent as much as men. Black and Hispanic women's earnings have more nearly equaled those of their male counterparts than white women's earnings compared with those of white men. In 2002, women earned 78 percent of what men earned (U.S. Department of Labor, 2003) Among Black and Hispanic men the ratios were about 91 and 88 percent, respectively; for Black women the ratio was 63 percent, and for Hispanic women 54 per-

TABLE 1.1 Women in the Labor Force, 1948–2002

Year	Women's Labor-Force Participation Rate	Women as a Percentage of Total Labor Force
1948	32.7	28.6
1952	34.7	31.0
1956	36.9	32.2
1960	37.7	33.4
1964	38.7	34.8
1968	41.6	37.1
1972	43.9	38.5
1976	47.3	40.5
1980	51.5	43.0
1984	53.6	43.8
1988	56.6	45.0
1992	57.8	45.4
1996	59.3	46.2
2000	60.2	46.6
2002	59.6	47.0

Source: U.S. Department of Labor, Bureau of Labor Statistics, *Handbook of Labor Statistics,* 2003.

cent. However, white workers of either sex earned more than their Black or Hispanic counterparts in 2002.

Median weekly earnings, 2002
White male	$702
White females	$549
Black males	$523
Black females	$474
Hispanic males	$449
Hispanic females	$396

Economic Status

In 1974 the Equal Credit Opportunity Act banning credit discrimination on the basis of sex became law. The credit industry had institutionalized discrimination against women because of their sex and marital status for many years. This discrimination was rooted in long-standing traditions, customs, beliefs, and attitudes that by the 1970s no longer reflected the realities of women's lives. Women were by that time a significant part of the workforce and less dependent than before on husbands and fathers for their livelihood. Yet, despite the changing social and economic role of women, the credit industry treated them as second-class citizens. Few banks and savings and loan associations granted full credit to a working wife's income. Single women also had difficulty qualifying for credit. Records tended to be kept in husbands' names, thus denying married women the ability to develop a credit history. To obtain credit, women often were forced to respond to humiliating questions regarding birth-control techniques and intent to bear children. Divorced and widowed women were subject to particular discrimination. Alimony and child support as well as other monetary resources were ignored as income when these women applied for credit (Gelb and Palley 1982). The Equal Credit Opportunity Act stated: "It shall be unlawful for any credit or card issuer to discriminate on account of sex or marital status against any individual with respect to the approval or denial of any extension of consumer credit or with respect to the approval, denial, renewal, continuation, or revocation of any open end consumer credit account or with respect to the terms thereof."

One group of women has benefited from economic prosperity, but the prosperity has missed another group completely. Although women have made substantial gains in their educational attainment and employment status during what might be called the feminist era, women are still more likely than their male contemporaries to be poor. According to Bureau of the Census figures, poverty rates were higher for females than for males at every age and among people of every race in the year 2000. In certain age groups, twenty-five to thirty-four and seventy-five and older, women are almost twice as likely as men to be poor. Overall, almost a quarter of Black and Hispanic women, compared with about 10 percent of white women, live in poverty.

The percentage of all households headed by women without a spouse present increased over the course of the latter part of the twentieth century. In 2000, 17.3 percent of households, including 13.8 percent of white households, 42.7 percent of Black households, and 22.6 percent of Hispanic households, fit that description. Female-headed families with children are far more likely to be poor than families of other types. Female householders with no spouse present had a median income of $11,884 in 2003, compared to a national median income of $21,273. Nearly 29 percent (28.8 percent) of people in families with a female head of household had household incomes that were at or below the poverty level. Nevertheless this percentage represented a continuing decline in the poverty rate of female-headed households.

Controversial Current Issues

Abortion

Two issues that have generated the most controversy and that have been central to the feminist movement have been the proposed Equal Rights Amendment (ERA) to the U.S. Constitution and abortion. The ERA would have guaranteed that state and national laws could not discriminate against women. In 1972, the equal rights amendment, which was first introduced in the years immediately following passage of the Nineteenth Amendment granting women the right to vote in 1920, finally obtained the necessary two-thirds vote in both the U.S. House of Representatives and the U.S. Senate to be sent to the states for ratification. Between 1972 and 1982, when it died for lack of adoption by three-quarters of the states, it generated mobilization by all of the national women's rights groups that had emerged in the 1960s and the older, more established women's organizations such as the League of Women Voters, the American Association of University Women, and the business and professional women's organization. It also fostered the development of organizations in opposition to it, which resulted in a major national debate on women's roles in society.

The issue of whether and when to permit women to terminate their pregnancies through abortion has become one of the most emotional and confrontational issues of contemporary politics. The issue has pitted opposing sets of women political activists against one another; women's rights activists have often carried signs stating, "If men got pregnant, abortions would be legal."

Feminists argue that only the woman affected can make what is often a difficult moral judgment, and that the fetus is part of a woman's body until birth. Feminists believe that women must have effective choice in deciding when and if to bear a child. Effective choice means that legal barriers to contraception and abortion must be removed and public and private agencies must provide full access to information and services. Feminists believe women must be full participants in making decisions about their health care, and to do this, women need complete and accurate information. Feminists also believe continuing research for safe contraceptive and abortion methods are necessary. Only with such a policy can women exercise their civil rights, have legal equality, and take advantage of opportunities for achievement in all aspects of their lives. Feminists see reproductive choice as the substance of independence and freedom for women in family and sexual relationships. It is crucial to empowerment in all social relations (Stetson 1991).

Religious conservatives argue that from the time of conception the fetus is a person with a soul and that abortion is therefore murder. Thus, the abortion debate has been framed as a clash of absolute rights, the right to choose versus the right to life. Pro-life groups have sought to restrict access to contraceptive information and services, to prevent abortions from being performed, and to make abortion illegal.

Reproductive rights, including the right to abortion, were an early but controversial demand of the women's rights movement in the late 1960s and early 1970s. In 1973, the U.S. Supreme Court ruled in *Roe v. Wade* that a woman's right to privacy was broad enough to encompass a decision to terminate a pregnancy. The Court invalidated restrictive abortion laws across the country. States could no longer categorically proscribe abortions or make them unnecessarily difficult to obtain. The promotion of maternal care and the preservation of the life of a fetus were not sufficiently "compelling state interests" to justify restrictive abortion laws. The Court ruled that throughout the first trimester, or the first three months of a pregnancy, the decision whether to have an abortion is that of a woman and her doctor. During the second trimester, states may regulate abortions, but only in ways reasonably related to their interests in safeguarding the health of women. In the third trimester, states' interests in preserving the life of the unborn become compelling, and they may limit or even ban abortions, except when necessary to save a woman's life.

This decision making abortion legal stimulated a political clash that continues more than thirty years later between what became to be called the pro-life movement and the pro-choice movement. Women's rights organizations have led the pro-choice movement, with the National Abortion Rights Action League (now called NARAL Pro-Choice America) being the point group and Planned Parenthood reproductive clinics the most immediate target of pro-life groups.

Activists on both sides have engaged in the full range of political tactics to affect public policy. In the early 1980s, with a conservative Republican administration in the White House, pro-life activists introduced a human life amendment in Congress, but it lacked broad enough support to make it through the legislative process. On the other side, in the early 1990s, pro-choice forces sought national legislative action with a freedom of choice act, but with the more conservative membership in Congress since 1994, this strategy has not been pursued.

Changing the composition of the Supreme Court became a second strategy of abortion opponents, and potential justices' stands on the abortion issue have become litmus tests of their fitness to serve on federal benches. Legislative restrictions on abortion have been a third tactic used by the pro-life movement to minimize abortions and lessen the scope of *Roe v. Wade*. Legislative enactments to restrict abortions have included requiring teenaged girls to inform at least one of their parents before obtaining an abortion, imposing waiting periods, requiring that spouses be notified, and instituting bans on the use of Medicaid funds for abortions.

These enactments have generated major Court decisions that, though continuing to uphold the principle of *Roe v. Wade*, have limited its reach. The two most prominent cases since *Roe* have been *Webster v. Reproductive Health Services*, decided in 1989, and *Planned Parenthood of Southeastern Pennsylvania v. Casey*, decided in 1992. *Webster* involved aspects of a Missouri law that prohibited the use of public facilities or employees in the performance of abortions, a prohibition against the use of public funding for abortion counseling, and a requirement that physicians conduct viability tests on fetuses of twenty weeks or more before aborting those pregnancies. The Supreme Court upheld the constitutionality of each of these sections of the law. Four justices also voted to overturn *Roe*, but five would have been needed to accomplish that end. In that same year, Pennsylvania passed the Abortion Control Act, which among other things included sections mandating lectures by doctors on fetal development before performing an abortion, a twenty-four-hour delay after the lecture, reporting requirements that could subject providers to harassment, spousal notification, and more-stringent parental consent rules requiring parents to come to a clinic with the minor or, if the parents would not come, judicial approval.

In its 1992 decision, the Supreme Court upheld a woman's right to an abortion but gave states even greater leeway than *Webster* had to limit abortions. The justices redefined what *Roe* stood for, rejecting its trimester approach to balancing the interest of women and the state. The Court overturned portions of several other abortion rights cases that had struck down informed consent, parental consent, and abortion counseling requirements as unconstitutional infringements of *Roe*. Seven justices rejected the idea that a woman's right to an abortion was a fundamental right. Instead, the plurality opinion redefined that "central principle" of *Roe* and replaced it with a lesser standard. States could enact abortion restrictions as long as they did not place an "undue burden" on a woman's right to an abortion. In *Casey,* none of the state's impediments to abortion except the one requiring spousal consent was deemed an "undue burden."

In 2003, Congress passed and President George W. Bush signed into law a ban on what pro-life advocates called a "partial birth" procedure and what pro-choice advocates called "late-term" abortions, a medical procedure that is conducted late in a pregnancy when the mother's life or health is at stake and traditional procedures used at earlier stages in the pregnancy can no longer be used. Congress had tried to pass such a law four times prior to this successful attempt. However, President Bill Clinton vetoed such a bill twice, and once the Supreme Court struck down a state law similar to the one proceeding through Congress. In 2002, the U.S. House passed a bill, but the Senate did not take it up. Opponents of the 2003 bill, argue that the language is vague and could be interpreted to ban other types of abortions earlier in a pregnancy. In June 2004, a California federal judge held this law was unconstitutional, ruling that it placed an undue burden on women seeking the procedure, its language was vague, and it failed to provide an exception for the health of the woman (Liptak 2004). It will be up to the Supreme Court to determine whether the "partial birth" abortion ban enacted into law is constitutional. It ruled in 2000 that a Nebraska law similar to the federal law was unconstitutional.

In 2004, President George W. Bush signed the Unborn Victims of Violence Act, a federal law that confers legal status to fetuses injured by crimes against pregnant women. Pro-choice activists worry that by granting embryos and fetuses full human rights it may create a precedent for those seeking to overturn *Roe v. Wade.* They also say the law may be used to prosecute pregnant women for drug or alcohol abuse. Both sides in the abortion debate have engaged continuously in electoral campaigns in support of pro-choice and pro-life legislators, governors, and presidents. Women's rights political action committees, such as EMILY's List and the WISH List, have been established with a commitment to a woman's right to choose as a litmus test for receiving monetary support. At the same time groups such as Feminists for Life and the Susan B. Anthony Group have sought to provide support to candidates who, while advocating greater equality for women in the political process, have opposed abortion. Finally, groups opposed to abortion have blocked entrances to abortion clinics and destroyed clinic property and equipment. A fringe element of the abortion opposition movement has even resorted to killing doctors who perform abortions and clinic workers.

Title IX

The issue of sex equality in intercollegiate sports, mandated by Title IX, has generated major conflict that continues into the twenty-first century. The act was aimed at ensuring equal opportunity for men and women athletes. Feminists wanted women to share equally in the resources of college and high-school athletics. The National Collegiate Athletic Association (NCAA), objecting to federal interference, lined up against the National Organization for Women (NOW), the Women's Equity Action League (WEAL), and the National Coalition for Women and Girls in Education members. At stake was a potential redistribution of financial resources from males to females. Feminists looked at the enormous imbalance of resources in such areas as scholarships, coaching staff, facilities, and supplies between men's and women's teams. They wanted equal spending. Major universities and the NCAA wanted to exclude the big-ticket men's sports of football and basketball from the provisions.

Regulations adopted in 1979 did not demand equal spending but required that "institutions must provide reasonable opportunities for award [financial assistance] for members of each sex in proportion to the number of students of each sex participating in . . . intercollegiate athletics" (*Federal Register* 44, no 239). Schools would primarily show that they were not discriminating by demonstrating that the percentage of women in their sports programs was roughly equivalent to the proportion of women in the student body (Stetson 1991).

In 2002, Rod Paige, secretary of education in the George W. Bush administration, convened the Commission on Opportunity in Athletics. The commission was charged with determining whether Title IX was "working to promote opportunities for male and female athletes." The commission advised the Department of Education to tell schools that cutting men's programs to achieve equity for women is a "disfavored practice." At the conclusion of the commission's tenure, Secretary of Education Paige issued a statement saying that he was not inclined to enforce its recommendations. One can assume that the support for women's and girls' sports among the many female voters contributed to his disinclination to implement the commission's recommendations. A group of national lawmakers, concerned that the Bush administration would weaken the provisions of

Title IX, introduced legislation in March 2003 stating that "Congress and women around the country will not tolerate attempts to weaken Title IX" and that any change to established Title IX policies would "contradict the spirit of athletic equality and gender equality."

Women in the Military

That women might be drafted was an issue opponents of the equal rights amendment used in their campaign to defeat it. But women's presence in the military has greatly expanded in recent decades.

In 1948, Congress limited women's presence to 2 percent of the military force and banned them from serving on warships and combat planes. Ground combat was not even considered. The 2 percent limit was lifted after the Vietnam War, but women were not allowed on warships or combat planes until after the Persian Gulf War, in which about 7 percent of the half-million soldiers were women.

In the mid-1990s, Congress repealed the laws that prohibited women from serving on combat ships and aircraft, ending the last statutory barriers to women's full participation in the defense of the country. In 1998, women flew in air-combat missions for the first time in U.S. history. The repeal opened the pathway to the top enlisted and officer positions for women in the Navy and the Air Force. Defense Department policies, however, continue to keep women from participating in the full range of military duties. By policy, women cannot serve on Navy submarines or in the SEALS and cannot serve in units whose primary mission is ground combat—infantry, armor, special forces, and most artillery units—or in units that routinely interact with ground-combat units. This policy effectively denies women access to most top positions in the Army and Marine Corps (Costello and Stone 2001).

By the time of the Iraq War in 2003, women made up 15 percent of the 1.4 million active-duty force and about 14 percent of the officers. Roughly 90 percent of military jobs have been open to women, though infantry, armor, special operations, and most artillery units remain closed. The Air Force has the largest percentage of women, and the Marine Corps has the smallest percentage. Women now constitute nearly one-third of the graduates of the Coast Guard Academy and approximately 15 percent of the graduates of the Air Force and Naval Academies and West Point.

Federal law during the Iraq War continued to bar women from ground combat, but that barrier was effectively smashed when the war's shifting, chaotic nature put everyone at risk. The guerrilla nature of the Iraq War, in which insurgents were just as likely to attack a convoy of supply soldiers as a patrol of combat troops, put the entire military in danger. Americans have come to support the idea of women serving in the military. A Gallup Organization poll in December 2003 found that eight of ten Americans thought women should have the opportunity, or be required to, serve in the same combat jobs as men.

Women's political participation has not only involved lobbying and demonstrating to achieve legislative and judicial victories, it has also mobilized interest groups to make sure those decisions are implemented. Women's groups have worked to put women in political leadership positions to ensure that women's special interests and concerns are heard in debates and that concerns special to women are part of the national agenda.

References

Baumgardner, Jennifer, and Amy Richards. 2000. *Manifesta.* New York: Farrar, Straus and Giroux.

Bookman, Ann, and Sandra Morgen. 1988. *Women and the Politics of Empowerment.* Philadelphia: Temple University Press.

Costello, Cynthia B., and Anne J. Stone. 2001. *American Women 2001–2002: Getting to the Top.* Washington, DC: Women's Research and Education Institute.

Cott, Nancy. 1987. *The Grounding of Modern Feminism.* New Haven, CT: Yale University Press.

DeTocqueville, Alexis. 2004. *Democracy in America.* Translated by Arthur Goldhammer. New York: Literary Classics of the United States.

Evans, Sara. 1989. *Born for Liberty: A History of Women in America.* New York: The Free Press.

Flexner, Eleanor. 1974. *Century of Struggle: The Women's Rights Movement in the United States.* New York: Atheneum.

Ford, Lynne. 2002. *Women and Politics: The Pursuit of Equality.* Boston: Houghton Mifflin Company.

Gelb, Joyce, and Marian Lief Palley. 1982. *Women and Public Policies.* Princeton, NJ: Princeton University Press.

Gladstone, Leslie. 2001. "Women's Issues in Congress: Selected Legislation 1832–1998." In *Women and Women's Issues in Congress 1832–2000.* Edited by Janet Lewis. Huntington, NY: Nova Science Publishers.

Ireland, Patricia. 1992. "Feminism Is Not Dead." *Washington Post,* February 1, A21.

Jull, Gloria T., Patricia Bell Scott, and Barbara Smith, editors. 1982. *All the Women Are White, All the Blacks Are Men, But Some of Us Are Brave: Black Women's Studies.* Old Westbury, NY: The Feminist Press.

Junn, Jane. 1997. "Assimilating or Coloring Participation?: Gender, Race, and Democratic Political Participation." In *Women Transforming Politics: An Alternative Reader.* Edited by Cathy J. Cohen, Kathleen B. Jones, and Joan C. Tronto. New York: New York University Press.

Kerber, Linda. 1980. *Women of the Republic: Intellect and Ideology in Revolutionary America.* Chapel Hill: University of North Carolina Press.

Kraditor, Aileen. 1965. *Ideas of the Woman Suffrage Movement, 1890–1920.* New York: Columbia University Press.

Liptak, Adam. 2004. "U.S. Judge in San Francisco Strikes Down Federal Law Banning Form of Abortion." *New York Times,* June 2.

Mason, Heather. 2004. "Are Americans Content with Status of Women?" *The Gallup Poll Tuesday Briefing,* March 30.

Norton, Mary Beth. 1980. *Liberty's Daughters.* Boston: Little, Brown and Company.

O'Connor, Karen. 1999. "Introduction: Women in American Politics." In *Encyclopedia of Women in American Politics.* Edited by Jeffrey D. Schultz and Lauren van Assendelft. Phoenix, AZ: Onyx Press.

Quinn, Sally. 1992. "Today's Feminist Movement Has Outlasted Its Usefulness." *St. Petersburg Times,* January 24, 12A.

Rupp, Leila J., and Verta Taylor. 1987. *Survival in the Doldrums.* New York: Oxford University Press.

Smeal, Eleanor. 2003. "The Art of Building Feminist Institutions to Last." In *Sisterhood Is Forever: The Women's Anthology for a New Millennium.* Edited by Robin Morgan. New York: Washington Square Press.

Stetson, Dorothy McBride. 1991. *Women's Rights in the U.S.A.: Policy Debates and Gender Roles.* Belmont, CA: Brooks/Cole.

U.S. Department of Labor, Bureau of Labor Statistics. 2003. *Highlights of Women's Earnings in 2002,* Report 972.

2
Protest Politics

> *It's not that I believe marches alone do the job, but once in a while you have to march for what you believe in.*
> —*Eleanor Smeal, President of the National Organization for Women, 1985*

Demonstrations, protests, and marches have been part of the activities women have engaged in to achieve their political goals. They have protested to demand equal rights for themselves as women and have engaged in this form of political activity to affect other types of public policies, such as gun control and nuclear proliferation, in the name of women.

Suffrage Protests

One of the first major demonstrations that focused on rights for women occurred at the centennial celebration of the Declaration of Independence in 1876. The National Woman Suffrage Association (which would later become the National American Woman Suffrage Association) in the summer of 1876 took advantage of the country's centennial celebration in Philadelphia to "draw attention to women's inequitable position in society and to bring women from all over the country together to exchange their experiences and knowledge." The

29

principal event of the centennial celebration in Philadelphia took place in Independence Hall, with the emperor of Brazil as guest of honor. The suffragists sought to present a Declaration of Rights for Women similar to the Declaration of Sentiments that the Seneca Falls convention had drawn up in 1848. They were denied permission to make this presentation but were given five tickets to attend the event. They took advantage of their presence to disrupt the ceremony. When the audience stood to greet the Brazilian monarch, Susan B. Anthony led her group of four women to the platform and "bore down on the chairman, president *pro tempore* of the United States Senate, Thomas W. Ferry" and handed him the Declaration of Rights. The women expected to be taken into custody. As they left the hall, they scattered throughout the room printed broadsides carrying their declaration. "There was great confusion as men stood on their seats reaching for the handbills and hundreds of arms were stretched out for them, while General Hawley shouted for order to be restored." Leaving the building, the five women took advantage of an empty bandstand that had been erected for the evening's program around which a large crowd was milling. Marching to the bandstand, Anthony read the declaration in a booming voice. More leaflets were distributed (Flexner 1974, 171).

The Congressional Union (CU), which became the National Woman's Party in 1916, led by Alice Paul, undertook militant action during the decade of the suffrage campaign. The Democratic Party was in power nationally, and the CU held it responsible for the failure of federal suffrage legislation to pass in Congress. The CU first planned a massive parade down Pennsylvania Avenue in Washington, D.C., to coincide with the festivities of Woodrow Wilson's inauguration as president in 1913. Sixteen "suffrage pilgrims" had walked from New York City to Washington to participate, newspaper photographers clicking all the way. Inez Milholland, dressed like Joan of Arc, on a white horse, led the parade. Women from countries where they were enfranchised came first, followed by groups of American nurses and doctors in uniform, actresses, homemakers, farmers, lawyers, teachers, and college women in academic gowns. There were large floats—"heralds" on horseback, reporter Nellie Bly among them—and all-female marching bands. Along the parade route, vendors sold "Votes for Women" banners, and 300,000 people, mostly men, stood watching.

At the Treasury Department building, covered bleachers held 20,000 spectators waiting for a performance of "The Allegory," an extravagant series of pantomimes set to music, with costumed women representing classical mythological figures, tying concepts of peace and justice to "the cause." Violence broke out early and frequently. Spectators spit on, cursed at, shoved, struck, and fondled the marchers. Milholland had to charge with her horse to clear the way. Ambulance drivers and physicians had to fight the opposing crowds to reach the injured, which numbered at least 100. The police, witnesses said, jeered. Eventually, the War Department called out the mounted cavalry. Educator Helen Keller was too traumatized to make her scheduled speech. With so much press attention, the story spread widely, bringing sympathy from a horrified public. A congressional inquiry later that month lambasted local authorities. Alice Paul had made her mark, and the whole world was watching (Bernikow 2004).

The CU targeted Democratic congressmen in close races and actively campaigned against candidates who did not support enfranchising women. President Woodrow Wilson became a target also. Alice Paul organized pickets in front of the White House and called on Wilson to pressure Congress to take up and pass an amendment to the Constitution. On January 10, 1917, the first "Silent Sentinels" appeared. These were women who stood motionless holding banners that read "Mr. President, What Will You Do for Woman Suffrage?" and "How Long Must Women Wait for Liberty?" These suffragists were the first picketers ever to appear before the White House.

The picketers initially attracted sympathy from the public. Women from around the country sent donations. However, in 1917, while other suffragists were debating how to respond to the country's war on Germany, Alice Paul heightened her efforts to call attention to women's disenfranchisement. Ignoring the war, the National Woman's Party picketers carried signs reading: "Kaiser Wilson, have you forgotten your sympathy with the poor Germans because they were not self-governed? Twenty million American women are not self-governed. Take the beam out of your eye." As the rhetoric intensified, police began arresting picketers, some of whom were physically attacked by daily crowds of onlookers. Each time police arrested a group of marchers or a woman was felled by attack, another woman was there to take her place. States sent delegations to the picket lines, and those who could not picket sent donations to support those marching in their place. When jailed, women refused to pay their fines and remained in jail. In an attempt to intimidate new picketers, prison terms of up to sixty days were imposed. The women engaged in several hunger strikes to protest their incarceration. Prison officials responded by force-feeding them through the nose, a dangerous and particularly painful practice. Public reaction was swift and overwhelmingly sympathetic to the suffragists, prompting early releases. Women released from prison took advantage of public sympathy by campaigning for suffrage in their prison clothes (Ford 2002).

Second-Wave Protests

Both branches of the contemporary women's rights movement, the radical liberation branch and the more moderate women's rights branch, engaged in protests, marches, and demonstrations to call attention to inequalities they believed women suffered in American society. In 1967, the New York chapter of the National Organization for Women picketed the *New York Times* to protest its sex segregation of advertisements for jobs. Dressed in old-fashioned costumes, NOW demonstrators protested the *New York Times* old-fashioned policies. Leaflets explaining the protest were distributed. The demonstration was featured on television news shows, and even the *New York Times* reported the story on an inside page, including a photograph.

In fall 1967, Shulamith Firestone and Pam Allen organized the New York Radical Women. The group's first public action took place during an antiwar demonstration in January 1968. The Radical Women, joined by 300 to 500 women from the Jeannette Rankin Brigade, a coalition of women's peace groups led by Jeannette Rankin, the 87-year-old former U.S. representative, staged "The Burial of Traditional Womanhood" in a torchlight parade at Arlington Cemetery.

In 1968 also, a group of women's rights activists organized a protest of the Miss America Pageant in Atlantic City, New Jersey. This protest was the first modern feminist activity to get front-page coverage in major newspapers. The purpose of the demonstration was to "protest the image of Miss America, an image that oppresses women in every area in which it purports to represent us." A "Freedom Trash Can" was set up into which protesters threw "bras, girdles, curlers, false eyelashes, wigs," and other such "woman's garbage," and a sheep was crowned Miss America, signifying that women "are appraised and judged like animals at a county fair." The protesters announced before the event that they would not speak to male reporters. They entered the hall where the pageant was being televised, unfurled a banner that read "Women's Liberation," and shouted "Freedom for Women" and "No More Miss America" before security guards ejected them.

In 1970, Betty Friedan, as president of NOW, called for a general strike on the fiftieth anniversary of the passage of the Nineteenth Amendment. Strike committees were set up in cities and towns across the country; most often these committees were local NOW chapters. The word "strike" was redefined from its usual meaning to one of "do your own thing" strikes to make it possible for some women to participate privately, in their own homes and offices, without having to take to the streets. Three central demands were drawn up—twenty-four-hour child-care centers, abortion on demand, and equal opportunity in employment and education.

As a prelude to Strike Day, New York NOW members, led by chapter president Ivy Bottini, organized a demonstration at the Statue of Liberty. They draped over a railing an enormous banner, which they had carried over to the island in sections. It read "Women of the World Unite!"

On Strike Day, women across the country, including some veterans of the suffrage movement, marched, picketed, protested, held teach-ins, staged rallies, presented guerrilla theater skits, and took the day off from work or housework. In addition, the mayors of some cities officially dedicated the day to women's equality. "Respectable housewives and 'hippie' students, secretaries and women lawyers marched together carrying signs that read 'Don't Cook Dinner—Starve a Rat Today!' 'Eve Was Framed,' 'End Human Sacrifice! Don't Get Married!' 'Washing Diapers Is Not Fulfilling'" (Deckard 1979, 359).

The sponsoring coalition called on "women all over the country" to boycott four products whose advertising was termed "offensive and/or insulting to women . . . and degrading to the image of women." The four products were Silva Thins, a brand of cigarette produced by the American Tobacco Company, a subsidiary of American Brands; Ivory Liquid, a detergent product of Procter and Gamble Manufacturing Company; Pristeen, a "feminine hygiene deodorant" made by Warner-Lambert Pharmaceutical Company; and *Cosmopolitan*, a magazine published by the Hearst Corporation (Charlton 1970a).

August 26, 1970, marked the largest demonstration for women's rights ever held until then. It was the first time the "potential power of the movement became publicly apparent" (Hole and Levine 1971, 92–3). In describing the day in the *New York Times,* journalist Linda Charlton (1970b) began her review stating, "They have marched down Fifth Avenue, they have at other times burned bras and written books and pressured Congressmen and made speeches. They are the

Women's Liberation Movement, and whatever that is, almost everyone's heard of it."

That same year, twenty NOW members led by Wilma Scott Heide and Jean Witter also disrupted U.S. Senate hearings on the vote for eighteen-year-olds, demanding hearings on the equal rights amendment. At a signal from Heide, the women rose and unfolded posters they had concealed in their purses. Committee Chair Birch Bayh later credited this demonstration with prompting the hearings on the ERA held later in the year.

NOW organized a 1969 Mother's Day demonstration at the White House for "Rights, Not Roses" as part of "Freedom for Women Week." Other demonstrations took place in Chicago, Albuquerque, and Los Angeles. In 1971, the New York NOW formed a "Baby Carriage Brigade" for a demonstration in support of Elizabeth Barrett, a widow who was fighting in the U.S. tax courts defending her right to deduct child-care expenses. Their slogan: "Are Children As Important As Martinis?"

In 1973, in a park across the street from the U.S. Supreme Court, NOW members, dressed in judicial robes, conducted a mock session of the Court. The skit dramatized what the Court would be like if it were composed exclusively of women interpreting the laws that applied to men's lives. In 1975, NOW sponsored the first "Take Back the Night" action and an "Alice Doesn't Day" women's strike.

Case Study: The Clarence Thomas Hearings

In July 1991, President George H. W. Bush nominated Clarence Thomas for a seat on the U.S. Supreme Court. Hearings on his nomination galvanized women's rights supporters in opposition. Initially, his appointment to the bench had been fought by women's rights groups that believed that he would provide the fifth and deciding vote to overrule *Roe v. Wade*, the abortion rights case that declared women's right to privacy included the right to have an abortion. Federal judicial nominees must be approved by the U.S. Senate. First the Senate's Judiciary Committee holds hearings and votes on a nominee. If the nominee is approved by the Judiciary Committee, the nominee's name is then sent to the full Senate for a vote. By October 6, 1991, the Senate Judiciary Committee had voted to forward Thomas's nomination to the full Senate. On that date, however, Nina Totenberg, of National Public Radio, announced that the committee had suppressed allegations of sexual harassment that University of

Oklahoma law professor Anita Hill had brought against Thomas. Thomas had employed Hill when he had chaired the Equal Employment Opportunity Commission (EEOC). On October 8, Democratic congresswomen marched from the House to the Senate to demand an investigation. The Senate gave in, and new hearings were called with Anita Hill as the primary witness.

Maureen Dowd of the *New York Times* (1991) captured the event:

> The group of seven women, all Democratic members of the House, marched purposefully up to the Capitol room where the Democratic senators were in their regular Tuesday caucus. They knocked on the door, hoping to give their colleagues in the room, all men except for Senator Barbara A. Mikulski of Maryland, "the woman's point of view," as Representative Louise Slaughter of upstate New York, put it. They wanted to state their case about why the vote on Judge Clarence Thomas should be delayed to give a thorough airing to Prof. Anita F. Hill's accusations of sexual harassment. But they were told they could not come in. "Nobody Ever Gets In." They knocked again. They were told again that they could not come in. They waited in the hall, looking chagrined and angry. Finally, an aide to Senator George J. Mitchell, the Senate majority leader, told the women that Mr. Mitchell would meet with them for a few moments in his office around the corner. "We were told that nobody ever gets in there," said a disgusted Representative Slaughter as she strode from the caucus room to Mr. Mitchell's office, adding sarcastically, "certainly not women from the House."
>
> "There's no monolithic way that women respond to this," she said. "But we are the people who write the laws of the land. Good Lord, she should have some recourse here." Mr. Mitchell told the women of the House to go back and lobby the thirteen Democratic Senators who favored the Thomas nomination, noting that if five or six of them said that they were no longer sure how they would vote the confirmation vote could be delayed.

Anita Hill was then allowed to testify. Her testimony before the Judiciary Committee was nationally televised. Many women around the nation sat quite stunned watching their televisions as the all-male and all-white Senate Judiciary Committee questioned African American Anita Hill for hours during this hearing. As white male senator after white male senator questioned law professor Anita Hill's veracity, mental stability, and morals, many white women around the country were outraged, while Black women struggled to cope with this public battle. It was clear to many women, regardless of race, that most of the members of the all-male Judiciary Committee "just didn't get it." Many women decided on the spot to run for public office; others decided to get involved in politics.

Emboldened by their ability to block an immediate Senate vote on Supreme Court nominee Clarence Thomas, women sought to seize the initiative on a host of other legislative issues, from family leave to expanded breast cancer research, and to launch a new push for sensitivity toward women in the workplace. "Things are really popping around here, and it is incredible," said Harriet Woods, executive director of the National Women's Political Caucus (NWPC). "There is an incredible wave of women who were initially furious but are now saying, 'Terrific'" (Frisby 1991). Hoping to tap into the resentment, the NWPC bought an advertisement in the *New York Times* on October 25 featuring a drawing of the Senate Judiciary Committee grilling Justice Thomas. In the caricature, all of the senators were women. Among other things, these hearings led to the "Year of the Woman" in American politics. The hearings also stirred around a hundred women in New York City to form the Women's Action Coalition (WAC), which soon spread to thirty-five other cities.

Case Study: Marches for Women's Lives

Marches have been a central organizing tactic for pro-choice groups regarding abortion rights. On most anniversaries of the *Roe v. Wade* decision (January 23), pro-choice and pro-life groups have clashed in front of the Supreme Court in Washington, D.C. In addition, on a number of occasions when it seemed the Supreme Court might overturn its decision in *Roe v Wade,* pro-choice groups have organized large marches in Washington. The largest marches occurred in 1989, 1992, and 2004. Pro-life groups have countermobilized at each of these events.

On April 9, 1989, NOW organized the first demonstration, called the March for Women's Equality/Women's Lives, which attracted approximately 300,000 people, according to U.S. National Park police estimates. As described in news media accounts, the abortion rights advocates, many wearing coat hangers around their necks and chanting "Never again," filled the capital and declared the birth of a "new political army" aimed at maintaining safe, legal abortion in the United States. Doctors marched in laboratory coats, young parents strolled with their babies, and college students who had never attended a rally gathered at the Ellipse, near the Washington Monument. Many wore white in the tradition of the suffragists early in the century who had fought for the right of women to vote. Organizers warned the marchers that those who favored legal abortion had fallen into complacency despite the growing antiabortion movement in recent years. Now, they said, the tables would be turned. "This is like the Boston Tea Party. We're in the same mood," said Molly Yard, president of NOW. "We won't accept the tyranny of men and the church." A three-foot-high replica of a coat hanger symbolized the crude self-abortion techniques used by women before 1973; an effigy of Chief Justice William H. Rehnquist, a dissenter in the *Roe* decision, was held up; and signs offered messages such as the one to President Bush that declared: "Bush, Get Out of My Bedroom."

Several hundred opponents of abortion held a counterdemonstration. As the abortion rights group began the march from the Ellipse up Constitution Avenue and past the Supreme Court, the abortion foes walked by, holding up signs saying, "The child killing must stop"; "Operation Rescue will prevail," a reference to the antiabortion movement that demonstrates outside abortion clinics; and "What about the Babies?" Toward the end of the route, marchers had to pass a makeshift graveyard labeled the "Cemetery of the Innocent," which abortion foes had erected at the foot of the Capitol. The cemetery contained 4,400 crosses to symbolize the number of abortions performed on an average day in the United States. Numerous foreign delegations took part in the march. Organizers said demonstrators marched outside U.S. embassies in several foreign capitals, including Ottawa, Paris, and London. Yvette Roudy, former minister for women's rights in the French government, told the crowd: "What happens here reverberates around the world. . . . International sisterhood is powerful. We shall overcome." Hundreds of groups cosponsored the march, including trade unions and religious organizations. Patricia Hussey and Barbara Ferraro, two former nuns from Massachusetts who had defied the church in 1984 by signing an abortion rights advertisement, were among a number of honored guests. Norma McCorvey, the woman who went by the pseudonym of Roe in the decision legalizing abortion, participated in the demonstration. "Our law's in jeopardy," she said, wearing a blue sweatshirt with the words "Roe v. Wade" and bearing a drawing of the Supreme Court. Then she shook and cried. In later years, McCorvey would become a strong opponent of abortion rights (Bronner 1989; Toner 1989).

A second, even larger, national rally took place on April 5, 1992: the March for Women's Lives. Approximately 750,000 women, men, and children turned out for this NOW-organized march in Washington, D.C. They massed behind a banner that declared, "We Won't Go Back! We Will Fight Back!" It has been called one of the largest marches and rallies ever held in the nation's capital to that time. In addition to the leadership and delegations from pro-choice organizations and hundreds of celebrities, thousands of students from six hundred campuses across the country participated, with the aim of impressing lawmakers and the public with their political influence. On April 22, 1992, the Court was to hear arguments on a Pennsylvania law that sought to limit access to abortion through a variety of regulations, including a twenty-four-hour waiting period and a requirement that women seeking abortions notify their husbands. Many people on both sides saw the case as a potential vehicle for overturning *Roe v. Wade,* the 1973 Supreme Court decision establishing a nationwide right to abortion.

The march was about twice the size of the abortion rights demonstration that had filled the Mall three years previously. In planning the march, Patricia Ireland, president of NOW, stated, "We have a very, very serious threat against abortion and reproductive rights," estimating that 44 million women in the United States had already lost their abortion rights or had seen them seriously restricted, including poor women, rural women, and women in the military or living on American Indian reservations. "Women can no longer count on the Supreme Court's recognition of the fundamental, constitutional right to abortion," she said. "We have to deliver a clear message to the Supreme Court, to the Bush administration and to Congress: The women of this country won't go back. We will fight back."

The marchers came from across the country. They included mothers and daughters, Hollywood stars, teachers, preachers, and doctors, Republicans for Choice, Catholics for Choice, and two presidential candidates, Bill Clinton and Jerry Brown, according to media accounts. As in the March for Women's Equality/Women's Lives, most of the marchers wore white, the color favored by suffragists and their successors in the women's rights movement. The crowd carried signs such as "We Won't Go Back" and "I Have a Uterus and I Vote." One woman marched with two infants in a stroller bearing a sign that said, "In Vitro Babies for Choice." They invoked the names of Carol Moseley Braun of Illinois and Representative Barbara Boxer of California, strong proponents of abortion rights who were running for the U.S. Senate that year in an election in which women were seen as prominent players. The three women in the singing group Betty suggested that marchers passing the White House yell, "We're feminist, we're fierce, and we vote." Some demonstrators also tossed tennis balls on the White House lawn bearing the message, "Are you ready to be a mother?" Antiabortion groups held counterdemonstrations on the Mall shouting "Shame" and held up signs of aborted fetuses along the parade route. Others set up a graveyard of 2,200 crosses representing aborted fetuses on the Mall below the Washington Monument.

In July, after the Supreme Court handed down its ruling in *Pennsylvania v. Casey*, NOW kicked off a nonviolent campaign of civil disobedience. At an illegal speak-out in front of the White House protesting the U.S. Supreme Court decision, NOW president Patricia Ireland, Feminist Majority president Eleanor Smeal, Urvashi Vaid of the National Gay and Lesbian Task Force, Kay Ostberg of the Human Rights Campaign Fund, Ruby Sayes of Women of All Colors, Jane Pennington of the Older Women's League, and Aida Bound of the Women's International League for Peace and Freedom were arrested for demonstrating without a permit. Meanwhile, several hundred abortion rights demonstrators cheered them on. Ireland had said beforehand that the protest was civil disobedience "in the tradition of Margaret Sanger, arrested for distributing birth control, Susan B. Anthony, arrested for voting, and Rosa Parks, arrested for refusing to give up her seat in the front of the bus." All seven demonstrators, who had arranged with the police for their arrests, were later released in their own recognizance.

Once again, on April 25, 2004, a Women's March for Lives, centering on the issue of abortion rights, was organized in the national's capital. The march was sponsored by NARAL Pro-Choice America, the American Civil Liberties Union, the Feminist Majority, the National Organization for Women, the National Latina Institute for Reproductive Health, and the Black Women's Health Imperative; more than 1,300 health and activist groups nationwide endorsed the Women's March for Lives. The National Association for the Advancement of Colored People, which had never publicly supported a pro-choice rally, signed on as an endorser. Originally the demonstration was to be called the March for Choice, but that was not a title that resonated with many people of color. So it was changed to be the March to Save Women's Lives, and then the March for Women's Lives, which was the issue for poor and minority women. Advocating the change, Eleanor Smeal, president of the Feminist Majority, stated: "We've cracked something huge—I can feel it. The civil rights movement will be there, students from colleges and high schools will be there, women of color will be there. The environmental movement is coming—the Sierra Club has endorsed the march for the first time. We have more celebrities than I've seen before. We just have much more depth in so many communities."

Silvia Henriquez, executive director of the National Latina Institute for Reproductive Health and member of the steering committee, predicted that the focus on reproductive rights as part of a broader context would attract substantial numbers of Hispanic women: "Hispanics are the fastest-growing ethnicity in the country, and in the next twenty years millions of Latinas are going to be looking to raise their families in safe, healthy environments with full access to education and healthcare," she said, adding, "it's not that Latinas don't support abortion, or don't care about that issue. They do—but they tend to think of reproductive rights as part of their overall human rights and those of their families."

The SisterSong Women of Color Reproductive Health Collective in Atlanta planned to be prominent at the march. It had asked anyone who wanted to walk with its delegation in the march to wear red, yellow, and orange. The group had made sure to invite the many unseen organizations and advocates who have historically fought for reproductive justice in communities of color, as well as dozens of organizations from the antipoverty and antiracist movements, and those who work on HIV/AIDS, environmental justice, immigrants' rights, violence against women, and criminal justice issues. Bringing new faces to the march, women-of-color advocates hoped to create more awareness of the ways women of color and white women could differ in their definition of reproductive justice.

Although focused on defending a woman's right to choose from any further restrictions, organizers also rallied demonstrators around several issues: justice and equality for women in all socioeconomic strata around the world; access for all women to the full range of contraceptive services and family planning options; the need for better health services for women of all races, incomes, and ages; and the effect of the federal government's foreign aid policies on women worldwide.

Counterdemonstrators focused on the rally's pro-choice identity and theme. On the Saturday preceding the march, members of the Florida-based Operation Witness protested at Washington-area abortion clinics such as Planned Parenthood Federation of America, Greater Washington Health Center, and Washington Surgi-Center. On Sunday, Operation Witness members created "an ocean" of anti-choice signs and banners along eight blocks of the route to protest what they call the "Death March." Meanwhile, members of the National Silent No More Awareness Campaign, with offices in the Northeast, held signs reading "I Regret My Abortion" and "I Regret Lost Fatherhood."

According to reports, approximately 800,000 people filled the Mall and marched from the Washington Monument down Pennsylvania Avenue to the White House and then to the U.S. Capitol building. They were led by Gloria Steinem, Representative and Minority Whip Nancy Pelosi, U.S. Senator and former first lady Hillary Rodham Clinton, actresses Whoopi Goldberg, Kathleen Turner, and Cybill Shepherd, and former secretary of state Madeleine Albright. The march included activists from fifty nations. The Republican Pro-Choice Coalition drew 500 representatives from twelve states. In an act of what participants called civil disobedience, a group of approximately fifteen physicians stood near the beginning of the march dispensing prescriptions to those who asked for morning-after pills (see news media accounts: Gibson 2004, Stuever 2004, Toner 2004a, 2004b).

Peace Activism

Peace activism has been the focus of much of the political activism of women's groups. The history of women's special relationship to peace advocacy in the United States goes back to the nineteenth century. Julia Ward Howe, author of the "Battle Hymn of the Republic," appealed to mothers of the world in 1870 to unite across national boundaries "to prevent the war of human life which they alone bear and know the cost" (Swerdlow 1993, 28). She organized a Mothers' Peace Day, which was celebrated in 1873 in several U.S. cities. Women's clubs, benevolent societies, and social-reform groups from the late-nineteenth century until World War I promoted world peace. Women, they believed, would play a decisive role in ending war because world peace could be achieved only if men behaved more like women. In 1891 the National Council of Women conducted a petition drive calling on the U.S. government to avoid war with Chile. Women's groups also issued a call for arbitration during the Venezuelan border controversy with England in 1895. They pressured President William McKinley to reject war with Spain in 1898 and opposed the annexation of the Philippines on moral and political grounds. A women's peace campaign was waged in support of the 1899 Hague conference on international disarmament and arbitration. To bolster support for the Hague conference, women initiated a Peace Day that was celebrated nationally and continued as a national day for years.

The Women's Peace Party was established in 1915 to oppose the war in Europe, begun in 1914. The women founded this separatist peace organization because the male pacifists with whom they were working would not make any effort to stop the war. The head of the suffragist movement, Carrie Chapman Catt, said, "When the great war came and the women waited for the pacifists to move, and they heard nothing from them, they decided all too late to get together themselves and try to do something at this eleventh hour" (Swerdlow 1993, 30).

Case Study: Women Strike for Peace

On November 1, 1961, an estimated fifty thousand women walked out of their kitchens and off their jobs, in an unprecedented nationwide strike for peace after Russia had set off a number of atom bomb tests. Banning nuclear testing was the dominant theme of this strike. The women demanded that their local officials pressure President John Kennedy, on behalf of all children, to end nuclear testing at once and begin negotiations for nuclear disarmament. Many women pushed baby carriages, holding aloft placards that read "Save the Children," "Testing Damages the Unborn," and "Let's Live in Peace Not Pieces" in protest marches in cities around the country. They marched in front of the White House. They sent letters to Jacqueline Kennedy, wife of the president, and to Nina Khrushchev, wife of Nikita Khrushchev, leader of the Soviet Union. The women wanted to show that they were angry with the leadership of both countries. They were responding to the Women Strike for Peace (WSP) call, announced on September 22, to women across the nation, urging them to suspend their regular routine of home, family, and jobs for one day, in order to "Appeal to All Governments to End the Arms Race—Not the Human Race." The organizational call declared: "We strike against death, desolation, destruction and on behalf of life and liberty. . . . Husbands or babysitters take over the home front. Bosses or substitutes take over our jobs!" (Swerdlow 1993). The strike turned into a movement working for nuclear disarmament and protesting the Vietnam War. The movement lasted until 1973.

The WSP used noninstitutional means of getting its point across, as exemplified by the group's "unladylike" bestowal of raspberries upon members of the House Un-American Activities Committee at a hearing investigating the movement in December 1962. At this meeting the group also conducted a "procession of gardenias, carnations and roses" (*New York Times Observer,* December 15, 1962). On Easter that same year, New York members had paraded with brilliantly colored paper daisies to distinguish themselves in the annual Easter Day Parade down Fifth Avenue. They were described by a *New York Times* reporter in the following manner: "To judge by the participants in the New York areas, Women Strike for Peace is a heterogeneous group that cuts across barriers of age, economics, education, race and religion. Most of the women are mothers, others are grandmothers, and some, it would be fair to say, present the more formidable appearance of mothers-in-law" (Molli 1962).

In 1967, WSP activists joined with former congresswoman Jeannette Rankin, who was then eighty-six years old, to organize a new women's antiwar coalition called the Jeannette Rankin Brigade. In May 1967, she had a addressed a meeting of women peace protesters in Atlanta, Georgia, declaring that it was unconscionable that ten thousand "American boys" had already died in Vietnam and proposed that if ten thousand women were willing to raise their voices against the war and were sufficiently committed to the task to go to jail, they could bring war to an end, "because you can't have war without women." Those who took up her challenge decided not to engage in civil disobedience but rather to march on Congress, and to meet the crisis in America, they would convene their own Congress of American Women, which would develop programs to "express the political power, reason, and conscience of America." "This Is Woman Power," their publicity declared. On January 15, 1968, the opening day of the Ninetieth Congress, five thousand women from across the country, most of them clad in black, walked silently through fresh snow to the foot of Capitol Hill, led by former congresswoman Rankin. A law passed in 1946 forbade them from entering the Capitol, but a small delegation headed by Rankin was permitted to present the petition to the Speaker of the House and the majority leader of the Senate. Judy Collins led the women in song. The petition began, "We, United States women of all races, political, religious faiths have gathered together to petition Congress for a redress of intolerable grievance, exercising herein our fundamental right under the first amendment to Peaceably Assemble and to Petition the Government."

The petition went on to demand that the pledge Franklin Delano Roosevelt made during World War II, that women would sit on all the committees and commissions "to win the peace," become an immediate reality (Swerdlow 1993, 138–39). Adherents of the women's liberation movement initially were attracted to the Jeannette Rankin Brigade but ended up dismissing it because they viewed it as protesting in the name of wives, mothers, or sisters instead of as citizens. The women's liberation and peace movements clashed over the tactics, strategy, and philosophy.

In 1970, the WSP issued the "Declaration of liberation from military domination of our lives and the lives of our families by the warmakers in the Pentagon and their spokesmen in Congress and the White House." They demanded "the birthright that our forefathers pledged to all Americans in 1776. We women declare our liberation from military domination which deprives us and our loved ones of life, liberty and the pursuit of happiness" (Swerdlow, 1993, 141).

In April 1972 approximately one hundred women conducted a "die-in" at the headquarters of International Telephone and Telegraph (ITT), the maker of Wonder Bread as well as military equipment for the bombing of Cambodia. Later that year WSP women staged a sit-in outside congressional offices, demanding that Congress cut off funding for the war. In June, two thousand women formed a human ring around the Congress demanding an end to the war (Swerdlow 1993, 142).

Case Study: The Million Mom March

On Mother's Day 2000, hundreds of thousands of women marched to the U.S. Capitol in Washington to demand strict gun control legislation in what was billed as the "Million Mom March." The organizers of the Million Mom March hoped to draw mothers, stepmothers, grandmothers, godmothers, and "honorary mothers" to the Capitol on Mother's Day weekend to call upon Congress to enact what they called "commonsense gun control legislation." The organizers said that more than 700,000 people participated in the Washington rally; other rallies occurred in cities across the country.

The Million Mom March was the brainchild of Donna Dees-Thomases, a part-time publicist for CBS, the sister-in-law of Susan Thomases, a close friend of First Lady Hillary Clinton, and a New Jersey mother, who said her maternal instincts kicked in after the shooting the previous August at a Jewish Community Center in Los Angeles. The march supported an array of gun legislation, notably registration for all handguns and licensing of all handgun owners.

Many of the women came to the march through their churches or synagogues, or heard about the march on television or on the Internet. The organizers said there were 5 million hits on the Million Mom March Web site in the six days before the march.

President Clinton greeted some of the marchers at the White House that morning, urging them to keep fighting. "Don't be deterred by the intimidation, don't be deterred by the screaming, don't be deterred by the political mountain you have to climb," he said. "You just remember this: There are more people who think like you in America."

Longtime advocates for gun control urged them to make themselves felt on Election Day. "You are the future now," said Sarah Brady of Handgun Control Inc., who became an activist on gun control after her husband, James S. Brady, a former White House press secretary, was seriously injured in the assassination attempt on President Ronald Reagan. "We must either change the minds of lawmakers on these issues or, for God's sake, this November let's change the lawmakers."

In Los Angeles, politicians read the names of children killed by guns in Los Angeles County in 1999. Ann Rice Lane, chairwoman of Women Against Gun Violence, which was the program's host, said: "Today is an event. Tomorrow the work begins." And in Chicago, amid protests from counterdemonstrators shouting "Ban the gangs, not the guns," women gathered at Grant Park. Obrellia Smith, fifty years old, said, "I hope we will send a message to the legislators that they have to do something about this gun epidemic or they will lose their seats. We're losing too many babies" (Toner 2000).

In 2001, however, unable to sustain its momentum, the Million Mom March merged with the Brady Campaign and Brady Center to Prevent Gun Violence. It did sponsor a second march on Mother's Day in 2004, drawing approximately 2,500 to the Mall in Washington. The aim in 2004 was to win extension of the assault rifle ban. The event served as a kickoff for the organization's national campaign to extend the gun ban. The leaders of the march boarded a twenty-six-foot-long pink recreational vehicle, announcing their intention to sponsor similar demonstrations in the subsequent four months in cities nationwide.

Organized in opposition to the Million Mom March's advocacy of gun control is the Second Amendment Sisters, Inc. As the name suggests, the group promotes the right of people to own guns. Members believe that guns protect people and that a woman who owns a gun is equalized when it comes to crime and victimization. The group's mission is to preserve "the basic human right to self-defense, as recognized by the Second Amendment." Members "believe in personal responsibility, education, and enforcement of laws against violent criminals" (www.2asisters.org). On Mother's Day 2004, approximately a hundred members organized a counterdemonstration to the 2004 Million Mom March in Washington. The demonstration was billed as the Second Amendment Freedom for Everyone Rally (SAFER).

Case Study: CODEPINK

"Bush Says Code Red, We Say Code Pink!" CODEPINK describes itself as a woman-initiated grassroots peace and social justice movement that seeks positive social change through proactive, creative protest and nonviolent direct action. Its name is a play on the Bush administration's development of color-coded security alerts in the aftermath of the September 11, 2001, terrorist attacks on the World Trade Center in New York, the Pentagon, and the airplane hijackings. CODEPINK initiated a Women's Peace Vigil in front of the White House on November 17, 2002. Journalist Rachel Smolkin (2003) described the vigil, "From 9 AM to 5 PM, the fiery and pale pinks clash with the stately people's house, demanding the eye's attention: pink berets and pink jackets, pink mittens and pink scarves, pink turtlenecks and, most of all, pink peace buttons."

The vigil was maintained until March 8, 2003, International Women's Day. Several thousand women and men ended the vigil with a march on Washington. Other CODEPINK antiwar activities have included sending a delegation of fifteen women to Iraq to meet with Iraqi women and presenting "pink slips" to people in leadership positions who, according to CODEPINK, are not doing their job of representing the people. The targeted leaders are presented with pink slips (women's lingerie), demanding they do their jobs or the people will fire them. CODEPINK's tactics have included disruption of a press conference held by Charlotte Beers, a public relations expert hired by the State Department to promote support for the war on terrorism, especially in Islamic countries. In the middle of the event CODEPINK activists unfurled a pink banner that read "Charlotte, Stop Selling War." First Lady Laura Bush was targeted in New York City on Martin Luther King Day with signs urging her to "Tell George Not to Go to War." Local CODEPINK chapters have been formed around the country.

References

Bernikow, Louise. 2004. "March 3, 1913: Suffragists Assaulted in Nation's Capital." *http://www.womensenews.org,* February 29.

Bronner, Ethan. 1989. "Throngs Rally in D.C. to Keep Abortion Legal; 'Political army' Vows Action." *Boston Globe,* April 10.

Charlton, Linda. 1970a. "Women Seeking Equality, March on 5th Ave. Today." *New York Times,* August 26.

———. 1970b. "The Feminine Protest." *New York Times,* August 28.

Deckard, Barbara Sinclair. 1979. *The Women's Movement: Political, Socioeconomic, and Psychological Issues.* New York: Harper and Row.

Dowd, Maureen. 1991. "Seven Congresswomen March to Senate to Demand Delay in Thomas Vote." *New York Times,* October 8.

Flexner, Eleanor. 1974. *Century of Struggle: The Women's Rights Movement in the United States.* New York: Atheneum.

Ford, Lynn. 2002. *Women and Politics: The Pursuit of Equality.* Boston: Houghton Mifflin Company.

Frisby, Michael K. 1991. "Women Bring Their Issues to the Fore: the Thomas Nomination." *Boston Globe,* October 10.

Gibson, Gail. 2004. "Thousands Rally for Abortion Rights: March for Women's Lives in D.C. Protest Limits on Reproductive Freedom." *Baltimore Sun Times,* April 26.

Hole, Judith, and Ellen Levine. 1971. *Rebirth of Feminism.* New York: Quadrangle Books, Inc.

Molli, Jeane. 1962. "Women's Peace Group Uses Feminine Tactics." *New York Times,* April 19, 26.

Smolkin, Rachel. 2003. "A Vigil in Pink: Outside the Gates of the White House, Women Stage a Daily Protest for Peace." *Chicago Tribune,* February 5.

Stuever, Hank. 2004. "Body Politics: Today's Feminist, It Turns Out, Looks Like a Lot of People—Maybe a Million." *Washington Post,* April 26.

Swerdlow, Amy. 1993. *Women Strike for Peace: Traditional Motherhood and Radical Politics in the 1960s.* Chicago: University of Chicago Press.

Toner, Robin. 1989. "Right to Abortion Draws Thousands to Capital Rally." *New York Times,* April 10.

———. 2000. "Mothers Rally to Assail Gun Violence." *New York Times,* May 15.

———. 2004a. "A Call to Arms by Abortion Rights Groups." *New York Times,* April 22.

———. 2004b. "Rights Marchers Vow to Fight Another Bush Term." *New York Times,* April 26.

3
Women's Movements and Organizations

More than forty years passed between the time the first women's rights' movement culminated in the passage of the Nineteenth Amendment to the Constitution, granting women the right to vote, and the initiation of what has variously become known as the feminist movement, the second women's rights movement, or the contemporary women's liberation movement. This movement for women's rights, which emerged in the 1960s, became a major political, social, and economic phenomenon of the latter decades of the twentieth century, manifesting itself in a wide variety of groups, styles, and organizations and having a significant impact on the political involvement of women.

This movement for women's rights emerged out of many changes in women's lives. Over time, sociopolitical conditions and technological innovations had transformed the role of women as mothers and homemakers. The technological innovations included advances in medical science, especially contraception, which lowered birthrates and consequently the time devoted to raising children. Additionally, labor-saving devices freed women from housework, so that they had more time to perform other tasks. In the two decades from 1950 to 1970, female labor-force participation almost doubled, reaching 40 percent by the end of the 1960s. These trends and others helped reinforce an environment of changing lifestyles, later marriage, more-frequent divorce, greater sexual freedom, and the changed (if not diminished) role of the family, providing a favorable context for the resurgence of feminism. Women's contributions to the war effort in World War II also had a lasting legacy.

In 1963, Betty Friedan created a stir with the publication of *The Feminine Mystique*, in which she exposed "the problem that had no name." "The problem lay buried," she wrote, "unspoken, for many years in the minds of American women. It was a strange stirring, a sense of dissatisfaction, a yearning that women suffered in the middle of the twentieth century in the United States." The book described the psychological costs to overeducated women being consigned to the role of homemaker and mother. She debunked the myth that women, particularly housewives, were totally fulfilled by marriage and motherhood. Friedan argued that the American home had become a "comfortable concentration camp" for women, which led to "unhappiness and discontent" and said it was time for women "to stop giving lip service to the idea that there are no battles left to be fought for women in America."

Her work struck a chord with many middle-class women, becoming an immediate best seller. In addition, participation in the civil rights movement and antiwar protests led younger women into the feminist movement. Existing organizations of women also served as catalysts for efforts to promote greater equality for women.

Suffrage and the National Woman's Party

The National Woman's Party (NWP) grew out of the Congressional Union (CU), which was founded in 1913 as an auxiliary of the National American Woman Suffrage Association (NAWSA), with a focus on the passage of a federal suffrage amendment. The NAWSA had been taking a state-by-state approach to gaining the vote for women, a tactic with which the members of the CU had grown impatient. CU members engaged in militant actions that offended some of the more conservative members of NAWSA. In their efforts to obtain a national suffrage amendment, CU members chained themselves to fences, picketed the White House, engaged in hunger strikes in prison, and burned President Woodrow Wilson in effigy. The two groups split in 1914, and the CU changed its name to the NWP in 1916. Throughout the party's history, NWP membership consisted primarily of middle-class business and professional women.

After the suffrage for women was won in 1920, the NWP headed by Alice Paul, minimized the value of that victory. In 1921 Paul declared, "Women today . . . are still in every way subordinate to men before the law, in the professions, in the church, in industry, and in the home." Rejecting the plea of other women's groups to build a reform coalition on behalf of disarmament, birth control, and social-welfare legislation, the NWP pledged itself to work exclusively for the goal of total equality for women. Its members reasoned that any expenditure of energy on issues extraneous to women's rights would only impede progress toward their primary objective. American women were still enslaved, these feminists believed, and nothing less than complete dedication to having equal rights codified in the Constitution could bring about their emancipation (Chafe 1972, 114). In the 1920s, the NWP pursued three avenues toward this goal. It initiated the equal rights amendment (ERA); championed the equal rights treaty, its international equivalent; and promoted the equal nationality treaty, which dealt in a more limited way with citizenship rights. In the decades that followed, its single-minded dedication to seeing an ERA enacted into the Constitution caused the NWP to clash repeatedly with progressive reformers who fought for protective legislation for women workers. In 1940, the NWP succeeded in getting the Republican Party to endorse an ERA in its platform, and the Democrats followed suit in 1944. It remained in the party platforms until 1980, when the Republicans removed it.

The NWP played a central role in the women's rights movement, such as it was in the post-1945 period. A small, exclusive single-issue group, hardly popular even within the women's rights movement, it brought together individuals and groups interested in the ERA and other issues of concern to women, issued information on the status of the ERA, attracted publicity, and, perhaps more important, provided a continuous feminist presence through these years. The NWP mainly lobbied Congress and coordinated letter-writing campaigns to win support for the ERA from politicians and women's organizations (Rupp and Taylor 1987, 24). Year after year, the party worked to have the ERA introduced in Congress, questioned candidates on their position on the amendment, built a list of congressional sponsors, fought to keep the ERA in national party platforms, lobbied senators and representatives, sought the endorsements of other organizations, pressured appropriate subcommittees and full committees, and lobbied—always, until 1972, to no avail, but always without losing hope. "Our work is confined entirely to obtaining the passage of the Equal Rights Amendment," the leaders stated. The NWP continued to be composed largely of white, middle- or upper-class, well-educated, and older women.

In the years leading up to the second women's rights movement, the NWP played a role in the women's rights movement disproportionate to its size or even its political effectiveness. It managed this in part because it established a reputation as a feminist organization with a militant past at a time when other women's organizations were disassociating themselves from feminism, and in part because it simply persevered in a "very one track" way (Rupp and Taylor 1987, 43). It was the only organization during the years between the passage of the Nineteenth Amendment and the creation of the National Organization for Women (NOW) in 1966 that explicitly identified itself as feminist (Ryan 1992).

Other women's groups did grow in their influence during the time period immediately preceding the emergence of the second women's rights movement on national and state governments to adopt policies in a wide array of issue areas including traditional women's concerns such as child-labor legislation as well as broader civic concerns such as environmental conservation. The League of Women Voters (LWV), for example, tripled its membership between 1945 and 1969. In the mid-1950s, the General Federation of Women's Clubs boasted a membership of 826,000 and over 15,000 local clubs across the nation (Mathews 2001).

The League of Women Voters

The 1919 convention of the NAWSA created the LWV. Carrie Chapman Catt, the president of the NAWSA, felt that women should take their votes and become active in the political parties. Jane Addams, however, urged women to work in more nonpartisan efforts reforming their communities. She believed party membership was not as important as social reconstruction. The LWV was closer to Addams's vision. It adopted a mission of the education of women for citizenship, training them to assume a full share of governing and party membership, reforming the electorate, and promoting a more just society (Lemons 1975). The league coordinated the formation of the Women's Joint Congressional Committee (WJCC) in 1920 to work on legislative initiatives.

The league joined with other women's organizations in the 1970s to campaign for passage of the ERA as we have seen. In recent years, it has sponsored presidential debates and worked for campaign-finance reform as well as continuing to educate potential voters and conduct programs to get people registered to vote.

The Women's Bureau

Congress established the U.S. Department of Labor Women's Bureau in 1920 as an outgrowth of women's work during World War I. The mandate of the Women's Bureau at its creation was to assist states in setting workplace standards and policies to "promote the welfare of wage-earning women, improve their working conditions, increase their efficiency, and advance their opportunities for profitable employment." The Women's Bureau was not given the power to enforce laws, but it was to gather data on labor legislation passed and share this information among the states. It would provide information on these laws and on how to file a complaint, and initiate model programs to benefit women workers. The bureau also conducted investigations into the working conditions of women in various occupations in different states and assisted states that lacked the resources to conduct such investigations (Martin 2003, 52).

In the 1920s, for example, it carried out at least six studies challenging the idea that women worked only for "pin money," showing rather that they were contributors to families' basic income. The bureau found that approximately 90 percent of employed women worked outside the home because of economic need and used their income for support of themselves and their dependents; one out of every four women was the principal wage earner for her family. The majority of female wage earners came from immigrant and Black families (Chafe 1972). The Women's Bureau was a leader in promoting and maintaining protective legislation for women workers. Thus, for many years it strongly opposed an equal rights amendment to the Constitution and engaged in political conflict with the NWP. The bureau worked to have women included in the Fair Labor Standards Act of 1938. That act for the first time set minimum wages and maximum working hours for workers in general.

Over the course of its existence, the Women's Bureau has carried out numerous studies documenting the status of women in the workforce. The bureau promotes itself as the only federal agency mandated to represent the needs of wage-earning women in the public-policy process.

The Mission Statement of the Women's Bureau in 1999 stated:

> Central to its mission is the responsibility to advocate and inform women directly and the public as well, of women's rights and employment issues.
>
> To ensure that the voices of working women are heard, and their priorities represented in the public policy arena, the Women's Bureau:
>
> Alerts women about their rights in the workplace
>
> Proposes policies and legislation that benefit working women
>
> Researches and analyzes information about women and work
>
> Makes appropriate reports on its findings

In 2004 the Women's Bureau stated its mission as being "to promote profitable employment opportunities for women, to empower them by enhancing their skills and improving their working conditions, and to provide employers with more alternatives to meet their labor needs."

The vision of the Women's Bureau is to empower women to enhance their potential for securing more satisfying employment as they seek to balance their work and home-life needs. Its initiatives at the beginning of the twenty-first century included "Women and Technology," "Strengthening the Family," and "E-Government Initiatives." Its "Girls E-Mentoring in Science, Engineering, and Technology" program linked young women with women mentors in these fields. A similar program was undertaken in the nursing field. Other programs involved entrepreneurships for women with disabilities; the NEW project, for nontraditional employment for women; and an employee-driven older women worker project.

The Second Wave: Equal Rights under the Law

The contemporary women's rights movement had two origins, from two different strata of society, with two different styles, orientations, values, and forms of organization. In many ways there were two separate movements often referred to as the younger and the older branches or the more radical branch and the more moderate branch (Freeman 1975, 49).

The younger, more radical branch primarily emerged from young women's involvement in the civil rights and anti–Vietnam War movements in the 1960s. Extensive use of sit-ins, marches, and other unconventional tactics by pressure groups, as well as the tendency to question traditional authority, power relations, economic arrangements, and social values were distinctive in the politics of the 1960s. Most prominent among protest groups of the time were Blacks and youths who challenged establishment politics and expanded the scope of political conflict and negotiation from the halls of government to the streets. Women helped to shape these protests, and they in turn saw their lives reshaped by their involvement in the Black freedom struggle, the Chicano movement, welfare rights activism, student protests, and movements against the Vietnam War.

In the early 1960s, many women working in the civil rights movement, a significant number of whom were college students or recent graduates, began to sense that men in these organizations failed to value their contributions and treated them as second-class citizens. Although the rhetoric of these movements espoused equality, women were relegated to subordinate roles within them. The women came to see their position as analogous to that of the Blacks for whom they were seeking expanded rights. In the article "To the Women of the Left" they asked: "What is the role of women in the organization and in the movement and how would that relate to our concerns about democracy? Realizing that this is a social problem of national significance not at all confined to our struggle for personal liberation within the Movement, we must approach it in a political manner. Therefore it is incumbent on us, as women, to organize a movement for women liberation" (Evans 1979, 193).

At a 1965 meeting of Students for a Democratic Society (SDS), for example, "catcalls, storms of ridicule, and verbal abuse" were hurled at women who broached the women's issue. When a women's rights plank was introduced at the next annual SDS meeting, its sponsors "were pelted with tomatoes and thrown out of the convention" (Deckard 1979, 327). A similar situation occurred the next year at the national Conference for a New Politics. When two women—former civil rights activists Jo Freeman and Shulamith Firestone—took to the podium to demand that the convention address issues of sexism, they were patted on the head and told to "calm down a little." The conference then decided not to deal with these women's "trivial complaints." Freeman left to found a radical women's group in Chicago; Firestone did the same in New York City. Subsequently, often without knowledge of what was happening in other areas of the country, women began to hold meetings in cities across the United States. During 1967 and 1968 groups formed spontaneously and independently in five different cities—Chicago, Toronto, Detroit, Seattle, and Gainesville, Florida. They formed groups including the Feminists, New York Radical Women, the Chicago Women's Liberation Union, the Furies, and the Women's International Terrorist Conspiracy from Hell (WITCH) (Ferree and Hess 1994).

This new idea of women's liberation was spread mainly through the existing groups and the communications network of the student movement and counterculture. SDS women and those from other New Left groups, in particular, were well suited to the task of organizing the women's groups that were springing up in many parts of the country. This experience "radicalized" some women and led them to organize a variety of newer groups—women's liberation groups—that stressed, along with other concerns, consciousness-raising, reflecting the shared experiences and discrimination women suffered. These groups provided the opportunity to spread the idea that the problems they experienced were not the result of individual failures or situations but instead had roots in the dominant culture and were therefore common to all women.

During the 1960s and 1970s, radical feminists created alternative institutions such as battered-women's shelters, rape crisis centers, feminist health centers, and feminist bookstores. Many feminist activists began to question the validity of existing societal practices. Such women formed the core of the more radical segment of the women's movement, which emphasized nonhierarchical, democratic, virtually leaderless (anti-)structures.

Although the composition of both branches of the women's movement was predominantly white, middle-class, and college-educated, the median age of the activists of the initial movement was middle-aged (Freeman 1975). The women who came from the older branch were trained in and had used traditional forms of political action such as lobbying public officials and seeking positions within government. Their activism emerged in the public sector in networks of mainstream women's organizations such as the LWV, the National Federation of Business and Professional Women's Clubs (BPW), the National Council of Negro Women, and the American Association of University Women (AAUW), as well as almost one hundred different organizations and caucuses of professional women. Their style of organization is traditionally formal, with elected officers, boards of directors, bylaws, and the other trappings of democratic procedure. All started as top-down organizations lacking a mass base. Only NOW and the National Women's Political Caucus (NWPC) subsequently developed a mass base, though not all wanted to.

The most prominent and pervasive organization of the older branch of the women's movement is NOW, but it also encompasses such groups as the NWPC, Federally Employed Women (FEW), and the self-defined "right-wing" of the movement, the Women's Equity Action League (WEAL). Although the programs and aims of the older branch span a wide spectrum, their activities have tended to be concentrated on legal and economic problems.

The vanguard of feminist reform included WEAL (founded in 1968) and the National Abortion Rights Action League (NARAL) (created in 1973 through a reorientation of an earlier group)—both leadership groups that eventually developed mailing-list membership of modest size. WEAL was founded by women who had left NOW over the issue of abortion. It was active in cases of sex discrimination in higher education and in the ERA campaign. It established a tax-exempt arm, the WEAL Fund, to support lawsuits and to monitor implementation and enforcement focusing primarily on Title IX and academic discrimination. FEW was founded in 1968 for the purpose of pressuring the Civil Service Commission to enforce the executive order banning sex discrimination in federal employment.

In 1961, President John Kennedy had selected Esther Peterson to head the Labor Department's Women's Bureau. She was the only woman he appointed to a high-level position when he entered office, much to the dismay of women party members. At Peterson's urging, President Kennedy established the President's Commission on the Status of Women in December 1961. The commission was created in part seemingly to repay the many other women who had worked in his campaign. It has also been speculated that Kennedy saw the commission as a way of finessing or sidetracking the ERA, which he opposed. The amendment has been included in the platforms of both major parties in every election since 1944. But the major labor unions, which were an important base of President Kennedy's support, opposed its enactment.

Acting as the first official body to make a thorough study of women in the United States, the commission documented women's second-class status. Its report, *American Woman,* was made public in October

1963. The report included recommendations in seven areas: education and counseling, home and community, women in employment, labor standards, security of basic income, women under the law, and women as citizens. To further the proposed objectives in the report, the commission called for an executive order designating a cabinet officer to be responsible for implementing the commission's recommendations; that an interdepartmental committee be formed to "assure proper coordination and action"; and that a citizens' committee be established to serve as an advisory unit to the interdepartmental committee. Primarily, the report called for women to be encouraged to run for public office, for the enhancement of continuing education efforts for women, and an increase in child-care services for families at all economic levels. The report called for equal opportunity for women in hiring, training, and promotion in the workforce and the encouragement of more part-time employment opportunities. The Fair Labor Standards Act, enacted in the Roosevelt administration, needed to be extended to include more types of work and to bring more jobs under minimum wage standards, the report argued. The states were encouraged to establish the principle of equal pay for comparable work and paid maternity leave. The report called for laws to be scrutinized regarding the ways in which they discriminated against women.

The most concrete response to the activity of the president's commission was the eventual establishment of fifty state commissions and citizens' advisory councils to do similar research on a state level. The activity of the federal and state commissions laid the groundwork for the future women's rights movement in three significant ways: (1) it brought together many knowledgeable, politically active women who otherwise would not have worked together on matters of direct concern to women; (2) the investigations unearthed ample evidence of women's unequal status, especially their legal and economic difficulties, and in the process convinced many previously uninterested women that something should be done; (3) the report created a climate of expectations that something would be done.

In 1963, Congress also passed and President Kennedy signed into law the Equal Pay Act (EPA). At the time of passage of the EPA women earned merely fifty-eight cents to every dollar earned by men. This law was the first piece of federal legislation prohibiting discrimination on the basis of sex. The law amended the Fair Labor Standards Act of 1938 to require that men and women receive equal pay for equal work performed under equal conditions; a drive to obtain such legislation had begun during World War I. The act was passed as an alternative to an equal rights amendment. "Opponents of the ERA had long argued that the proper legislative route was 'specific bills for specific ills,' not blanket prohibitions" (Freeman 1990, 464). The language of the law prohibited paying women less than men. It did not prohibit paying men less than women. In this sense it could be viewed as a form of sex-specific protective legislation for women. This law by itself might not be particularly helpful to women to gain employment opportunities, as businesses would have little incentive to hire women if they had to pay them the same wages as men. More was needed. Discrimination in employment had to be deemed illegal. This happened with the passage of the Civil Rights Act of 1964.

The Equal Pay Movement

In 2002, the median annual earnings of women fifteen and older were $30,203, compared to $39,429 for their male counterparts. Women working full-time earned only about seventy-seven cents for every dollar earned by men, though more than in 1963, when the EPA was passed. This discrepancy has led members of Congress to introduce the paycheck fairness bill. The provisions of the act are aimed at updating and strengthening the EPA. They would toughen the remedy provisions of the EPA by allowing prevailing plaintiffs to recover compensatory and punitive damages. Gender-based wage discrimination would be put on an equal footing with wage discrimination based on race or ethnicity, for which full compensatory and punitive damages are already available.

The National Committee on Pay Equity (NCPE) has been organizing an annual Equal Pay Day that symbolically marks the point in a new year that woman would have to work to earn the wages paid to a man in the previous calendar year. Thus, in 2004, Equal Pay Day fell on April 20, meaning that women would have to work an extra three months and twenty days to have wages equal to what men had earned by December 31 of the previous year. The NCPE was founded in 1979 as a national membership coalition working to eliminate sex- and race-based wage discrimination and to achieve pay equity. Its membership includes labor unions; women's and civil rights organizations; religious, professional, educational, and legal associations;

commissions on women; state and local pay equity coalitions; and individuals.

Title VII of the Civil Rights Act (1964)

The Civil Rights Act of 1964 is one of the most substantive pieces of legislation enacted in the area of civil rights in contemporary times. It outlaws discrimination in voter registration and public accommodations, and Title VII of the act bars employment discrimination. The act was aimed at racial discrimination, but Title VII included a ban on sex discrimination in employment. Most interpretations of the process by which Title VII came to include sex-based as well as race-based discrimination emphasize the fact that the civil rights bill's opponents hoped to divide its supporters by adding an amendment to include sex discrimination in an attempt to ridicule and defeat the Civil Rights Act. As it made its way through the House of Representatives, Title VII did not include sex as a prohibited basis for discrimination in employment. Representative Howard Smith (D-VA), chairman of the powerful Rules Committee, who opposed the bill, added sex to the language of the bill as a tactic to defeat it. (The NWP had lobbied Representative Smith to include sex in this section of the bill, wanting white women have the same redress regarding job discrimination as Black women would have in the bill.) The aim of this tactic among southern conservatives, observers believed, was to bring so much controversy to the bill as to kill it entirely. However, Congresswoman Martha Griffiths (D-MI), a women's rights activist, had planned to introduce the amendment herself. Thus, although many liberal members of the House opposed the amendment, believing it would kill the bill, Representative Griffiths got all but one of the other congresswomen to support it and, in a curious coalition with southern members of the House, managed to pass the amendment and keep it in the bill. The amendment banning employment discrimination based on sex and the entire bill including it were passed and enacted into law.

When the law went into effect in July 1965, it became illegal to discriminate against women in hiring and promotions. But this section of the law was not taken seriously and not rigorously enforced. The Equal Employment Opportunity Commission (EEOC), the federal agency charged with eliminating discrimination in employment under Title VII, considered the sex provision, in the words of its director, "a fluke . . . conceived out of wedlock." Newspapers at that time often advertised job openings under "Help Wanted Male" and "Help Wanted Female" headings. Sex-segregated help-wanted advertisements became a central point of contention for women's rights activists in their battle to get the EEOC to deal seriously with the sex discrimination provision of the law.

> Segregated Help Wanted Ads, *New York Times,* 1964
> Schrafft's
>
> | Help Wanted—Female | Help Wanted—Male |
> |---|---|
> | GAL FRIDAYS | FOOD BACTERIOLOGIST/ |
> | TYPIST CLERK | CHEMIST |
> | FIGURE CLERK | Exp'd or Assoc. degree. |
> | STENO TYPIST | Good Salary |
> | Excellent oppty for gals with good skills generous company benefits including free lunches | |

The lack of seriousness with which the EEOC took the sex discrimination section of Title VII of the Civil Rights Act was a catalyst that led to the founding of NOW. NOW became the major women's rights organization of the second wave of feminism. The EEOC's lackadaisical attitude led to the recognition that an organization was needed to speak on behalf of women in the way civil rights groups had done for Blacks, an "NAACP for women." Only that kind of pressure, supporters felt, would force the EEOC and the government to take sex discrimination as seriously as race discrimination (Hole and Levine 1971, 82). The third annual meeting of the National Conference of State Commissions on the Status of Women, which opened in Washington on June 28 of 1965, provided an opportunity to create such an organization. This meeting, held under the sponsorship of the Citizens' Advisory Council and the Interdepartmental Committee on the Status of Women, brought together a large number of concerned women. An informal meeting of some of them to discuss the possibility of an independent women's group produced no results. Some of the state commissioners present felt that such an organization was not necessary, that it would be better to work through the official bodies already established. But when Kathryn Clarenbach, head of the Wisconsin commission, found that the conference was not allowed to pass resolutions or take action and, thus, that she could not introduce a resolution against the EEOC's position on want ads, it became clear to her and to many others that working through the state commissions would not be sufficient. Many of the people involved in these organizations, dissatisfied with the lack of progress made on their recommendations, joined with Betty Friedan in 1966 to found NOW.

The National Organization for Women (1966)

With 300 charter members, male and female, NOW announced its incorporation at a press conference in Washington, D.C., on October 29, 1966. The stated purpose of NOW was "to take action to bring women into full participation in the mainstream of American society *now*, exercising all the privileges and responsibilities thereof in truly equal partnership with men." Betty Friedan was elected its first president. In 1967, NOW adopted a Bill of Rights calling for:

1. An equal rights constitutional amendment
2. Enforcement of laws banning sex-based employment discrimination
3. Maternity-leave rights in employment
4. Tax deductions for child-care expenses for working parents
5. Child-care centers
6. Equal and unsegregated education
7. Equal job training opportunities and allowances for women in poverty
8. The right of women to control their reproductive lives

Two of these planks—the ERA and abortion rights—engendered major controversies and were adopted only after bitter debate. Women from the United Auto Workers objected to the inclusion of the ERA plank because their union still officially opposed it. Their secretarial services to the organization were withdrawn when this plank was passed. Passage of the abortion plank led to a walkout. Opponents argued that abortion was not a women's rights issue and that taking such a controversial position would destroy the organization's effectiveness.

In the years immediately following its founding, NOW became involved in a wide variety of feminist activities. In December 1967 it organized what was perhaps the first national demonstration on women's rights issues since the suffrage campaign, when it set up picket lines at EEOC offices in cities across the country. The following February, NOW filed formal suit against the EEOC "to force it to comply with is own governmental rules [i.e., Title VII]." NOW members picketed the *New York Times* to protest its sex-segregated want-ad policy. A questionnaire regarding women's rights issues was drawn up and presented to the major presidential candidates in the 1968 election. At the hearings in 1970 regarding the qualifications of Supreme Court nominee G. Harold Carswell, Betty Friedan testified against his being appointed to the Court because of his "antiwoman" position in a 1969 court case. NOW also filed formal charges of sex discrimination against the nation's 1,300 largest corporations. Its members testified at federal and local hearings on sex discrimination in education, employment, welfare payments, and public accommodations, and they disrupted a Senate committee hearing, demanding that hearings on the ERA be held (Deckard 1979). NOW took the lead in calling for and organizing a Women's Strike for Equality Day on August 26, 1970. This event was held to mark the fiftieth anniversary of women's suffrage and greatly contributed to the women's rights movement becoming a recognized national phenomenon.

NOW spent the early 1970s developing a grassroots organization. Its "guiding principles incorporated a commitment to remaining on the vanguard of the women's movement, to be an activist, rather than an educational group, to maintaining political independence from governmental institutions, to focusing on a diverse set of issues and tactics and to encouraging grassroots participation" (Barasko, forthcoming). Regional divisions were created, and several regional directors, as well as many local chapter officials, spent countless hours recruiting people into NOW and encouraging the formation of new chapters. NOW also attempted to form liaisons with the younger branch of the movement.

As NOW's membership expanded, the organization became more heterogeneous. Feeling the need for some national organization, many radical women joined NOW while still maintaining their roles in local autonomous groups. The logic of feminist analysis radicalized some NOW members. They began to see that major structural changes were required to make true equality possible. At the 1975 NOW convention, the brewing conflict between such women and the more conservative members came to a head. One group, which called itself the Majority Caucus, advocated a greater emphasis on improving the quality of life for masses of women through work-site organizing of women in stereotypic jobs; recognizing the bond linking oppression based on sex, race, sexual preference, poverty, and ethnic background; and struggling against all these types of oppression simultaneously. It called for greater recruitment of minority women and more militant tactics. Some opposition came from women who considered the caucus's program ideologically uncongenial, and some came from women who believed that because of the backlash, NOW should adopt a more moderate program, even though they themselves agreed with the Majority Caucus position. The caucus, led by Karen DeCrow, won a close but decisive victory. Considerable bitterness resulted from the conflict, and at first a lasting split within NOW seemed imminent. That this did not occur indicates that much of the opposition was based upon tactical rather than ideological considerations. At its 1977 national convention NOW was once again united. Ratification of the ERA was adopted as the top priority.

After 1975 NOW turned more to partisan and electoral engagement as a significant part of its action repertoire. Within NOW, the growing focus on electoral politics was not uncontested. At the 1982 national convention, Judy Goldsmith, the candidate for the presidency of NOW nominated by members committed to pursuing a pragmatic electoral strategy, only narrowly defeated a candidate advocating a return to more radical positions and unconventional political tactics. With Goldsmith's victory, however, the organization was poised to become more directly involved in the 1984 election campaign. For the first time, NOW became explicitly involved in the Democratic Party's nomination race, as NOW's Political Action Committee formally endorsed Walter Mondale's candidacy for the party's nomination.

Defeat of the Mondale-Ferraro ticket in 1984 forced a reevaluation of NOW's relationship with the Democratic Party. Claiming that Judy Goldsmith had turned NOW into a wing of the Democratic Party during her presidency, and promising a return to more radical tactics, Eleanor Smeal contested and won the organization's presidency in 1985. A central issue in this contested election was whether the equal rights amendment should be revived as a central organizing tactic. Smeal saw it, along with demonstrations and marches, as a way to infuse new life into the organization rather than focusing on electoral activities.

At its 1987 conference, a New York faction, the Progressive Action Caucus, ran against a Smeal-picked slate, United Feminist Action Campaign (UFAC). Molly Yard, the political director of NOW and a former labor activist, ran for president on the UFAC slate with the slogan the "Feminization of Power." This call symbolized a change from earlier references to women's economic powerlessness found in the slogan the "feminization of poverty." The call now was for women to take power by running for office. During the ERA campaign in the late 1970s, supporters had worn buttons saying fifty-nine cents, signifying the gap in earnings between women and men (women made only fifty-nine cents for every dollar a man earned). Similarly, the new symbol became a 5 percent button representing the percent of legislators in Congress who were women (Ryan 1992, 143).

But from 1980 on, electoral and partisan politics became an increasingly central component of the political strategy of the American women's movement. An extensive network of organizations and political action committees (PACs) emerged, with the common purpose of electing more women. Moreover, feminist organizations continued to engage with the presidential parties, particularly the Democrats, in an effort to further their policy agenda. Membership in NOW declined at both national and chapter levels after ratification of the ERA failed in 1982. At the national level NOW became a professionally structured organization that lobbied for legislation, supported candidates for elected office, and operated as a pressure group within the Democratic Party (Whittier 1995).

Hispanic Women's Movements

Other organizations were founded to support the interests of minority women, including the National Conference of Puerto Rican Women and the Mexican-American Women's Association. Chicana feminists have criticized what they considered to be exclusionary practices within feminist movements. "Chicana feminists have joined the voices of other feminist women of color in criticizing the movement's limited attention to differences among women on the basis of race, ethnicity, class, and sexual orientation. Chicana feminists are critical of any feminist analysis that treats race/ethnicity as a secondary source of oppression. Chicana feminist voices call for a reformulation of feminist theory and practice in order to establish a more inclusive framework for analyzing the experiences of all women and for bringing about meaningful political change" (García 1989, 230).

In the 1960s, a Chicana feminist movement that addressed the specific issues affecting Chicanas as women of color in the United States began to develop. Through their political organizations, activities, and writings, Chicana feminists assessed their participation in the larger Chicano social protest movement. In the same way that Chicano males were analyzing their unequal status in U.S. society,

Chicanas examined the forces shaping their own life circumstances as women.

Collectively, U.S. Latinas at various historical periods have been active in organizations focusing on different issues, at both grassroots and professional levels. As a largely working-class population, Latinas have shown their activism in labor union, education, health, and housing advocacy groups, voter-registration campaigns, and in combating violence against women and the civil rights abuses of some of the authoritarian regimes in their countries of origin. They also played major roles in the democratization processes in countries such as Chile, Brazil, Argentina, Guatemala, and El Salvador during the 1970s and 1980s, and in supporting political refugees from these countries seeking sanctuary in the United States (Acosta-Belen and Bose 2003).

As in other feminist movements, activity within the Chicana community was facilitated by the rise of a feminist press. The publication of Chicana feminist newspapers and newsletters provided a basis for the development of a feminist communication network for Chicanas. In 1971 in the first issue of the Chicana newspaper *Hijas de Cuauhtemoc* (Daughters of Cuauhtemoc), Anna Nieto Gomez called for the elimination of sexism in Chicano families, communities, and in the male-dominated Chicano movement. Similarly, Bernice Rincon, another voice of Chicana feminism, argued in her magazine-newsletter, *Regeneracion,* that Chicanas could no longer be relegated to a subservient status. Chicanas needed to have access to key leadership positions. Enriqueta Longeaux y Vasquez, founder of the New Mexico–based Chicana newspaper *El Grito,* wrote numerous articles calling on Chicanas to challenge sexism within their communities and racism in the larger society. Her articles addressed a variety of issues facing Chicanas. She examined the woman's role in the family, her experiences with discrimination in education and the workplace, her economic circumstances, and the development of survival strategies. Other publications that raised consciousness among Chicanas included *Encuentro Femenil, La Comadre,* and *Hembra.*

By the 1980s a small group of Chicanas had entered colleges and universities and started to produce research studies on Chicanas. A direct connection exists between the development of Chicana feminist thought and the rise of Chicana studies as an academic field. By emphasizing the interconnectedness of race, class, and gender, this scholarship has challenged many of the assumptions inherent in both ethnic studies and women's studies.

Chicana feminists have organized numerous regional and national conferences to address their concerns. The First National Hispanic Feminist Conference, which attracted a thousand Hispanic and non-Hispanic feminists, was held in 1980. These meetings were designed to draw attention to the most pressing needs of Chicanas, such as welfare rights, reproductive rights, health care, poverty, immigration, and education. Chicana feminist groups placed demands on many national Chicano organizations. As early as 1972 a group of Chicanas exerted pressure on the leaders of the National Chicano Political Conference, meeting in San Jose, California, in order to have their needs addressed by the entire organization. Similarly, in 1982 a Chicana feminist group organized by students from the University of California at Berkeley called for the National Association for Chicano Studies (NACS) to address feminist concerns. In 1984 women in NACS formed a Chicana caucus within the organization and succeeded in changing the theme for the national conference to "Voces de la Mujer" (Voices of Women) (García 1989).

The National Women's Political Caucus

The NWPC, founded in 1971 by Congresswoman Bella Abzug, Betty Friedan, and Gloria Steinem, has aimed at working more directly in the electoral area to increase the number of women and feminists in elective office, whereas NOW would continue to focus on expanding women's rights. The idea behind the organization was that women from the two major political parties, combined with feminists not identified with a party, could create an outside force that would move both parties to give women and women's issues more attention and significance in the political arena. The caucus would "help elect women and also men who declare themselves ready to fight for the needs and rights of women and all underrepresented groups." Its statement of purpose pledged to oppose sexism, racism, institutional violence, and poverty through the election and appointment of women to political office; the reform of political party structures to give women an equal voice in decision making and the selection of candidates; and the support of women's issues and feminist candidates across party lines. It pledged to work in coalition with other oppressed groups. The caucus developed specific Democratic and Republican Party task forces.

Within the overall goal of forming a feminist organization focused on electoral and partisan politics, NWPC founders disagreed on strategy. Betty Friedan envisioned an organization that would encompass women "representing all political elements," one that would extend beyond the membership of NOW or women's liberation groups to reach politically active women who had not yet identified themselves as feminists. She saw an organization that would unite women in caucuses within and across political lines to elect women and focus attention on women's issues. Bella Abzug and Gloria Steinem, in contrast, aimed to organize a coalition of the "outs"—the poor, Blacks, youth, women, and gays. They believed the organization's primary objective should be to build a political movement of women for social change that would simultaneously help elect more women, minorities, and other underrepresented groups, and build an electoral bloc strong enough to influence male politicians to support their programs. Friedan would work to elect women with a broader range of ideological perspectives than Abzug and Steinem (Young 2000). That tension between supporting a woman candidate over a profeminist male candidate has been a long-standing one with the caucus. There have been occasions when NWPC has endorsed one candidate and NOW has endorsed another in the same race.

The caucus was instrumental in getting the Democratic Party in 1972 and later years to change its nomination procedures to mandate equal representation of men and women among its national convention delegates. Although not mandating equal representation, the Republican Party also instituted measures to encourage greater representation of women among its convention delegates. Beyond influencing the leadership structure and internal processes of the major political parties and working to elect women's rights supporters to public office, the NWPC has led efforts to expand the number of women being appointed to high-ranking, policy-making federal jobs. After every presidential election, it has convened the Coalition for Women's Appointments, composed of representatives from more than seventy women's and public-interest groups, to identify qualified female candidates, collect and send their resumes to the White House, and then lobby for their appointment (O'Connor 1999).

Women-of-Color Organizations

Public opinion polls have shown that Black women have been the most supportive of feminist ideology and equal rights ideas. For example, the 1972 Virginia Slims American Women's Opinion Poll showed that support for efforts to strengthen or change women's status in society was highest among Black women, 62 percent of whom favored such efforts, compared to an overall support of 48 percent.

But minority women have faced not only gender concerns in seeking equality but also race and class issues. Women of color have seen the leadership of contemporary women's rights movement as being predominantly white, middle-class women with seemingly narrower concerns than those of minority women. Black feminists' priorities, for example, differed from those of the white feminists. A minimum wage for domestics and safeguarding the rights and improving the position of welfare mothers have been the major goals of Black feminists (Deckard 1979, 345).

Black women's participation in the civil rights movement during the 1950s and 1960s had been crucial for its success, although few women were recognized for their leadership. Frustrated with male dominance in the civil rights and Black nationalist movements, Black women have felt that they had to choose—they could either become feminists or support their brothers. They had to decide whether their basic identity was racial or sexual. But ideological tendencies within parts of the Black movement eventually led many Black women to decide that a Black feminist movement was necessary. Black women found that too many Black men were blaming them for their situation. Black matriarchy and the "castration" of the Black male by the Black female became accepted tenets of "revolutionary" rhetoric. Black men were telling Black women to take a subordinate position so as to build up the damaged Black male ego. In effect, women were being told that the Black liberation movement could succeed only at their expense (Deckard 1979, 344).

The National Black Feminist Organization

Many Black women felt that neither the white women's movement nor the male-dominated Black movement addressed some of their basic concerns. A Black woman's organization was the obvious solution, but because women feared that such a group would be considered divisive, it was not until 1973 that a national group was formed. In August 1973, thirty African American women, all of whom had been active in the women's movement, formed the National Black Feminist Organization (NBFO). It was the first national Black women's organization that was explicitly feminist and dedicated to eliminating the dual oppression of racism and sexism. Approximately thirty African American women had held an all-day gathering in May of that year, using the donated offices of the New York chapter of NOW. These women had a diverse set of politics, and they met with no specific agenda other than to bond, honor, and recognize one another, and to share histories. Participants who called themselves feminists decided to organize a conference to reach out to other Black feminists. The conference organizers agreed upon the need to speak out to declare that (1) there was indeed a Black feminist politics; (2) racism and sexism needed to be addressed by the Black community and the larger women's movement; and (3) there was a need for an organization to address those issues, led by those who were victimized by those dual oppressions. The group's membership grew to more than a thousand by the end of 1973. Four hundred women attended its first convention.

In November 1973, in New York City, the first Eastern Regional Conference on Black Feminism was held, drawing more than five hundred African American women from across the country. Many journalists and activists took special note of the diversity of participants at the conference: they included Black women from all walks of life, from lawyers to domestic workers, welfare rights organizers to polished elected officials.

Later, chapters of the NBFO were founded in numerous major U.S. cities. The NBFO became an active part of feminist coalitions in New York City, confronting media stereotypes, fighting for minimum wage for domestic workers, raising consciousness about rape and sexual abuse, and working with political candidates who supported NBFO issues. The NBFO's emphasis continued to be on combating sexist and racist discrimination against Black women and struggling for greater involvement in the political process. By 1977 independent chapters of the NBFO were continuing to work on local and regional issues, but the national structure had dissolved.

The Combahee River Collective

In 1974, the lesbian community within the Black women's movement had come to believe that the NBFO had abandoned the movement's initial goals. Partly in response to the NBFO's shortcomings, and partly in response to a series of unsolved murders of African American women in Boston during the early 1970s, a group of Black feminists in Massachusetts formed the Combahee River Collective (CRC) in 1974. The group split from the NBFO and developed a radically different political philosophy. The CRC was more radical and less mainstream than the NBFO in its anticapitalist position and its explicit concern about class and homophobia. For the CRC, Black women could not be completely liberated until racism and homophobia were annihilated, and unless capitalism was replaced by socialism. Equality with men under the current economic arrangements was not enough, they argued.

The CRC took its name from the South Carolina river that was the site of a military action led by Harriet Tubman that freed hundreds of slaves. The CRC described itself as "a Black feminist group in Boston whose name came from the guerrilla action conceptualized and led by Harriet Tubman on June 2, 1863, in the Port Royal region of South Carolina. This action freed more than 750 slaves and is the only military campaign in American history planned and led by a woman." The CRC was founded to work on African American women's issues, including violence against women, racism, sexism, heterosexism, and reproductive rights. The Combahee collective was a small core group that met for six years, reading, writing, and organizing in Boston. They were at the forefront of articulating the parameters of Black feminism (Breines 2002).

Black feminists' autonomous organizing began to influence strongly other parts of the women's movement in the 1980s. Black feminists challenged white feminists to eradicate racism, to broaden the scope of what they defined as women's issues, to integrate their organizations, and to share leadership with women of color. In 1991, a grassroots effort, African American Women in Defense of Ourselves, gathered more than sixteen hundred signatures for a widely circulated ad in response to the Anita Hill–Clarence Thomas hearings. In 1995, amid controversy, Black feminists spoke out about the patriarchal assumptions of the male-only Million Man March. However contested, Black feminism, rooted in the struggles of generations of Black women, continues to play a vital role in the sociopolitical life of the United States.

The National Women's Conference (1977)

In 1972, the United Nations declared 1975 International Women's Year and an International Women's Year Conference was held in

Mexico City. As part of the year, President Gerald Ford appointed a Commission on the Observance of International Women's Year, with thirty-nine members, to gather statistics, make recommendations, and participate as delegates in the conference. Stimulated by this international effort, Congresswomen Bella Abzug and Patsy Mink introduced a proposal for a public, government-funded conference in every state and territory that would identify issues and elect delegates to a U.S. National Women's Conference. "As a kind of Constitutional Convention for women and a remedy for the founding fathers who had excluded all women from the first one, this national elected body would then recommend to Congress and the president those changes in laws, government procedures, and the Constitution itself that would remove barriers to women's equality" (Steinem 1986, 166). Congress appropriated $5 million to fund the conference.

To determine the focus of the national meeting and to select delegates to it, women first convened a series of open "town meetings" in each state and territory of the United States. Some of these meetings involved as many as 10,000 to 20,000 women and were the biggest political meetings ever held in their states. In some of the state meetings conservative women vied with feminists to become delegates to the national meeting. But feminists prevailed in most of the state meetings, and the resolutions passed were strongly feminist. The 1,442 delegates chosen to go to Houston were a diverse group—17.4 percent were Black, 8.3 percent Hispanic, and almost 10 percent were members of other minority groups.

The National Plan of Action adopted at the conference included twenty-five planks. The planks are listed in the Documents section. To understand the evolution of the contemporary women's rights movement, it is instructive to consider these planks alongside the report of the President's Commission on the Status of Women in 1963 with its seven recommendations. The National Plan of Action was much broader in the areas it covered and also was able to respond to a host of laws that had been added to the books that the earlier commissioners did not have reference to.

The 1963 report, for example, in its Education and Counseling plank, had stated that "the education of girls and women for their responsibilities in home and community should be thoroughly reexamined with a view to discovering more effective approaches." The Education Resolution in the 1977 report called for the "vigorous and expeditious enforcement of all laws prohibiting discrimination at all levels of education," leadership programs for women employed in postsecondary schools to be upgraded and expanded, and action to be taken to remove race and sex stereotyping in state school systems.

The Campaign for the Equal Rights Amendment (1970s to 1980s)

Ratification of the ERA became the primary goal of the contemporary women's rights movement in the 1970s and early 1980s. The ERA to the Constitution had been first proposed in 1923. Its text read: "Men and women shall have equal rights throughout the United States and in every place subject to its jurisdiction. Congress shall have power to enforce this article by appropriate legislation."

In the years between the ratification of the Nineteenth Amendment and the founding of NOW, the proposed equal rights amendment greatly divided women's organizations. Social reformers opposed the amendment. They had worked hard to get special protection laws enacted for the benefit of women and children and believed that an equal rights amendment would make these protective laws unconstitutional and hurt rather than help women. They wanted to help women in the positions they were then in. Beginning in the late nineteenth century, protective legislation had established maximum hours, minimum wage laws, and working conditions for women. Initial protective legislation had attempted to curb sweatshop conditions and the mistreatment of both male and female workers. But the Supreme Court declared them a violation of the right to contract. Progressives and feminists then joined together in the 1880s to help women workers only. States enacted two types of protective labor laws: One type prohibited women from being employed in certain occupations considered dangerous to their health or morality or unsuitable to their primary role as mothers; the second type regulated work conditions for women. Women, for example, could not be employed in mining jobs and jobs related to alcoholic beverages. They were also kept from being lawyers. Protective labor legislation restricted the number of hours women could work and the amount of weight they could lift, and occasionally required special benefits such as rest periods. Night work was sometimes prohibited.

As opposed to protective legislation affecting all workers, protective laws for women survived the test of constitutionality in 1908. In

Mueller v. Oregon, the Supreme Court upheld an Oregon law that restricted the employment of women in factories, laundries, or other "mechanical establishments" to ten hours a day on the grounds that women's "physical structure and a proper discharge of her maternal functions—having in view not merely their own health but the well-being of the race—justify legislation to protect her" (Freeman 1990, 458–59).

At issue in the debate over an equal rights amendment was whether women would fare better in society if they had the same legal rights and responsibilities as men or whether their biological and social differences from males required laws tailored to meet their special needs. This philosophical disagreement split women's groups into two often-warring camps around the issue of adoption of an equal rights amendment after women had obtained the vote. Pro-amendment forces, led by the NWP, argued that if women were equal under the U.S. Constitution, they would have the greatest opportunity for individual achievement and full participation in all aspects of American life. An equal rights amendment would eliminate laws that assigned individuals to separate categories simply on the basis of gender. Women could no longer be barred from such occupations as bartending and police work or forced to resign from jobs if they married or became pregnant. A males-only military draft would probably become unconstitutional under an equal rights amendment, as would Social Security benefits that paid more to men than women.

Antiamendment groups accused amendment supporters of a lack of realism about the conditions most women experienced. They argued that women desperately needed the protective laws that were already on the books. Women would be worse off if their right to be supported by their husbands were taken away, or if maximum hours, lifting limitations, and other labor laws that safeguarded the health and safety of working women became unconstitutional, they reasoned. They accused the NWP of being insensitive to the needs of women. The NWP countered that protective labor legislation hurt women workers by protecting them out of higher-paying jobs. Passage in 1964 of the Civil Rights Act effectively removed protective legislation from the controversy over the ERA when it banned discrimination on the basis of sex in employment.

To become part of the Constitution, the ERA needed to pass both houses of Congress with a two-thirds vote in each body and be ratified by three-fourths of the states (thirty-eight states). In 1971, the House of Representatives voted 354 to 23 to adopt the ERA. Then on

March 22, 1972, the ERA passed the Senate on an 84 to 8 vote. Within forty-eight hours of congressional passage, six states ratified the ERA, and by the end of 1972, it had been ratified in twenty-two states (Steiner 1985). (Not all state legislatures were in session in 1972.) Ten years later, the proposed amendment died, three states short of the thirty-eight needed to ratify it. But during those ten years women's groups undertook national and state campaigns to obtain ratification. Initially, Congress allowed for seven years for ratification, but in 1978, in a controversial move it voted to extend the deadline for ratification until 1982.

Janet Boles (1982) has suggested that the campaign for ratification involved three phases. In phase 1, which covered 1972–1977, advocates engaged in legislative lobbying, presenting research and giving testimony at hearings. They also undertook letter-writing and telegram campaigns, public education, and election activities, such as contributing time or money to a pro-ERA candidate's campaign. NOW, the LWV, and the BPW "participated on a roughly equal basis during these years. State groups were reactive and were created or mobilized only in response to anti-ERA activity. While pro-ERA groups were able to defeat some state legislators who opposed ratification, only five states ratified the ERA after 1973" (Boles 1982, 573).

By 1977, Boles reports that 70 percent of Americans were living in states that had ratified the amendment. ERA supporters in these states were urged to "adopt" one or another of the unratifying states by providing financial and tactical assistance; however, this effort met with little success. In 1977, NOW initiated phase 2 by adopting different tactics, which marked its ascendancy as the leading proponent of the ERA. NOW's rise to the forefront was triggered by the adoption of two campaigns. First, NOW called for an economic boycott of states where ratification had not yet occurred. Generally, this boycott took the form of having large national associations cancel or threaten to cancel conventions scheduled in cities in unratifying states. By late 1977, more than forty-five organizations—ranging from the American Association of Law Librarians to the American Home Economics Association—had joined the boycott, and cities such as Chicago, Atlanta, and St. Louis were losing millions as a result. The state of Missouri sued NOW, but in 1979 the convention boycott was ruled a legitimate political tool. By mid-1980, almost two hundred organizations had joined the boycott.

Given the impending deadline for ratification—March 1979—a resolution to extend the ratification deadline an additional seven years was introduced in Congress at the urging of numerous women's groups. Two California law students who were members of NOW first suggested this precedent-setting strategy. In addition, these groups, as suffragists had done before, sponsored a march on Washington, D.C., that attracted more than 100,000 participants. Many dressed in white as suffragists had done long before in their quest for the Nineteenth Amendment. These well-planned efforts ultimately led Congress, over the strong objections of amendment opponents, to approve a thirty-nine-month extension period for ratification. During this phase, NOW shifted its focus to a national campaign instead of one centered on the legislatures in unratifying states.

Phase 3 began in 1980 when NOW committed itself to full implementation. At its October national conference NOW pledged a total mobilization for the ERA and agreed to increase the size, diversity, and range of its ratification campaign. The funds it raised for the ERA campaign dramatically increased to nearly $1 million in 1981. During this final period, Boles reports, groups supporting the ERA utilized almost all conceivable tactics. Conventional lobbying techniques through state coalitions continued, several national groups were formed, more research was presented on the anticipated impact of a federal ERA and of the states with their own ERAs, and national political action committees raised money to elect pro-ERA candidates to state legislatures. The LWV in 1980 formed the National Business Council for ERA, composed of 155 corporate leaders who personally lobbied and spoke for the ERA in unratifying states.

In addition, new strategies were devised: mass gatherings in all states, which often brought together supporters from all over the country; campus tours to urge students to take a leave of absence to work for the ERA; door-to-door canvassing by NOW "ERA missionaries" in states that had not yet ratified the amendment; and an increasing reliance on personal appearances by pro-ERA entertainers to capture media and public attention. The LWV, NOW, and the BPW each sponsored media projects. Though most ads ran primarily in unratified states, NOW aired a series of commercials on national television.

ERAmerica was formed as a national alliance of more than two hundred organizations that supported the ERA. These groups included the American Bar Association, the Girl Scouts, and the National Council of Senior Citizens, with NOW playing a key leadership role. The AFL-CIO labor union joined, as did the BPW, the General

Federation of Women's Clubs, the LWV, and a number of religious organizations.

ERA supporters pursued a variety of strategies. In the electoral arena they attempted to replace opponents with supporters. Legislators who had declared themselves supporters and had won with movement backing but then voted against the ERA came under attack, and a number were defeated. NOW and other women's groups urged organizations not to hold conventions in unratified states.

According to public opinion polls, the public supported passage of the ERA during the years of the ratification campaign. In 1974, nearly three-quarters of Americans favored the ERA (74 percent) versus just over one-fifth who opposed it (21 percent). When the ratification period ended in 1982, 62 percent favored it, whereas 23 percent opposed it (Daniels, Darcy, and Westphal 1982).

One might wonder why groups opposed the ERA and how they successfully defeated its ratification. The main groups that actively opposed the ERA were the Eagle Forum, founded in 1972 by Phyllis Schlafly, and Concerned Women for America (CWA), founded in 1979 by Beverly LaHaye. CWA developed a national network of anti-ERA prayer chains that weekly sought God's direct intervention. Stop-ERA, a Schlafly spin-off from the Eagle Forum, was dedicated specifically to the antiratification campaign in the states. Anti-ERA groups were organized on the principle of protecting what was perceived as traditional family values. They charged that the feminist agenda deliberately degraded homemakers and that unwilling mothers might even be forced to become employed. They argued that the amendment would mean that private schools would have to be coed; all sports, including contact sports, would be coed; and rest rooms and prisons would be desegregated. All persons would pay the same income tax regardless of their income; there would be government-funded abortions and homosexual schoolteachers, and women would be forced into combat, they argued (McGlen and O'Connor 1995).

Seventeen states have equal rights clauses or amendments. They are of three types: (1) two states, Utah and Wyoming, have clauses in their original constitutions that give women the right to vote and equal legal rights; (2) nine states have amendments to their constitutions similar to the proposed federal amendment; (3) in the other six states, constitutional amendments contain language that resembles the Equal Protection Clause of the Fourteenth Amendment. Between 1977 and 1990, no state adopted an ERA, and voters rejected such amendments in Florida (1978), Iowa (1980), Maine (1984), and Vermont (1986) (Stetson 1991).

Concerned Women for America

Concerned Women for America (CWA) is a public-policy women's organization that brings biblical principles into all levels of public policy. It focuses on six core issues that, according it its Web site (www.cwfa.org), the organization has determined need "biblical principles most and where we can have the greatest impact." The six core issues are definition of family, sanctity of life, education, pornography, religious liberty, and national sovereignty. The mission of the CWA is "to protect and promote biblical values among all citizens—first through prayer, then education, and finally by influencing our society—thereby reversing the decline in moral values in our nation." The vision of the CWA is for women and like-minded men from all walks of life to come together and restore the family to its traditional purpose and thereby allow each member of the family to realize his or her God-given potential and be a more responsible citizen.

CWA is the largest Christian Right organization targeted at women. It has a monthly newsletter, "Family Voice," with 200,000 subscribers, and a syndicated radio show, *Beverly LaHaye Live.* Women are encouraged to lobby from their "kitchen tables." The organizational structure of the CWA is based on a "prayer chain." Seven individuals, including a prayer leader, form a prayer group; seven such groups form the chain; and seven chains form a local chapter of CWA, which is run under the direction of a chapter leader. Each chapter thus consists of fifty members. CWA has more than 2,500 local affiliates. Chapters are under the direction of a regional director who reports to the national CWA headquarters, which is located in Washington, D.C. CWA's core issues include a belief that modern feminism, which it claims has misused the United Nations to spread the agenda worldwide, has in fact harmed women and families (www.cwfa.org).

The National Political Congress of Black Women

Among other groups organized to promote greater equality and involvement in politics of minority women is the National Congress of

Black Women, formerly the National Political Congress of Black Women. It was founded in 1984, and Shirley Chisholm, former member of the House of Representatives, was elected its first president.

According to its Web site, the congress has served as an independent, nonpartisan political organization to encourage all Black women to participate in the political process as voters, political candidates, policy makers, fundraisers, and political role models for younger people. In its first years, the congress organized forty-two chapters across the country to press for more African American women in public office. The National Congress of Black Women has also mobilized a campaign to include Black suffragist Sojourner Truth in the monument commemorating the women's suffrage movement in the rotunda of the U.S. Capitol.

The Fund for a Feminist Majority

After Eleanor Smeal gave up the presidency of NOW, she established a feminist institute, the Feminist Majority Foundation, in 1987 to conduct research on politics and economics, including the construction of legislative districts and how that impacts who runs for public office and their likelihood of winning, as well as developing educational leadership. Its political action arm, the Fund for a Feminist Majority, also worked to flood elections with women candidates in a "feminization of power" campaign. The fund predicted that 1992 would be a breakthrough year for women candidates. It launched its 1992 Feminization of Power Campaign, spearheaded by the fund's national coordinator, Katherine Spillar, and the campaign's southwest coordinator, Dolores Huerta, to inspire record-breaking numbers of women to run for office. As part of the campaign, the fund released a report, "The Feminization of Power: 50/50 by the Year 2000," describing the severe underrepresentation of women in government. Women were only 5 percent of the members of Congress and held only 18.4 percent of all state legislative seats. The strategy of the campaign was to flood the ticket in the hopes that the more women who ran, the more women would win.

As it has developed over the years, the Feminist Majority has not only taken the lead in challenging the political process in order to elect feminist women to public office but also has engaged in a wide variety of activities in opposition to public policies that it views as hurting women. The fund fought to bring the abortion pill RU 486 into the country and worked to improve political and civil rights for women in other countries. For example, in 1992 the Feminist Majority set up an emergency Western Union hotline and urged the public to flood the Kuwait Embassy and the U.S. State Department with letters urging immediate action on the widely reported accounts that hundreds of Asian women workers were being raped or beaten by their Kuwaiti employers and had taken refuge in their countries' embassies.

The Feminist Majority sponsored a conference on domestic violence immediately after the March for Women's Lives in 1992. Feminist Majority organizers met with the leadership of forty-eight state domestic violence coalitions and strategized to increase funding for programs to combat the mounting epidemic of violence against women. The conference was cosponsored by the National Woman Abuse Prevention Center and focused on sharing information on legislation, developing a federal policy agenda, and implementing the Feminist Majority's campaign to achieve gender balance in the police force.

The year 1992 also saw the Feminist Majority's campaign for gender balance break new ground with the unanimous vote by the Los Angeles City Council in favor of proposals for gender balancing the Los Angeles Police Department (LAPD). The proposals, drafted by the Feminist Majority in conjunction with the California Women's Law Center and Los Angeles City Council member Zev Yaroslavsky, sought to increase the percentages of women in the LAPD from 14 percent of the force to 44 percent. Katherine Spillar, who spearheaded the police project in Los Angeles, pointed out: "Well over half of all 911 calls are calls of violence against women. Research shows that women officers tend to respond more effectively to incidents of violence against women. And women officers are more convinced of the importance of responding to family fights as a crucial police duty" (1991).

The Independent Women's Forum

In addition to profamily, religious Right groups, such as CWA and the Eagle Forum, a leading group challenging the Feminist Majority and other feminist organizations is the Independent Women's Forum (IWF), which was founded as a conservative women's think tank in 1992 in reaction to the Clarence Thomas hearings. It is a nonprofit, nonpartisan policy organization dedicated to research and public education on policy issues concerning women. The mission of the IWF is to "advanc[e] the spirit of enterprise and self-reliance among women, and supporting the principles of political freedom, economic liberty, and personal responsibility." In 2004 it issued a report, "Dependency Divas: How the Feminist Big Government Agenda Betrays Women." The purpose of this report, IWF asserts, is to raise awareness that the traditional feminist agenda is inconsistent with independence for women. The feminist agenda is replacing dependence on men with dependence on government. And often, these big government proposals have serious unintended consequences that make women worse off. The IWF promotes itself as providing "a voice for responsible, mainstream women who embrace common sense over divisive ideology . . . to make that voice heard in the U.S. Supreme Court, among other decision makers in Washington, and across America's airwaves, to counter the dangerous influence of radical feminism in the courts, to combat corrosive feminist ideology on campus and to change the terms of the debate on quality of life issues affecting American women." Its programs, including legal, campus, and work/family projects, aim to "educate women on the benefits of the free market and the danger of big government, challenge conventional feminist myths with accurate information and lively debate, and provide a forum for women who are not represented by radical feminist groups" (www.iwf.org). Lynne Cheney, wife of Vice President Richard Cheney, is on the board of the IWF. It has a "sister group," the Independent Women's Voice, which lobbies government officials on public policy. Neither entity takes a position on abortion.

The IWF has opposed the administration of Title IX, the statute that guarantees equal treatment for male and female athletes, as substituting one form of discrimination against women for another form of discrimination against men. The IWF filed friend-of-the-court briefs urging the Supreme Court to find the University of Michigan's use of preferences unconstitutional in the 2004 affirmative action case. It has challenged the idea of a wage gap that shows that women earn less on average than men. Rather, the IWF supports policies such as reductions in the tax rate and deregulation of business that it believes will create more job opportunities and higher take-home pay for women and men.

The IWF started a "Take Back the Campus" crusade, in which an array of well-known conservative women are brought to colleges by activist conservative clubs to explore such questions as "whether women's-studies programs actually harm women with misleading feminist myths of women as victims." Speakers suggest that the preponderance of women's-studies classes and the proliferation on campuses of "Take Back the Night" marches, sex and dating rules, and rape-awareness lectures, activities that are aimed at making women feel empowered on campus, in fact do precisely the opposite. They infantalize women.

The Rise of Feminist Interest Groups

In regard to contemporary feminist activity, Ferree and Hess (1994) have suggested that the period 1963–1970 represented the emergence of the movement, that 1971 and 1972 were the most active years of the movement, and that 1973–1980 saw the transition from social movement to interest group politics. Two directions were pursued by activists as a means toward equal rights. On the one hand, large, formal organizations such as NOW and the NWPC pursued reform through political advocacy. On the other hand, a companion strand of smaller, often less formal groups opted to pursue more-radical action and direct resource provision to women as well as engaging in consciousness-raising activities. NOW picketed the EEOC and filed complaints against the *New York Times,* whereas the New York–based WITCH hexed the New York Stock Exchange. Subsequently, the EEOC ruled that sex-segregated job advertisements violated Title VII of the Civil Rights Act, and the stock exchange dropped 5 points.

Since the mid-1970s the women's movement has undergone a transition from social movement to interest group, in the process forming a dense and diverse field of organizational activity. There are five types of groups: (1) mass-based membership organizations, such as NOW and the NWPC; (2) specialized groups, such as litigation and research groups, (3) single-issue groups, such as NARAL; (4) traditional women's groups; and (5) an "electoral campaign sector" comprising PACs sponsored by large women's organizations such as NOW along with a number of campaign-oriented groups such as the Women's Campaign Fund.

From 1980 on, electoral and partisan politics increasingly became a central component of the women's movement's political strategy. The formation of PACs became a major method of influencing electoral politics. PACs are groups formed to contribute money to the campaigns of candidates for public office. The number of women's PACs active at the national level grew from five PACs in 1978 to a high of twenty-two in 1994. Women's PACs include PACs that contribute money only to female candidates such as EMILY's List and the WISH List, PACs that contribute to both female and male candidates using the candidate's record or position on feminist issues as the criterion for funding, and PACs that contribute to both female and male candidates' positions on issues that are not necessarily feminist issues. Such groups include the American Nurses Association's PAC and the Women's Action for Nuclear Disarmament. All of the major organizations and PACs maintain permanent offices with professional staffs in the Washington, D.C., area (Young 2000).

The activities of feminist organizations have greatly impacted the women's rights movement. Such diverse organizations as the National Congress of Neighborhood Women, created in 1974 in support of working-class women, and the Coalition of Labor Union Women, founded in that same year, add to the mix. The groups have worked for change in the law, the courts, universities, corporations, local communities, and in individual women's lives. "Few people have remained untouched, directly or indirectly, by these organizing efforts" (Ferree and Martin 1995, 4).

Kay Lehmann Schlozman's 1984 study of organizations that represent women in Washington located eighty-nine such organizations with their own offices in the capital. They included women's rights organizations such as the Center for Women Policy Studies and the Older Women's League; associations of women professionals such as the National Association for Women Deans, Administrators and Counselors; and groups of women of a particular ethnic or religious derivation such as the Organization of Pan Asian American Women. In addition, they include organizations that are not specifically women's organizations but that have a high proportion of female members: unions and professional associations in fields such as nursing and occupational therapy having a disproportionate share of women. These organizations can be grouped into four categories: women's rights organizations and caucuses or organizations of women from particular occupations or religious or ethnic backgrounds; occupational groups; and a heterogeneous residual group that includes one New Right organization whose expressed purpose is to represent women's interests. She estimated that that these women's organizations accounted for only 1 to 2 percent of all organizations with representation in Washington (Schlozman 1990).

Case Study: NARAL Pro-Choice America and Feminists for Life

NARAL Pro-Choice America, formerly the National Abortion and Reproductive Rights Action League, is the preeminent organization nationally defending a woman's right to choose an abortion. NARAL Pro-Choice America leaders testify at congressional hearings, engage in national advertising campaigns, work to expand access to clinics providing abortions, and protest and march in the streets. It supports pro-choice candidates as well as a PAC to provide financing to endorsed candidates. In the 2004 presidential election, at a time in which abortion rights have been considerably narrowed with the passage of the Partial Birth Abortion Act in 2003, NARAL Pro-Choice undertook a multimillion-dollar campaign of television and print advertising in highly competitive states to try to make abortion a critical issue in the campaign for the White House.

The organization was founded in 1969 as the National Association for the Repeal of Abortion Laws. The group became the National Abortion Rights Action League after the 1973 Supreme Court decision *Roe v. Wade* overturned many legal restrictions on abortion. Reproductive Rights was added to its name in 1993. In recent years, abortion rights' activists have framed the issue in terms of big government and government intrusion in people's lives rather than in terms of women's rights and have not worked publicly to expand support for abortion to poor women. The change in name to emphasize "pro-choice" is part of this effort. "Through our name change we are underscoring that our country is pro-choice," said Kate Michelman, president of the organization. "It is the right name for this moment in history." In 2004, NARAL Pro-Choice America had affiliates in twenty-five states.

Feminists for Life of America was established in 1972. According to its mission statement, it is a "nonsectarian, nonpartisan grassroots organization that seeks real solutions to the challenges women face. Its efforts are shaped by the core feminist values of justice, nondiscrimination and nonviolence." It traces itself back to suffragists Susan B. Anthony and Elizabeth Cady Stanton. It was founded by former NOW members Pat Goltz and Catherine Callaghan, who opposed NOW's decision to advocate the legalization of abortion.

Feminists for Life works on other issues besides abortion, such as the Violence Against Women Acts, pay equity for women and minorities, welfare reform, as well as eliminating sexual harassment, capital punishment, and euthanasia. Feminists for Life is headquartered in Washington, D.C., with chapters throughout the country. Feminists for Life is particularly engaged in a college outreach program because so many abortions are performed on college students. Its president frequently lectures on college campuses.

References

Acosta-Belen, Edna, and Christine E. Bose. 2003. "U.S. Latinas: Active at the Intersections of Gender, Nationality, Race, and Class." In *Sisterhood Is Forever: The Women's Anthology for a New Millennium.* Edited by Robin Morgan. New York: Washington Square Press.

Barasko, Maryann. Forthcoming. *Governing NOW: Grassroots Activism in the National Organization for Women.* Ithaca, NY: Cornell University Press.

Boles, Janet. 1982. "Building Support for the ERA." *PS* 15(4) (Fall): 572–77.

Breines, Wini. 2002. "What's Love Got to Do with It? White Women, Black Women, and Feminism in the Movement Years." *Signs* 27(4): 1095–1133.

Chafe, William. 1972. *The American Woman: Her Changing Social, Economic, and Political Roles, 1920–1970.* New York: Oxford University Press.

Charlton, Linda. 1970a. "Women Seeking Equality, March on 5th Ave. Today." *New York Times,* August 26.

———. 1970b. "The Feminine Protest." *New York Times,* August 28.

Daniels, Mark R., Robert Darcy, and Joseph W. Westphal. 1982. "The ERA Won—At Least in the Opinion Polls." *PS* 15(4) (Fall): 578–584.

Deckard, Barbara Sinclair. 1979. *The Women's Movement: Political, Socioeconomic, and Psychological Issues.* New York: Harper and Row.

Evans, Sara. 1979. *Personal Politics: The Roots of Women's Liberation in the Civil Rights Movement and the New Left.* New York: Knopf.

Ferree, Myra Marx, and Beth B. Hess. 1994. *Controversy and Coalition: The New Feminist Movement Through Three Decades.* Revised edition. New York: Twayne.

Ferree, Myra Marx, and Patricia Yancey Martin. 1995. "Doing the Work of the Movement." In *Feminist Organizations.* Edited by Myra Marx Ferree and Patricia Yancey Martin. Philadelphia: Temple University Press.

Freeman, Jo. 1975. *The Politics of Women's Liberation.* New York: David McKay Company.

———. 1990. "From Protection to Equal Opportunity: The Revolution in Women's Legal Status." In *Women, Politics, and Change.* Edited by Louise A. Tilly and Patricia Gurin. New York: Russell Sage Foundation.

Friedan, Betty. 1963. *The Feminine Mystique.* New York: W. W. Norton.

García, Alma M. 1989. "The Development of Chicana Feminist Discourse, 1980." *Gender and Society* 3(2): 217–38.

Gelb, Joyce, and Marian Lief Palley. 1982. *Women and Public Policies.* Princeton, NJ: Princeton University Press.
Hole, Judith, and Ellen Levine. 1971. *Rebirth of Feminism.* New York: Quadrangle Books, Inc.
Lemons, J. Stanley. 1975. *The Woman Citizen: Social Feminism in the 1920s.* Urbana: University of Illinois Press.
Martin, Janet. 2003. *The Presidency and Women: Promise, Performance and Illusion.* College Station: Texas A&M University Press.
Mathews, A. Lanethea. 2001. "'Between Diapers and Dishes': The General Federation of Women Clubs and Public Policy in the Mid-20th Century." Paper presented at the Annual Meeting of the Midwest Political Science Association, Chicago, IL, April.
McGlen, Nancy E., and Karen O'Connor. 1995. *Women, Politics, and American Society.* Englewood Cliffs, NJ: Prentice Hall.
Minkoff, Debra C. 1995. *Organizing for Equality: The Evolution of Women's and Racial-Ethnic Organizations in America, 1955–1985.* Philadelphia: Temple University Press.
———. 1997. "Organizational Mobilization, Institutional Access, and Institutional Change." In *Women Transforming Politics.* Edited by Cathy J. Cohen, Kathleen Jones, and Joan C. Tronto. New York: New York University Press.
Murphy, Irene. 1973. *Public Policy on the Status of Women.* Lexington, MA: Lexington Books.
O'Connor, Karen. 1999. "Introduction: Women in American Politics." In *Encyclopedia of Women in American Politics.* Edited by Jeffrey D. Schultz and Lauren van Assendelft. Phoenix, AZ: Oryx Press.
Rupp, Leila J., and Verta Taylor. 1987. *Survival in the Doldrums.* New York: Oxford University Press.
Ryan, Barbara. 1992. *Feminism and the Women's Movement: Dynamics of Change in Social Movement Ideology and Activism.* New York: Routledge.
Schlozman, Kay Lehmann. 1990. "Representing Women in Washington: Sisterhood and Pressure Politics." In *Women, Politics, and Change.* Edited by Louise A. Tilly and Patricia Gurin. New York: Russell Sage Foundation.
Smolkin, Rachel. 2003. "A Vigil in Pink; Outside the Gates of the White House, Women Stage a Daily Protest for Peace." *Chicago Tribune,* February 5.
Some of Us Are Brave: A History of Black Feminism in the United States (http://www.mit.edu:8001/activities/thistle/v9/9.01/6blackf.html).
Spillar, Katherine. 1991. Testimony before the Independent Commission on the Los Angeles Police Department.
Steinem, Gloria. 1986. "The First National Women's Conference." In *Women Leaders in American Politics.* Edited by James David Barber and Barbara Kellerman. Englewood Cliffs, NJ: Prentice-Hall, Inc.
Steiner, Gilbert Y. 1985. *Constitutional Inequality: The Political Fortunes of the Equal Rights Amendment.* Washington, DC: The Brookings Institution.
Stetson, Dorothy McBride. 1991. *Women's Rights in the U.S.A.: Policy Debates and Gender Roles.* Belmont, CA: Brooks/Cole Publishing Company.

Whittier, Nancy. 1995. *Feminist Generations: The Persistence of the Radical Women's Movement.* Philadelphia: Temple University Press.

Young, Lisa. 2000. *Feminists and Party Politics.* Vancouver: University of British Columbia Press.

4
Participation in Electoral Politics

The first women's rights convention took place in 1848 in Seneca Falls, New York, when approximately 350 people met in the Wesleyan Chapel to discuss "the social, civil and religious rights of women." Among other resolutions, participants at this convention resolved that "it is the duty of the women of this country to secure to themselves their sacred right to the elective franchise."

This resolution was one of twelve resolutions adopted at the convention, which was led by Elizabeth Cady Stanton and Lucretia Mott. It was the only resolution not to pass unanimously. Many of the participants thought it was too bold a move, one that would make them appear ridiculous, as one leader argued. Only the endorsement by the Black abolitionist Frederick Douglass led to that resolution's achieving a majority of the votes. Douglass wrote in the *North Star* immediately following the convention, "All that distinguishes man as an intelligent and accountable being, is equally true of woman, and if that government only is just which governs by the free consent of the governed, there can be no reason in the world for denying to woman the exercise of the elective franchise, or a hand in making and administering the laws of the land" (Foner 1976, 51).

In the years immediately following the Seneca Falls Convention, the women's rights community focused on a wide array of issues, but obtaining the vote was not a significant aim of these early activists. "Of more immediate concern were the control of property, of earnings ... guardianship, divorce, opportunity for education and employment, lack of legal status (women still could not sue or bear witness), and the whole concept of female inferiority perpetuated by established religion" (Flexner 1974, 82).

Women's rights activists channeled their energies into the Civil War, especially since many in the movement had been active abolitionists. They believed that "when peace came, a grateful country would reward them spurred on by the Republican Party" (Flexner 1974, 142). They would be very disappointed. Voting rights became central to their movement when, after the war, Congress supported a constitutional amendment that granted Black men the right to vote but refused explicitly to include women in the amendment. The Republican leaders in Congress who advocated the civil rights amendments feared that including woman suffrage with the enfranchisement of Black men would assure that amendment's defeat. Susan B. Anthony and Elizabeth Cady Stanton, angered by the actions of their former partners, began a campaign for a constitutional amendment to give women the vote.

Some argued that the privileges and immunities clause of the Fourteenth Amendment, which stated that "[N]o state shall make or enforce any law which shall abridge the privileges or immunities of citizens of the United States," gave women the right to vote, and they tested that belief by attempting to cast ballots. In 1872, Susan B. Anthony led a group of sixteen women in Rochester, New York, to register and then vote. Consequently, she was charged with "knowingly, wrongfully and unlawfully voting for a representative to the Congress of the United States." She was convicted and fined $100, which was never paid. In another case resulting from women attempting to vote, *Minor v. Happersett,* the Supreme Court in 1875 ruled unanimously that suffrage was not a right of citizenship. The plaintiffs in that case had argued that Virginia Minor's rights under the Fourteenth Amendment were violated because she was denied "the privileges and immunities of citizenship, chief among which is the elective franchise."

In 1920, after more than seventy years of advocacy, the right of women to vote became a constitutional amendment. According to the suffragists' accounting, it took 480 campaigns to get state legislatures to submit amendments to their electorates; 277 campaigns to persuade state party conventions to include woman suffrage planks in their platforms; 19 campaigns with 19 successive Congresses; and the ratification campaign of 1919 and 1920 to achieve this goal (Kraditor 1965).

Women's suffrage had not been wholly dependent on passage of a federal amendment. The National Woman Suffrage Association, founded in 1869, devoted its energy to a federal amendment, but an opposing organization, the American Woman Suffrage Association, also formed in 1869, focused on gaining the right to vote from state legislatures. In addition local struggles attempted "to increase women's political influence by winning a fragment of the franchise that fell indisputably within state control," such as "school suffrage," that is, votes on public education or "home protection," for example, votes on liquor questions (Gordon 1995). Women gained suffrage in several states prior to the passage of the Nineteenth Amendment. By the time of the 1916 presidential election, 4 million women could vote for president in twelve states (Freeman 2000, 79). Seventeen additional states had limited women's suffrage for presidential elections (Cox 1996). Wyoming had led the way when as a territory it had granted women the vote, and it maintained that right when it became a state in 1890. Colorado voters passed an amendment to their constitution granting women the franchise in 1893 and in 1894 elected the first women to a state legislature. The two organizations, the National Woman Suffrage Association and the American Woman Suffrage Association, operated independently of each other for twenty years. In 1890 they combined to form the National American Woman Suffrage Association (NAWSA), with strategies aimed at getting the vote state by state and nationally.

The Impact of Suffrage

Contrary to the hopes of the suffragists, women did not rush out to vote in the 1920 presidential election and in elections in the years immediately following the passage of the Nineteenth Amendment. In 1920, only about one-third of the eligible women voted, whereas approximately two-thirds of the eligible men voted (Baxter and Lansing 1981, 17). Women's mobilization as voters in the 1920s varied according to socioeconomic status, with middle-class, native-born, urban women voting at higher rates than lower-class, immigrant, or rural women. Women's levels of participation also depended on political party efforts to bring them into the local voting universe. Variations in women's voting rates were related to "the extent to which one or both parties found it advantageous to mobilize women voters" (Andersen 1996, 66).

Women gradually increased their voting participation as it became a more accepted aspect of their citizenship. In the 1940s, the ability to conduct national opinion polls became more commonplace in American politics. According to the Roper surveys as reported by Louis Harris (1954), men and women turned out to vote at the following rates:

	Men	Women
1940	68%	49%
1948	57%	45%
1952	63%	55%

Conducted by the University of Michigan, the National Election Studies (NES), which began in the 1950s, showed that "the vote participation rate among women in our samples is consistently 10 percent below that of men, as an overall estimate." But as the authors point out, consistent with the characterization of variation in women's turnout in the 1920s, the overall difference masked "a good deal of variation among social groupings." Rural women, women in the South, and mothers with young children were substantially less likely to vote than their male counterparts. At the college level, women were more likely to vote than men in the 1950s (Campbell, Converse, Miller, and Stokes 1960).

In 1964, the Bureau of the Census initiated a national survey of voting participation that has continued since then. In the 1964 election, according to the Bureau of the Census figures, approximately 1.8 million more women than men voted, but the voting rate for men exceeded that for women, 72 percent to 67 percent. (Women are the majority of the population, so although more women than men might vote, it does not necessarily follow that their turnout rate will be higher.) It was not until four elections later that a higher percentage of eligible women voters turned out to vote than of eligible men.

In determining the impact of groups on election results, it is important to consider their population size, their turnout rates (i.e., the percentage of a group's members who are eligible to vote who actually turn out), and the presence of that group as a percentage of the whole population to have a complete picture of where a group stands in the portrait of the electorate. "To the extent that a group's impact

TABLE 4.1 Turnout Rates of Men and Women in Presidential Elections, 1980–2000

Year	% of Eligible Men Voting	% of Eligible Women Voting	% Difference (Women–Men)	Numerical Difference	Women as % of All Voters
1980	59.1	59.4	+.3	5,559,000	53.0
1984	59.0	60.8	+1.8	7,170,000	53.5
1988	56.4	58.3	+1.9	6,815,000	53.3
1992	60.2	62.3	+2.1	7,242,000	53.2
1996	52.8	55.5	+2.7	7,199,000	53.4
2000	53.1	56.2	+3.2	8,436,000	52.1

Source: U.S. Bureau of Census, Current Population Survey, Voting and Registration, available at www.census.gov. 2002.

on election outcomes is affected by its size, women [have] had an increasing potential to influence the distribution of the vote because of their sheer numbers" (Mattei and Mattei 1998, 412). Table 4.1 reflects women's presence as voters in U.S. presidential elections over twenty years, based on Bureau of the Census surveys. With each election since 1980 women's numerical and proportionate advantage has grown over that of men.

In the first Census Bureau report of voter participation in 1964, the authors noted that the difference in male and female voting percentages was related to age. They pointed out that the difference between the proportion of voters among men and women increased with age to the disadvantage of women. Age continues to affect the relation between sex and turnout, but now younger women turn out at higher rates than younger men. That advantage is reversed among older citizens (Table 4.2).

TABLE 4.2 Voting Turnout by Age and Gender, 1980–2000

Year	18–24 %M %F	25–34 %M %F	35–44 %M %F	45–54 %M %F	55–64 %M %F	65–74 %M %F	75+ %M %F
1980	39 41	53 56	63 66	67 68	73 70	73 67	66 53
1984	39 43	52 57	62 65	67 68	73 72	74 70	68 57
1988	34 38	37 46	50 46	61 62	66 67	69 70	59 50
1992	41 45	50 56	61 66	68 69	72 71	76 72	71 61
1996	30 35	40 47	53 57	61 64	68 68	73 68	68 59
2000	30 35	40 47	52 57	61 64	59 67	71 69	72 61

Source: U.S. Bureau of Census, Current Population Survey, Voting and Registration, available at www.census.gov. 2002.

The 2000 election provides a reference for looking at the relationship between sex and turnout among different racial and ethnic groups. As Figure 4.1 shows, white women, Black women, and Hispanic women all turned out at higher rates than their male counterparts in the 2000 election. The turnout rate for Asian American women was just under that of Asian men. Figure 4.2 shows each racial and ethnic group as a percentage of the overall electorate in the 2000 election. It is interesting, as Baxter and Lansing (1981) reported, that Black women increased their rate of voting faster than Black men and more than either white men or white women, even though their demographic profile of lower socioeconomic status would have suggested a different pattern.

After studying the evolution in voting participation on the part of women, it would be logical to ask what difference the participation of women has made. Related to the whole campaign for female suffrage and beyond has been the question whether women would form a distinct voting bloc or make voting decisions just as men do. How would they influence the electoral process and electoral outcomes? Along with their low turnout in the years following their obtaining the vote, women did not appear to constitute a distinctive voting bloc.

The impact of women in electoral politics became noticeable in the 1950s, however. Survey research has shown and political leaders have noted a gap in the voting decisions of men and women since the election of 1952, in which Republican Dwight Eisenhower defeated Democrat Adlai Stevenson. Women were 2.1 percent more supportive of Eisenhower than men in that election. According to pollster Louis Harris:

> In 1952, everything changed.... Women reacted sharply to the new pressures [as opposed to the economic pressures of the New Deal]. They reacted sharply to nearly everything about the 1952 election. They came out to vote in greater numbers than ever before. They voted differently than ever before. They reacted to different issues in different ways from their male counterparts. They became a political entity, significant in their own right, probably for the first time since they had been delivered from political bondage (1954, 108).

Harris reported the findings that women supported Eisenhower more than men did, and that they had as a group "broke[n] with the Democratic Party way of voting which they had taken to enthusiasti-

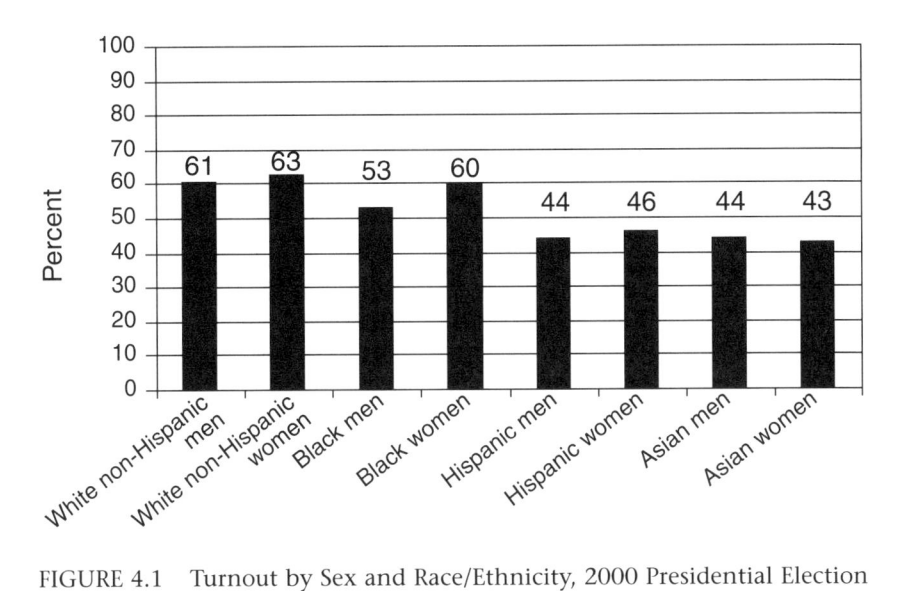

FIGURE 4.1   Turnout by Sex and Race/Ethnicity, 2000 Presidential Election

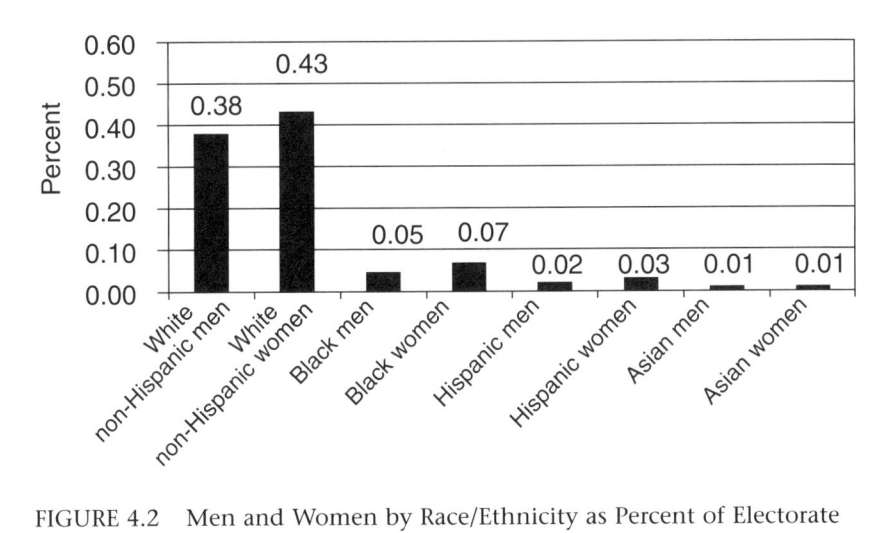

FIGURE 4.2   Men and Women by Race/Ethnicity as Percent of Electorate

cally under Roosevelt" for Democratic Party leaders. But even before Harris's warning, Democratic leaders were well aware of "the reported trend of women voters toward the Republican ticket," and had discussed this trend in party meetings held after their loss in 1952 (Harvey 1998, 211).

Harvey reports:

> The response of these leaders to the apparent emergence of a gender gap was *not to develop policy initiatives designed to appeal to this emergent group* [author's emphasis], but rather to discuss new techniques of attracting women's votes through the organizational auspices of the women's Democratic organization.... Following the Democrats' defeat in the 1956 presidential election, Chairman Paul Butler told the DNEC that women as an electoral group were the source of the Democratic party's woes: "the most important segment of the electorate, so far as the future plans of the Democratic party is concerned, is the women of America. I think that we have failed to keep pace with the Republican organization in our appeal to the women" (1998, 211–212).

John Kennedy was well aware of this problem for the Democrats and adopted a campaign strategy in 1960 aimed at women. In particular, he targeted suburban women with a campaign theme highlighting education issues. Harris polls in 1960 and responses to the "Calling for Kennedy Drives" showed that middle-class women and young suburbanites were especially concerned with the problem of educating their children. Thus, in his campaign for the presidency, John Kennedy pledged to make educating young Americans a priority of his administration (Silverberg, 1988, 47). Federal aid to education became a prominent campaign theme. But Richard Nixon, Kennedy's Republican opponent, still received a slightly higher percentage of women's votes.

The Gender Gap

The "gender gap" became a political phenomenon after the 1980 election. Ronald Reagan had handily won the 1980 election. But that election revealed an 8 percent gender gap in votes for the winning candidate: 46 percent of women voted for Reagan, as opposed to 54 percent of men. The votes of women had been noted during the campaign, but the idea of a women's bloc had primarily been ignored or dismissed. Adam Clymer was the first journalist to address the difference in Ronald Reagan's support between men and women in a post-election analysis piece in the *New York Times*. Clymer reported: "Mr. Reagan's long-standing difficulties in persuading women to vote for him . . . held down his percentages again Tuesday. . . . The [*New York Times*/CBS News] poll suggested that both fear about war and opposition to the Equal Rights Amendment handicapped Mr. Reagan's bid for their support" (Clymer 1980).

As recounted by Kathy Bonk (1988), Eleanor Smeal of the National Organization for Women (NOW) recognized the significance of Clymer's story. At that time, NOW and other women's rights organizations were discouraged over the failure of campaigns to get the equal rights amendment (ERA) passed. The gender gap in the 1980 election gave these groups a "hook" to get media attention and ammunition to press politicians to vote for the amendment. Building on Clymer's story, NOW headlined its December/January (1980–1981) issue of its newspaper: "Women Vote Differently Than Men, Feminist Bloc Emerges in 1980 Elections." The article went on to state, "The NYT/CBS poll reported that 8 percent fewer women (46 percent) voted for Reagan than did men (54 percent). ABC's poll was similar. This difference calculated in actual votes, amounts to a net loss of 3.3 million female votes for Reagan." The NOW article was reworked into op-ed pieces written by Smeal and reprinted in both the *Chicago Sun Times* and the *Chicago Tribune*. The target audience was Illinois legislators who would be voting on the ERA during the next fifteen months (Bonk 1988, 86).

The term *gender gap* first appeared in the media in a Judy Mann piece in the *Washington Post* in 1981. "Last November, there was a gender gap of 8 percentage points in the *New York Times*/CBS exit poll on the presidential election. . . . The gender gap has steadily increased since the election." Since that time the gender gap has been a major feature of electoral politics in the United States. In Figure 4.3 one can see the gender gap in votes in president elections from 1980 through 2000. The gap is measured as the difference in the percent of votes the Democratic presidential candidate obtained from women and the percentage obtained from men. The size of the gap varies by election year. The first presidential election in which a majority of women voted one way and the majority of men voted another was 1996. In other words, had only men voted in 1996, Robert Dole would have been elected president, at least in terms of the popular vote.

The story of political party identification vis-à-vis the gender gap has primarily focused on women's increasing affiliation with the Democratic Party; however, a look at trend data tell a somewhat different story. Some have examined public opinion data on party identification and proclaimed a "dramatic conversion of men to the Republican Party," noting that "changes in male partisanship have been the driving force behind increases in the gender gap" (Kaufmann and Petrocik 1999, 866). A national trend toward greater independence from political party identification is evidenced. Independence increased over the course of the latter part of the twentieth century from less than one-third of the populace to about 40 percent. Women have consistently been slightly less likely than men to consider themselves independents. In the 1950s over 45 percent of both men and women tended to consider themselves to be Democrats in the American NES surveys, and only about one-quarter to 30 percent identified with the Republican Party. Republican Party identification declined among both men and women in the 1970s; increased in the 1980s, returning to its earlier levels; and continued to increase somewhat among men but leveled off for women in the 1990s. Democratic Party identification shows a long-term decline among both men and women, but the decline has been greater for men than women (see Figures 4.4, 4.5, and 4.6). In an NES survey during the 2000 election, 37 percent of women compared with 30 percent of men identified with the Democratic Party; 41 percent of men were independent, compared with 38 percent of women; and 29 percent of men and 23 percent of women considered themselves Republican.

Political Involvement beyond Voting

Voting may be the ultimate election act, but campaigns for election can engage citizens in a variety of political activities. Perhaps if women are outvoting men, they also dominate other forms of participation in elections. Citizens can engage in political debate, trying to influence others in their vote choice, attend rallies and political gatherings, wear a campaign button or put a bumper sticker on their car, work for a party or candidate, and contribute money to a campaign, for example. Women's greater propensity than men to vote, however, does not seem to carry over into these other forms of political activity.

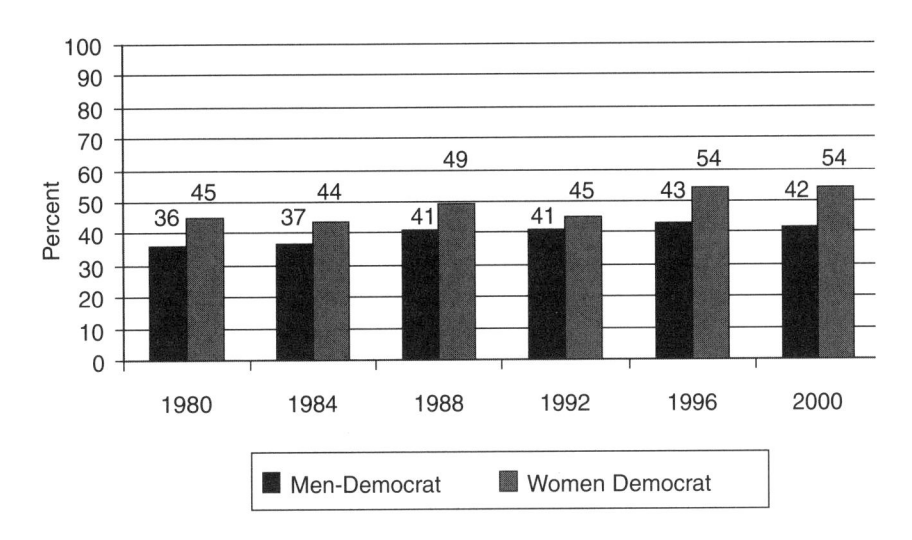

FIGURE 4.3 Democratic Candidate Gender Gap

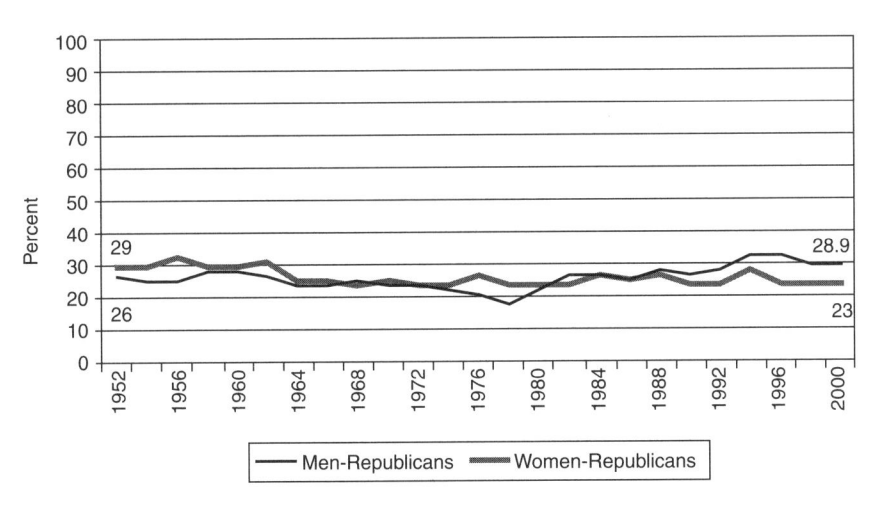

FIGURE 4.4 Republican Party Identification, Men and Women 1952–2000

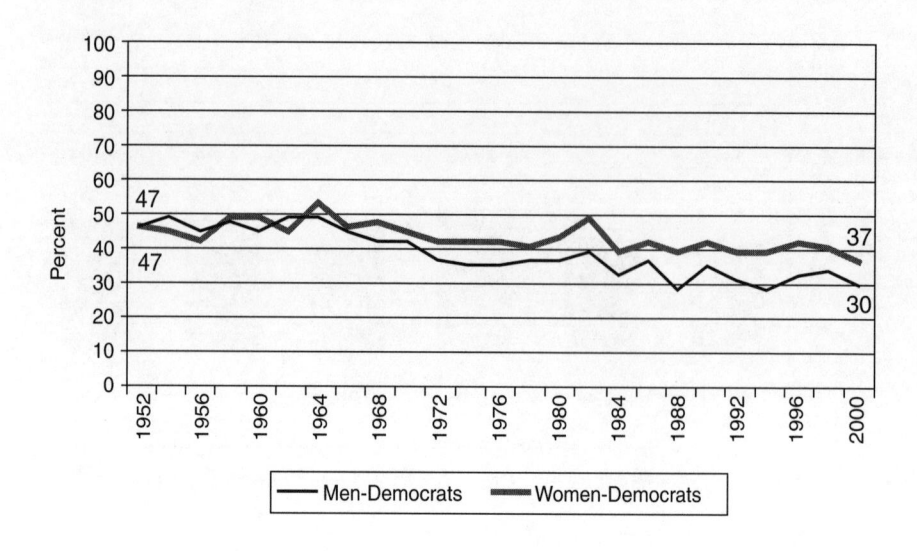

FIGURE 4.5 Democratic Party Identification, Men and Women, 1952–2000

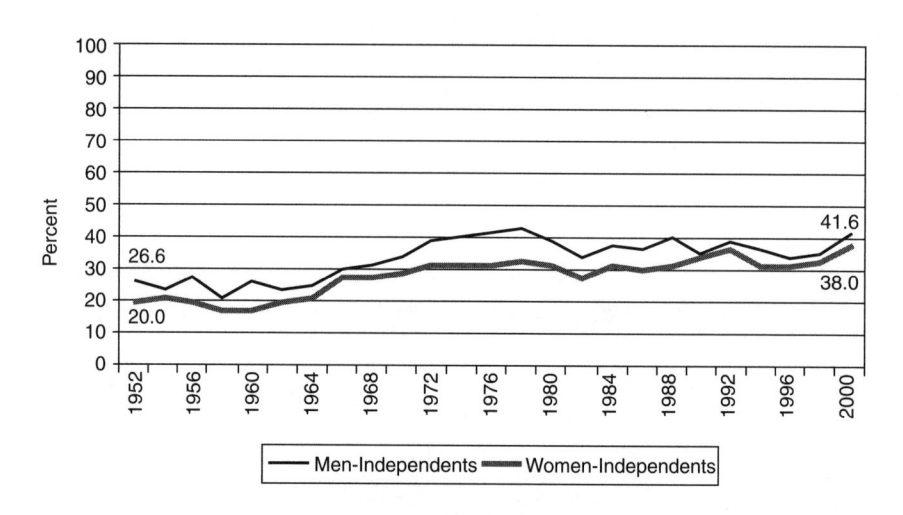

FIGURE 4.6 Independents, Men and Women, 1952–2000

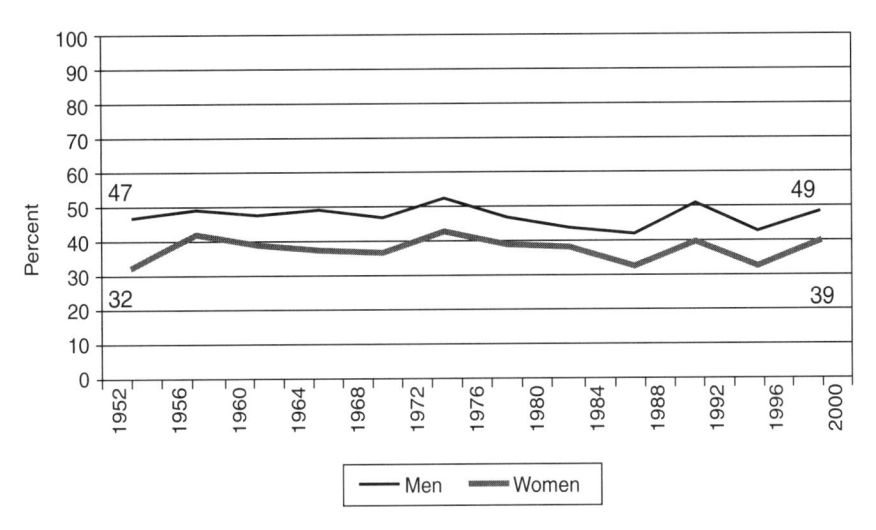

FIGURE 4.7 Participation of Men and Women in at Least One Campaign Activity, 1952–2000

The NES surveys have asked respondents since the 1950s if they have done any of these five activities. Women have consistently reported lower levels of involvement, and the gap has not diminished over the course of the contemporary era (Figure 4.7). With respect to the 2000 election, for instance, 48 percent of men and 39 percent of women reported having participated in at least one of these activities. Only very small percentages of men and women get actively involved in election campaigns beyond talking to others, trying to influence their vote, which 40 percent of men and 31 percent of women reported doing in the 2000 election. Men were slightly more likely than women to engage in the other activities, but the differences were small, and less than 15 percent of men or women reported having engaged in any one of them.

Very few people make substantial financial donations to political candidates. The Federal Elections Commission requires that all donations of $200 or more to candidates for federal office (i.e., U.S. representative, U.S. senator, or president) be individually reported. In the 2000 election, 0.5 percent of adult males gave $200 or more to candidates for federal office; 0.2 percent of adult women gave $200 or more. In the same election, donations of $1,000 or more were given to federal candidates by just over 0.2 percent of adult males (0.22 percent) and just under 0.1 percent of adult females (.09 percent).

A somewhat different picture of women's involvement emerges, however, if one compares the political participation of Black women with that of Black men. Overwhelmingly, Black women participate in more types of activities and participate more frequently than their Black male counterparts. A key to understanding these differences is the greater involvement of Black women in organizations and church activities. Additionally, Black women are more likely than Black men to be encouraged to participate, a factor that is very important to political participation (Alex-Assensoh and Stanford 1997).

Women and Political Parties

The Republican and Democratic Parties had disappointed activists for women's rights in the decades after the Civil War by their indifference and opposition to granting women the right to vote. As suffragist leader Carrie Chapman Catt put it in 1917: "It has been the aim of both parties to postpone woman suffrage as long as possible. Many of us have deep and abiding distrust of all political parties; they have tricked us so often that our doubts are natural" (Peck 1944, 283). But even without the vote, women were involved in partisan politics and engaged in electoral campaigns (see, for example, Freeman 2000.) As more states granted women the vote and the prospect of passage of a national amendment became more evident, the parties initiated efforts to establish more formal roles for women in their organizational structures. "The national party organizations, sensitive to the demands and the potential influence of a new element in the electorate, responded to the imminent granting of suffrage with organizational changes designed to give women nominally equal roles in the party hierarchy and to allow for the efficient mobilization of women voters by women leaders" (Andersen 1996, 80–81). Party leaders feared the independence of women on the rolls of the voters. They thought women would create a "petticoat hierarchy which may at will upset all orderly slates and commit undreamed of executions at the polls" (Chafe 1991, 25), and they viewed the formation of the nonpartisan League of Women Voters (LWV) as threatening.

The Democratic Party acted first, in 1916 creating a Women's Bureau to mobilize women voters in the western states where they had the franchise. In 1917, the Democratic National Committee (DNC) created a women's version of itself staffed by appointed female members from the fifteen full suffrage states (Harvey 1998). In 1919, the DNC adopted a plan for an Associate National Committee of Women. The DNC also agreed that year to appoint a woman associate member from each state, based on the nomination of the state committeeman. The DNC also recommended that Democratic state committees provide women with similar representation at the state and local level and equal representation of men and women on the executive committee. At the Democratic National Convention in 1920, delegates voted to double the size of their national committee, with "one man and one woman hereafter [. . .] selected from each state" (Andersen 1996, 85).

The Republicans in 1918 created a Republican Women's National Executive Committee. In 1919, they adopted a plan calling for state chairmen to appoint "a State Executive Committee of women numbering from five to fifteen members to act with the State Central Committee" (Harvey 1998, 113) and established a women's division. But in 1920, they rejected equal representation for women on the Republican National Committee (RNC), although eight women were appointed to its twenty-one-member executive committee. In 1924, Republican leaders agreed to the enlargement of the RNC and the election of male and female members from each state.

Women came to represent about 10 to 15 percent of the delegates to the parties' national conventions in the years following their obtaining national voting rights. Although they gained some measure of formal equality in the party organizations in the early days after suffrage was obtained, women struggled for many years to win respect and equal power within the parties.

The New Deal administration attracted women to the Democratic Party. Activist women, many of whom were colleagues and friends of First Lady Eleanor Roosevelt, came to Washington to take positions in the Roosevelt administration. Molly Dewson, appointed director of the DNC's Women's Division in 1932, transformed the division into a strong force within the party. The Women's Division became a full-time operation, among other things working to have women appointed to positions in the administration. The Republicans were prompted to form the National Federation of Republican Women (NFRW), a federation of state and local Republican women's clubs in 1938 (Young 2000, 86–87).

The NFRW developed into a major independent group within the Republican Party and continues to operate as a force for advancing the participation of women in politics. The Democratic Party does not have a parallel organization. The NFRW is run by a national president and has a membership of 100,000 women and 1,800 local units throughout the country. It is a completely self-sustaining organization within the Republican Party structure. Its president has a voting membership on the RNC chairman's executive council. The NFRW's mission is "to help women from all walks of life become players at the political table nationally, statewide and locally." It advocates "empowering women of all ages, ethnicities and backgrounds" (www.nfrw.org). The federation runs a campaign-management school in conjunction with its biennial convention. Students learn ways to raise money successfully, write winning campaign plans, organize volunteers for get-out-the-vote activities, and communicate with voters.

With the rise of the second women's rights movement in the 1960s, the unequal treatment of women in the party organizations once again became a prominent and contentious issue, especially within the Democratic Party. During the 1972 presidential campaign, political party organizational politics was the focus of concerted action. It was that year that the Democratic Party adopted the reforms the McGovern-Fraser Commission had recommended for the selection of nominating convention delegates. The commission's Guidelines A-1 and A-2 required each state's delegation to the national convention to include representation of minority groups, women, and young persons "in reasonable relationship to their presence in the population of the state" (Ranney 1975). The significance of this requirement for women's roles in party politics and by extension in elections cannot be understated. Beginning in 1972 and since then, women have far exceeded their earlier presence as national delegates. The average percentage of women delegates between 1948 and 1968 was 15 percent and 13 percent respectively for Republicans and Democrats. In 1972, women constituted 40 percent of the Democratic delegates and 30 percent of the Republican delegates. In 1978, the Democratic Party wrote equal representation for women and men as national convention delegates into its rules. In 2000, 48 percent of the delegates to the Democratic National Convention were women, and 35 percent of the Republican delegates were women.

In recent years the Democratic and the Republican Parties have each made efforts to be the party of women, although at the same time they have taken some diametrically opposing stances regarding women's rights, or feminism. The two political parties have now completely polarized around feminism and the reaction to it. On feminist issues and concerns, instead of following the traditional pattern of presenting different versions of the same thing, the parties are presenting conflicting visions of how Americans should engage in everyday life (Freeman 1993, 21). The Republican Party, which had for years endorsed the ERA, eliminated its support in its platform in the 1980 election and began to oppose women's right to choose on the abortion issue.

Even while the two major parties have taken divergent stances on feminism, both parties have sought to include more women in leadership positions and appear to be "women friendly." The status of women within the party organizations has changed, and women have become both "insiders" and leaders. In 2003, women were the elected chairs of Democratic state parties in twelve states and chairs of Republican state parties in thirteen states. In the 107th Congress (2001–2002), women headed the Democratic Party's campaign committees. These committees help the parties' candidates raise money and compete, with the goal of increasing the number of the party's representatives in the U.S. House of Representatives and the U.S. Senate. (The Republicans have similar committees.) Washington Senator Patty Murray chaired the Democratic Senatorial Campaign Committee and New York Representative Nita Lowey chaired the Democratic Congressional Campaign Committee. In that same Congress Nancy Pelosi of California was elected Democratic whip, the second-highest partisan position in the House of Representatives, and in 2003 she became minority leader.

Both the Democratic and Republican Parties have developed initiatives to woo women voters. In 2001, as support among women for the Republican Party continued to decline in national polls, the RNC announced a campaign called "Winning Women." The effort would highlight the number of women in high positions in the Bush administration and frame issues to appeal to women. The DNC initiated the Women's Vote Center in 2001 also. The Women's Vote Center listed three primary goals for the 2002 and 2004 election cycles, including (1) conducting voter research that helps design an effective, targeted message strategy; (2) training women activists to reach and motivate other women with appropriate messages on key issues through the Democratic Voices program; and (3) implementing effective women's vote initiatives in targeted states. In 1993, the DNC established the Women's Leadership Forum (WLF). The WLF is an effort among women to raise money for the party to fund such efforts as the Women's Vote Center.

Feminist Issues at the Polls

Initiated by Franklin Roosevelt and the Democrats in the 1930s, the New Deal ushered in a realignment in U.S. politics that centered on the role of the national government in economic affairs. The major dividing line between Democrats and Republicans was the extent to which the national government should be involved in regulating and managing the economy and providing welfare benefits to ease marketplace inequalities. In the latter decades of the twentieth century other issues have joined this economic cleavage in electoral politics. Public policy in U.S. elections has been divided into a number of issue domains such as social-welfare policy, civil rights, foreign policy, and defense. The gender gap phenomenon has focused on differences between the positions of men and women on these issues.

In its fact sheet "The Gender Gap: Attitudes on Public Policy Issues," the Center for American Women and Politics (CAWP) at Rutgers University reported in the mid-1990s that compared with men, women are:

- More likely to favor a more activist role for government
- More often opposed to U.S. military intervention in other countries
- More supportive of programs to guarantee quality health care and meet basic human needs
- More supportive of restrictions on firearms
- More supportive of affirmative action and efforts to achieve racial equality

Foreign and Domestic Policy Issues

The most enduring gender gap issues, eliciting the largest differences between the sexes, have involved women's greater opposition to the use of force in both the foreign and domestic domains, and their greater support for public policies of a compassionate nature. Pacifism has consistently divided the sexes. Women were less supportive than men of the Korean and Vietnam Wars and subsequent military actions (see Table 4.3.). In their early study of women's political participation, Baxter and Lansing reported: "A pattern stands clear over twenty-five years: women have been more opposed to the use of

TABLE 4.3 Men, Women, and Military Action

		Men	Women
1952	The United States has done the right thing in getting into the fighting in Korea	48%	32%
1964	U.S. has done the right thing by getting involved in Vietnam	42%	30%
1972	Favor troop withdrawal from Vietnam	54%	70%
1991	Approve of sending U.S. troops to Saudi Arabia in response to Iraqi invasion of Kuwait	78%	54%
1996	Approve of the presence of U.S. troops in Bosnia	52%	37%
2003	The U.S. should invade Iraq even if we have to go it alone	34%	23%

force and the support of warlike policies. When these measures are correlated with level of education and age, the younger, more highly educated women take the more 'dovish' position" (1981, 59). In 1986, *Public Opinion Quarterly* presented a review of policy preferences regarding force issues from the 1960s to the 1980s that showed gender differences averaging eight percentage points, with men almost always selecting more violent options across the range of issues over time (Shapiro and Mahajan 1986, 49). In the 2000 NES, 51 percent of women and 59 percent of men advocated an increase in defense spending rather than decreasing or maintaining spending at current levels.

The terrorist attack of September 11, 2001, on the World Trade Center and the Pentagon affected the gender gap on defense issues. Many polls have been conducted, exploring all aspects of the situation, especially Americans' response to the attacks. Generally women seemed to be as supportive as men regarding specific aggressive actions; the term *security moms* began to be used in the media to describe women's response to terrorism. The Program on International Policy Attitudes (PIPA) survey of January 2003, just prior to initiation of the war on Iraq, probed a number of aspects of foreign policy that showed women continuing, however, to be less militaristic than men. Women were less in favor of the United States going alone in attacking Iraq and more supportive of continued efforts to work with the United Nations (Table 4.4).

TABLE 4.4   PIPA Survey on Iraq Issues

Question	Men	Women
Do you think that a country, without UN approval, does or does not have the right to use military force to prevent another country that does not have nuclear weapons from acquiring them?		
Countries have the right	52%	41%
Do you think that the United States, without UN approval, does or does not have right to use military force to prevent a country that does not have nuclear weapons form acquiring them?		
United States has the right	54%	42%
There has been some discussion about whether the United States should use its troops to invade Iraq and overthrow the government of Saddam Hussein. Which of the following positions is closest to yours?		
Only with UN approval and the support of its allies	50%	59%
Do you think that for the United States to invade Iraq at this point, it is necessary or not necessary to get approval from the UN Security Council?		
Necessary to get approval	61%	72%

Source: Program on International Policy Attitudes, January 28, 2003, poll.

In her early analysis of the gender gap following the 1980 election, Kathleen Frankovic focused on issues of war, peace, and the environment to explain differences between men and women in their evaluation of President Ronald Reagan:

> Today, as before, women are more likely than men to fear a nuclear war and less likely to want the United States to be aggressive in its dealings with foreign countries. But the extent of sex differences on issues goes beyond war and peace to other life-preserving questions. Women are more likely than men to take a stronger position on the preservation of the environment. They are less likely than men to support off-shore drilling for oil . . . less likely to be in favor of the construction of nuclear power plants. . . . These issues appear to be directly related to the different evaluations women and men give Ronald Reagan" (1982, 444).

Although both men and women have tended to support the death penalty, women have been less supportive than men. In 1988, 76 percent of women and 86 percent of men supported the death penalty. Gun control has been a major issue of contention between men and women, too. A May 2000 Gallup survey asking, "In general, do you feel that the laws covering the sale of firearms should be more strict, less strict, or kept as they are now?" found that 72 percent of women and 52 percent of men favored stricter laws covering the sale of firearms. In 1998, the National Opinion Research Center at the University of Chicago did an extensive attitudinal poll on guns. On forty-one of forty-five questions, a statistically significant difference existed between men and women. In each case, women were more concerned about risk and violence and more supportive of safety steps and restrictions (Gilbert and Skiba 2000).

Women's Rights

NOW emphasized feminist concerns in the early 1980s as accounting for the rise in the gender gap. But the group's thesis is not supported by public opinion data. Men and women have consistently over time varied little in their endorsement of equality for women. Public opinion surveys have shown that a majority of men supported women's rights issues earlier than did a majority of women. The general public has been supportive of most issues regarding equality for women in the political and economic realm, and women and men have had similar levels of support for these issues extending back to the 1970s. From 1970 on, in response to questions whether they favored or opposed efforts to strengthen and change women's status in society, over 80 percent of both women and men have said that they favored such efforts. Figure 4.8 presents one example of the lack of a gender gap on equality issues. Presented with the statement: "Some people feel that women should have an equal role with men in running business, industry and government and others feel that a woman's place is in the home," a majority of both men and women have opted for equal roles. Furthermore, on the controversial issue of abortion rights, men and women have expressed similar views over time. Figure 4.9 shows the closeness of men's and women's positions on

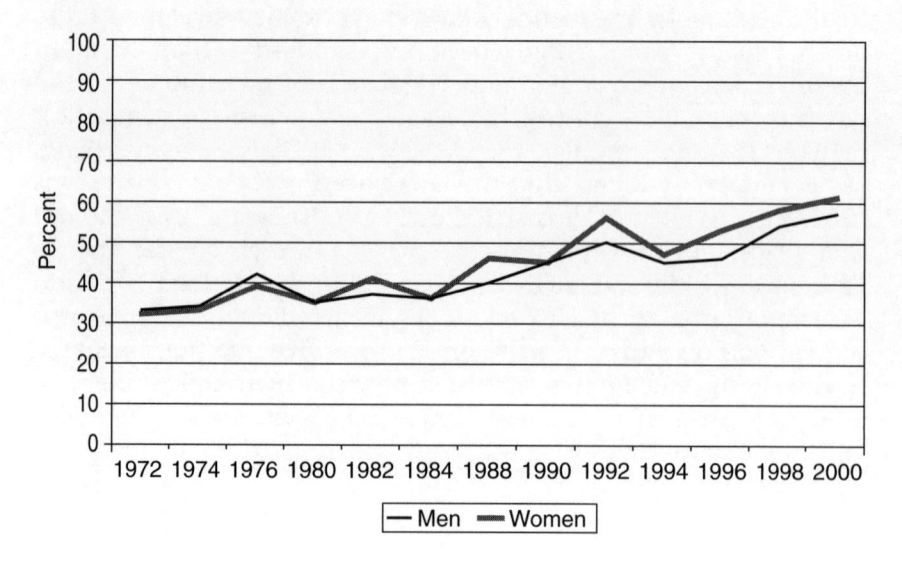

FIGURE 4.8 Percentages of Men and Women Favoring Equal Roles for Men and Women 1972–2000

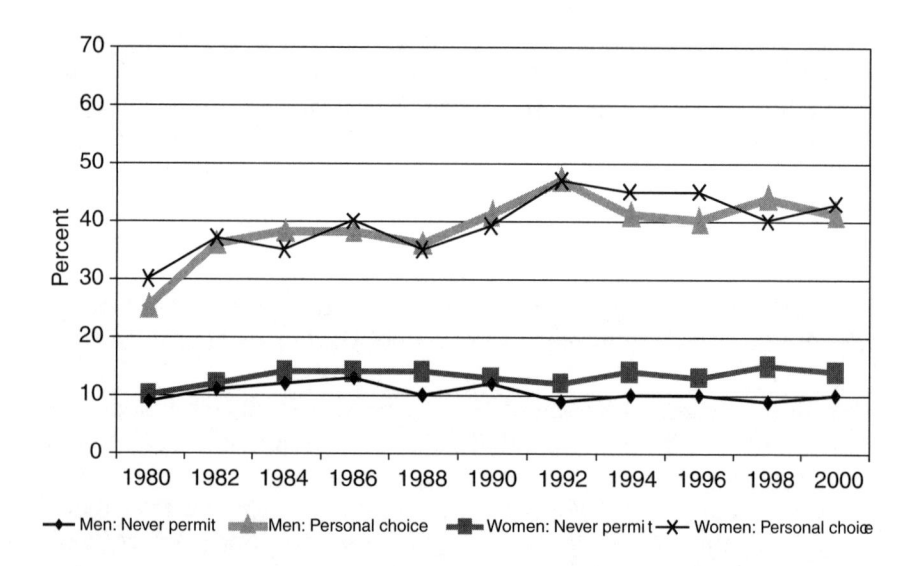

FIGURE 4.9 Opinion on Abortion, Men and Women, 1980–2000

the extreme opinions on the abortion statement: Abortion should never be permitted or abortion should be a matter of personal choice.

The second domain beyond issues of force in which a gender gap has emerged has been in the area of "compassion issues." Women tend to see government as a way to fix problems and make lives better; men tend to see it as obtrusive and meddling. Women are more likely than men to be caregivers of children and of aging parents, so they are more likely to see ways in which government can help people. Polls have consistently shown that women are more concerned than men about education, government spending on programs for the poor and needy, and issues like Social Security and Medicare; the polls show that men are more skeptical of government, whereas women have a more expansive view of what government can and should do. Women are the chief beneficiaries of programs such as Social Security and Medicare, or they are the caretakers of those beneficiaries. Women often work in government jobs, as teachers, social workers, or in libraries and arts councils, all of which probably contributes to their greater support for government services and an activist government. Figure 4.10 shows the difference between men and women in their support for government services.

Economic Issues

Women tend to place more emphasis on the national economy than men do. Sometimes political scientists consider this perspective a more sociotropic view of the economy, meaning that women consider how society as a whole is doing, regardless of their own financial situation, whereas men vote based on their view of their personal finances (pocketbook voting). Traditionally women have been socialized to emphasize values such as cooperation, nurturance, sacrifice, harmony, and moralism, whereas men are socialized to prize rationalism, competition, and objectivity. These distinctions may be exaggerated, but the extent to which women remain less imbued than men with the values of competition and aggression, "we might expect them to be less likely to select a candidate for personal economic reasons, since these values underlie economic criteria" (Welch and Hibbing 1992, 202). Women also tend to be more pessimistic than men as to the health of the economy, perhaps in part because they

112 ■ **Women and Political Participation**

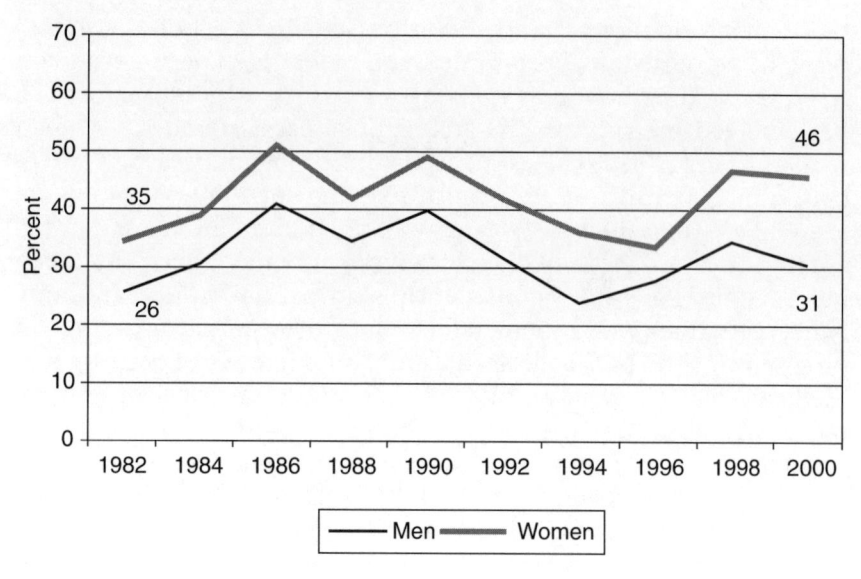

FIGURE 4.10 Men and Women's Support for Government Services, 1980–2000

are not as financially well off as men and more dependent on the welfare state.

The Effect of Gender on Elections

The gender gap has been a concern not only for presidential candidates but also in races for lower-level offices. Two features of the electorate are important here: differences in votes for candidates in general and differences in support for female candidates. Figure 4.11 shows that the voting tendencies of men and women in terms of the percent of their votes going to Democratic candidates in U.S. House of Representative races have tracked quite closely, as measured by the aggregated percent of the vote for one of the major parties' candidates. The gap grew somewhat in the 1990s.

This general measure may mask the impact of gender on individual races. Exit polls, surveys conducted at random samples of polling stations throughout the country asking people about their voting decisions as they exit the polls, allow us to determine the extent to

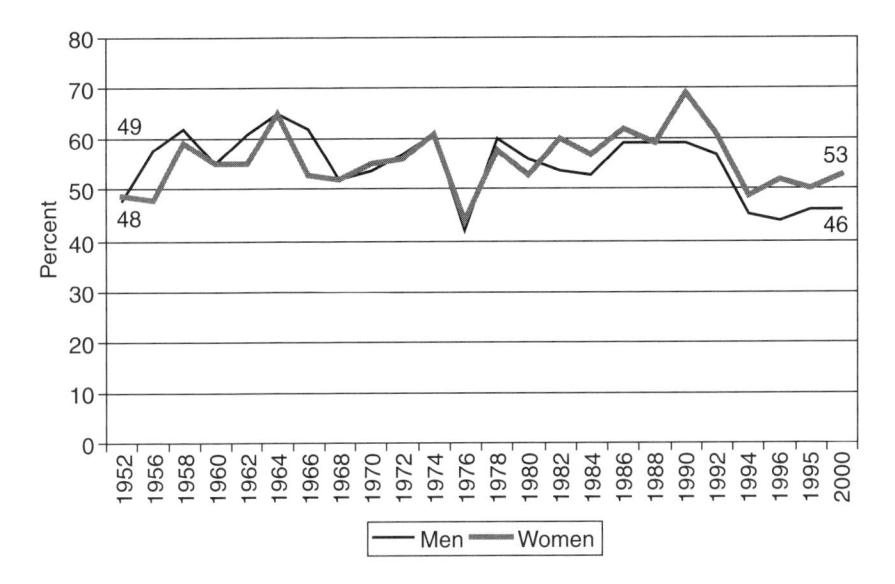

FIGURE 4.11 How Men and Women Voted for U.S. Representatives (% of Vote for the Democratic Candidate), 1952–2000

which gender has mattered in individual gubernatorial and senatorial races.

With respect to all elections there has been no definitive answer to the question whether women vote for women in the gender gap era. But exit poll data do show a tendency for women to support other women to a greater extent than men do. Democratic women candidates have been especially advantaged in this realm. Smith and Selfa reported in 1992 that "since 1980 Democratic candidates regardless of their gender have done better among women than have Republican candidates" (1992, 30). In the 1992 "Year of the Woman" voting, women candidates for the U.S. House and Senate won more votes from women than from men (Wilcox 1994). Examining gubernatorial and senatorial elections from 1990 through 1994, Seltzer et al. (1997) concluded: "[O]n average, women have been slightly more likely than men to vote for women candidates. The average gender gap (tendency for women to vote more Democratic than men) was several points greater when the Democratic candidate was woman and several points smaller when the Republican candidate was a woman than when both candidates were men." Kathleen Dolan's study of voting for women candidates in U.S. House of Representative races for six election years led her to conclude: "In some elections, women voters were more likely to support women candidates, but not in others. In some years, such issues as abortion or defense were related to choosing women candidates, but not always" (2004, 154).

In the 2000 New York senatorial election, women voters provided the margin of victory for Hillary Rodham Clinton. Men split their votes evenly between Clinton and her opponent (49 percent for Clinton and 49 percent for Rick Lazio), whereas women overwhelmingly preferred Clinton to Lazio (60 percent to 39 percent). Two other female Democratic senatorial candidates challenging Republican incumbents also won their elections thanks to the votes of women. Women voters provided the margin of victory for Debbie Stabenow against Senator Spencer Abraham in Michigan. A majority of women (54 percent) voted for Stabenow, and an equally large majority of men (54 percent) voted for Abraham. In Washington State a majority of women (54 percent) voted for Maria Cantwell, and an equally large majority of men (54 percent) voted for her opponent, Senator Slade Gordon.

Journalists capture political trends with catchy phrases. Political consultants like to divide the electorate into voting segments and focus on what have come to be called "swing voters," voters who could vote for either party and thus swing the election for one party or the other. Gender-related stories in recent elections have been part of this phenomenon. Thus, 1992 was "the Year of the Woman," and the 1994 election became known as the "Year of the Angry White Male." Two years later in 1996, "soccer moms" was the catch phrase, and in 2004, "NASCAR dads" emerged as a viable political group for candidates to appeal to, although a counterforce focusing on single women also appeared.

The 1992 election became known as the "Year of the Woman" because record numbers of women ran for public office and were victorious. In the 102nd Congress (1991–1992) only two women were U.S. senators. But in the 1992 election, four women won new seats in that body, tripling their numbers. Twenty-four new women were elected to the House of Representatives, increasing the number of women in that body from twenty-nine to forty-seven, the largest increase ever by far. Women also made gains in state legislative elections. A large number of seats in the U.S. House of Representatives were open (i.e., did not have incumbents running for reelection) that year because of redistricting after the 1990 Census; because several incumbents chose not to seek reelection, ambitious women politicians were provided with unprecedented opportunities. Special circumstances also motivated women to run in record numbers. Bank and post office scandals in the U.S. House of Representatives made the public less accepting of the status quo and contributed to a strong anti-incumbent movement. Women candidates, viewed as outsiders, were seen as attractive alternatives. Voter stereotypes of women candidates played to their advantage in that election. Women candidates were perceived as more likely than male candidates to have new ideas, to be honest, to stand up for what they believed regardless of the political consequences, to understand the voter needs, and to be moral and upright (Carroll 1994).

In addition, issues central in that election were ones on which women had been perceived as particularly competent, such as education, health care, and unemployment. Finally, the Senate Judiciary Committee hearings on the nomination of Clarence Thomas to be a justice on the U.S. Supreme Court stimulated some women to run and receive a positive reception from voters, particularly women voters. These televised hearings involved an all-white, all-male panel of senators grilling Anita Hill, a law professor, about her charges of sexual harassment by nominee Thomas. The existence of opportunities and a "large pool of skilled women politicians ready to exploit those opportunities" made 1992 a year in which women substantially increased their numbers in elective office (Wilcox 1994).

The election to the U.S. Senate in 1992 of Patty Murray, a Democratic state senator from Washington State, is representative of gender politics in U.S. elections. Running on the theme of "just a mom in tennis shoes," she won this high office. She was perceived as an outsider in a year in which such an image was very much a political plus. She had begun her activism in politics as a suburban mother when she organized a grassroots lobbying campaign to urge the state legislature to do something about pesticides that blew into her yard as her young son played. She also became involved in local education issues and served as a member and president of the Shoreline School Board.

Murray went on to beat an incumbent state senator through an aggressive door-to-door campaign. The story goes that upon arriving at the state Senate she was dismissed by another legislator as "just a mom in tennis shoes." However, she became minority whip, the fourth-ranking position in the Democratic leadership and became known for her hard work and powerful presence in the legislature. But after one term she announced her candidacy for the U.S. Senate initially in a primary against the Democratic incumbent senator, Brook Adams. Adams eventually dropped out of the race because of allegations of sexual harassment.

She adopted the "mom in tennis shoes" theme as "an intentional effort to cast herself as the underdog. That the slogan also evoked images of family, the middle class, and womanhood was more than a tangential benefit" (Schroedel and Snyder 1994, 56). Women were largely responsible for Patty Murray's victory, voting for her in large numbers. Public opinion polls indicated she had a two-to-one margin among women over her closest rival in the primary. The general election exit poll showed that women voted for Murray by a 58 to 42 percent margin, whereas only 51 percent of men voted for her. Women also supported her with their money. Most of her individual contributions came in amounts of less than $200. But the Federal Elections Commission reports also show that women gave $205,650, and men gave $173,900 in contributions of $200 or more. The large contribution category of $200 or more, 61 percent of which came from women, also indicated the disproportionate financial aid she received from women. She also received approximately $200,000 in campaign contributions from women nationally through EMILY's List. EMILY's List, NOW, and the National Women's Political Causcus (NWPC) all endorsed her, giving her campaign national exposure (Schroedel and Snyder 1994).

The 1994 national midterm election occurred in a very different context from the 1992 election regarding gender politics. Crime was the dominant issue in the 1994 policy debates. Public opinion polls repeatedly showed crime topping the list of voter concerns, and women were viewed as being soft on crime. According to pollster Celinda Lake, who had worked for many female congressional and gubernatorial candidates: "It's very hard for women to show toughness. I think women can get over that barrier but it's one of the biggest barriers facing them. Women are definitely hurt by the fact that crime is the number one issue" (Foerstel and Foerstel 1996, 51). Republicans took over the U.S. House of Representatives in 1994 for the first time since the 1950s, even ousting the Democratic Speaker of the House, Tom Foley of Washington State. The day after the election, the *Washington Post* wrote: "Two years ago, it was the Year of the Woman. This time around the elections may be know as the Year of the Man, or the Year of the Angry Man." White men voted Republican by a margin of 63 to 37 percent, whereas women disproportionately stayed home, leading to the description of the election as the revenge of the "angry white men." That phrase seems to have been coined by *USA TODAY* in its analysis of election results on November 11, 1994, in a pieced titled "Angry White Men: Their Votes Turn the Tide for GOP; 'Men Want to Torch Washington.'" Everett C. Ladd (1997) counted 1,500 stories about the "angry white male" on the Lexis-Nexis on-line news site through November 1995.

White men, according to news reports, were angry at President Bill Clinton because of his stands on issues like homosexuals in the military and health care. They felt they had not participated in the economic recovery. They were angry about crime, welfare, immigration, and affirmative action. Men have become more sympathetic to hardline Republican positions on issues like crime and taxes, which were central to political campaigns that year. Nationwide, 54 percent of men and 46 percent of women voted for Republican House candidates, according to the exit polls of voters, the largest gap since at least 1980. Among white voters, 62 percent of men voted for Republican congressional candidates, as did 55 percent of white women. Thus, control of the agenda in the U.S. Congress shifted from the Democrats, who wanted to expand social-welfare programs like national health insurance, to Republicans, who believed they had an electoral mandate to dismantle the welfare state the Democrats had constructed.

"Angry white men" were reported to feel devalued and displaced. From the ranks of the service sector to middle management, men saw the rights revolution on behalf of women and Blacks moving beyond a level playing field to a system of exclusionary favoritism, and they saw a present and a future of sharply declining wages and status. "For these men, the workplace, and often the home, are places where they are viewed as the illegitimate beneficiaries of a past patriarchal, white order. This external experience stands in direct contrast to their own dominant internal experience of descent and decline" (Edsall 1994, A31).

Case Study: Soccer Moms

The context of national elections changed again two years later. The media framed the 1996 presidential election in terms of "soccer moms." They became the key swing group on which candidates would focus. According to the research of Susan Carroll (1999), the term first appeared in the news media in a July 21 *Washington Post* article by E. J. Dionne Jr., where he defined the soccer mom as "the overburdened middle income working mother who ferries her kids from soccer practice to scouts to school." His article suggested that the term *soccer mom* was a creation of consultants involved in the presidential campaigns.

No clearly agreed upon definition of the soccer mom emerged in press coverage, but typically she was a mother who lived in the suburbs; was a swing voter; harried, stressed out, or overburdened; worked outside the home; drove a minivan, station wagon, or sports-utility vehicle; was middle-class, married, and white (Carroll 1999). The candidates in the presidential election therefore emphasized programs that would appeal to "moms," such as President Clinton's focus on school uniforms, teen curfews, and installing V-chips in television sets. He took credit for and urged expansion of the Family and Medical Leave Act and advocated longer hospital stays for childbirth. He expressed opposition to cigarette advertising aimed at teenagers. Families and children, especially women and children interacting, often appeared in ads encouraging the reelection of President Clinton. Women were "shown helping their children with homework, carrying in groceries with their children, and sending their children to school with lunch in hand" (Jamieson, Falk, and Sherr 1999, 15). The gender of the children in the ads also invited female identification. When individual children appeared in the advertisements, they were often girls. Clinton's opponent, Senator Bob Dole, took the stage with "soccer moms" and stressed tax relief aimed at helping mothers to stay at home or be employed at home. Thus, the 1996 election, while emphasizing the importance of women voters, stressed a certain type of woman in a certain situation.

Case Study: "W Stands for Women"

Women's votes and gender politics were central to the presidential election of 2000. Media reports during the election highlighted gender as "the most decisive battleground of the 2000 presidential election" and predicted that women might "decide the presidential race." Each campaign was reported as "tirelessly ask[ing] itself 'what do women want?'" On March 15, an article appeared in *USA TODAY* with headline "Women Hold the Key: In a Close Race, Female Vote Might Deliver Victory" (Page 2000, A1).

Early in the campaign season, George W. Bush, the leading candidate for the Republican nomination, decided not to cede women's votes to the Democrats. He developed a message of "compassionate conservatism," which suggested a humane approach to government.

He talked often about education, his favorite theme, with a pledge "to leave no child behind." He promised to ease the tax burden on single women with children and to end the tax penalty married couples paid. He discussed faith-based solutions to social problems, which injected into the campaign a tone of morality that some analysts say women like (Wilkie 2000). In a post–1996 election analysis, Bush, then governor of Texas, stated that "the Republican Party must put a compassionate face on a conservative philosophy. . . . The message to women . . . is we care about people. The message is: We care" (Balz 1996, 1).

Initially in the 2000 presidential campaign, women gave Republican George Bush more favorable ratings than presumed Democratic presidential nominee Al Gore. In January 2000, Bush led Gore among women 42 percent to 41 percent (WOMEN VOTE! Monitor poll, January 2000). But by the fall campaign, Bush's support from women had fallen greatly and presaged a defeat in the November election: "The most stunning development in the latest, post–Labor Day round of national polling is Al Gore's lead among women voters. The vice president not only erased the advantage Bush held earlier with women. With an appeal centered on social and economic security for working families, Gore also opened up a gender gap—call it a chasm—that appears to be the biggest since pollsters noted a Mars-and-Venus disparity in voting behavior in the 1980 presidential race—20 points in the CNN/USA Today/Gallup poll, 57 percent of women favored Gore compared with 37 percent of men" (Leonard 2000, 1).

The significance of women's votes for the two presidential candidates in 2000 can be seen in the activities they engaged in and the time they spent talking to women. "Both Bush and Gore are wooing women in every way they can: the words they use, the issues they emphasize, the audiences they choose to appear before and the ads they air" (Page 2000, 1). Both parties' national conventions were structured to appeal to women voters. Women speakers were prominent at the convention, and issues noted to be of special concern to women were highlighted. The famous Gore kiss of his wife on the podium at the Democratic National Convention worked to dispel his image of being cold and mechanical. The title of his acceptance speech was "Lessons from his Mother." At the Republican convention, U.S. Representative Jennifer Dunn served as master of ceremonies, and women were prominent as speakers, often focusing on issues perceived to be of special concern or interest to women. Both nominee Bush and his wife, Laura, emphasized education in their convention speeches. Republicans also added a section on women's health care to their platform.

During the fall campaign, both candidates appeared on the Oprah Winfrey and the Regis Philbin shows, TV shows that have a particularly large audience of women. Al Gore's campaign developed a special Web site devoted to women entitled, "Al Gore: Fighting for Women." The site stressed the vice president's accomplishments and positions relating to such issues as equal pay, the Family and Medical Leave Act, the Civil Rights Act of 1990, the Women's Health Equity Act, breast cancer legislation, domestic violence, choice, and child care. Gore campaigned heavily on quality-of-life issues. He cast himself as "the defender of women's health-care needs against powerful, profit-driven health maintenance organizations and insurance companies" (Poole and Mueller 2001, 6).

The Bush campaign distributed a pamphlet, the "Blueprint for the Middle Class," that featured a picture with a woman on every page (Poole and Mueller 2001). And when it became clear that Bush was failing to win female voters, it was decided to "bring out the big guns." Notable women like former first lady Barbara Bush, the presidential candidate's mother, his wife, Laura, and vice presidential candidate Richard Cheney's wife, Lynne, were sent on a "W Stands for Women" tour, W being the middle initial in the candidate's name. "The women embraced the issue of education. They danced cautiously around the issue of abortion. And they returned time and again to the issue of integrity" (Bruni 2000, A30).

A second Bush bus tour was planned around the theme of a metaphor for life. Each day of the one-week tour represented a new stage in development from birth to retirement. Different issues relating to each stage were emphasized. For example, on the first day of the tour, Bush, while visiting a maternity ward in a hospital, stressed his plan to double the child-care credit. On subsequent days, the campaign focused on the issues of school safety, the marriage penalty, Social Security, and health care for the elderly (Poole and Mueller 2001). He used a health center for women and children in Little Rock, Arkansas, to argue that his domestic programs would benefit a wider range of middle-income voters than the programs of his Democratic rival.

As one journalist noted during the 2000 presidential campaign, "the campaigning on what were once considered 'women's issues, such as education, has become more sophisticated because these issues are "now near the top of the agenda for voters in general. Some analysts in fact, talk of the 'feminization' of politics'" (Toner 2000).

The 2002 election was very different from a gender perspective from the 1992 "Year of the Woman" election. Whereas the 1992 elections focused on domestic issues, the 2002 election centered on national security and war against terrorism after the September 9, 2001 attacks. Whereas in 1992, in the wake of scandals in the House of Representatives, "Washington outsiders" enjoyed a favorable atmosphere, in 2002 pollsters talked about the decisiveness and effectiveness of the incumbents, and women candidates were experiencing tougher races (Leonard 2000, A3). Redistricting that had occurred as a result of the 2000 census did not create as many open seats in the U.S. House of Representatives as in 1992, and new districts were drawn in a highly partisan manner, creating little competition between the parties.

The 2002 election *was* promoted, however, as the "Year of the Woman Governor." Term limits that opened up a several gubernatorial seats provided a particularly opportune election season for newcomers seeking governorships. Only five of fifty states had women governors going into 2002, but ten women obtained their party's nomination for the election including both a Democratic woman and a Republican woman who ran against each other in Hawaii. In the end, however, the number of women governors only increased by one. The number of women in the U.S. House of Representatives decreased from sixty to fifty-nine. While Democratic Senator Jean Carnahan was defeated in her reelection bid in Missouri, former secretary of labor and transportation Elizabeth Dole won a U.S. Senate seat in North Carolina, keeping the number of women in the U.S. Senate the same at thirteen.

Gender continued to play a prominent role in the 2004 presidential election. Both President George W. Bush and challenger John Kerry targeted women voters with messages about health care, education, and homeland security. The prominence of gender to the campaign strategies of the two major parties is noted in a *Congressional Quarterly Weekly* Special Report titled "Erasing the Gender Gap Tops Republican Playbook." The article lists a number of legislative initiatives Republicans have undertaken in Congress to appeal to women voters, such as the "Healthy Mothers and Healthy Babies Access to Care Act," which addressed tort reform. Democrats in return worked to protect their base by trying to increase voter registration and turnout among unmarried women, who had been known to seldomly vote, but when they did vote, to vote Democratic. Senator Hillary Rodham Clinton went door to door in New York and South

Florida for "Voices for Working Families," a coalition of labor unions, civil rights advocates, and women's organizations with a goal of registering 1,000,000 women, particularly minority women in battleground states (Martinez and Carey 2004). In an interesting twist, the efforts to energize different groups of voters along gender lines involved the Republicans reaching out to so-called NASCAR dads.

Case Study: NASCAR Dads

The 2004 election saw a new group taking on political significance in the campaign process as swing voters, challenging soccer moms for candidates' attention: "NASCAR dads." Pollsters, political consultants, and journalists have defined this potentially key voting group in the 2004 campaign in a variety of ways, just as soccer moms in the 1996 election took on a number of defining characteristics. They have been described as:

- Blue-collar wage earners disaffected with politics and parties and willing to throw a vote to the candidate who speaks to his needs
- Working-class men who place more emphasis on values than on party labels
- Auto-racing fans, usually anti–gun control, who tend to live in more rural areas of the country
- Hard-working, average tax-paying Americans that are raising their families and putting their kids through school; patriotic gun owners who hunt, go shooting, love the Second Amendment
- Conservatively orientated men, but often aligned with Democrats on economic issues
- Churchgoers, love to hunt and fish, and may wear a T-shirt with the slogan "Guns, God, and guts: That's what made America great"

For Democrats, the NASCAR dad strategy was a conscious effort to regain some of that lost constituency, to reach out and connect with voters whose fathers never voted Republican in their lives and whose grandfathers certainly never did. In the Democratic campaign leading up to its caucuses and primaries in the 2004 presidential election, Senator Robert Graham of Florida, a candidate for his party's nomination for president, sponsored a truck in NASCAR's Craftsman series in a bold publicity endeavor to draw the attention of the NASCAR dads.

President George W. Bush made a point of attending the 2004 NASCAR season-opening Daytona race in Florida. Bush's plane did a flyby over the Daytona International Speedway, and after he landed, his motorcade took a spin around the track. Clad in a black racing jacket, he mingled with the drivers before the race. "I'm thrilled to be here," Bush said. "This is more than an event, it's a way of life for a lot of people." Asked if he would like to ride in one of the stock cars, Bush said, "I'd like to, but I'm afraid the agents wouldn't let me. I flew fighters when I was in the Guard and I like speed." Bush announced to the forty-three drivers, "Gentlemen, start your engines." More than 200,000 people saw the race in person, and an estimated 40 million watched on television (Bohan 2004).

The parties' attention to this group, however broadly defined, instead of to women's issues, suggests that women's participation may not mean as much as before. The idea that women's votes should be considered more important than men's votes because of their higher turnout may be fading. But the attention to these different gender groups suggests the continued centrality of gender in U.S. electoral politics. Furthermore, the gender battle in the 2004 presidential election is highlighted by groups organized to mobilize women such as EMILY's List and the Wish List, Mainstream Moms Oppose Bush (the MMOB) and 1000 Flowers. The MMOB registered as a political action committee with the Federal Election Commission and sponsored "Adopt-A-Swing-State" letter-writing parties around the country, targeting undervoting and unregistered women in the battleground states with issues-based, personal letters and mail-in voting information (www.themmob.com.). 1000 Flowers described itself as a group of ordinary citizens who came together to get more from our democracy. They launched a nonpartisan "Nail the Election" campaign to encourage unregistered women to register to vote. They produced beauty kits with counter displays, voter registration materials, and nail files with fun, encouraging slogans for distribution to nail and beauty salons across the country (www.1000flowers.org).

Case Study: Women's Voices, Women Vote

The group Women's Voices, Women Vote also emerged in the 2004 election to challenge the election's focus on NASCAR dads. Women's

Voices, Women Vote is a project to determine how to increase the share of unmarried women (women who were never married or who are divorced, widowed, or separated) in the electorate and develop a set of messages to motivate their participation. Based on Census Bureau figures, this nonpartisan organization estimated that close to 22 million unmarried women were eligible to vote in 2000 but did not and that if unmarried women voted at the same rate as married women, there would have been 6 million more voters in the 2000 presidential election. According to the U.S. Census, unmarried women are 46 percent of all voting-age women and 56 percent of all unregistered women. As of 2000, there were 16 million unmarried, unregistered women and 22 million unmarried, registered women who did not vote.

The project is designed to "change the culture of unmarried women" when it comes to voting. The organization planned to develop messages to engage these women, emphasizing that, in fact, they are able to affect the policies that influence their lives and that voting is a powerful way to do that. According to its Web site (www.wvwv.org), Women's Voices, Women Vote would develop models for "innovative and integrated campaigns with research tested messages, visuals, and voices, be they celebrities or ordinary people. In addition to the research about how to communicate with these women, we will also determine exactly where they are and how to reach them through sophisticated microtargeting in a number of key states."

A national survey that Women's Voices, Women Vote undertook in its early days found that unmarried women were more likely to describe themselves as liberal and were more pro-choice, by a substantial margin compared with married women; believed the country is going in the wrong direction; wanted government to play a prominent role in taking on the most pressing domestic problems, most particularly health-care costs and education; and supported a right to privacy and a woman's right to choose.

References

Alex-Assensoh, Yvette, and Karin Stanford. 1997. "Gender, Participation, and the Black Urban Underclass." In *Women Transforming Politics*. Edited by Cathy J. Cohen, Kathleen B. Jones, and Joan Tronto. New York: New York University Press.

Andersen, Kristi. 1996. *After Suffrage: Women in Partisan and Electoral Politics Before the New Deal.* Chicago: University of Chicago Press.

Balz, Dan. 1996. "Stands on Education Cost GOP among Women, Governors Told; New Message Urged as Surveys Find Larger Gender Gap." *Washington Post,* November 27.

Baxter, Sandra, and Marjorie Lansing. 1981. *Women and Politics: The Invisible Majority.* Ann Arbor: University of Michigan Press.

Bohan, Caren. 2004. "Bush Courts 'NASCAR Dads' at Daytona 500." http://news.myway.com.

Bonk, Kathy. 1988. "The Selling of the 'Gender Gap': The Role of Organized Feminism." In *The Politics of the Gender Gap: The Social Construction of Political Influence,* ed. Carol M. Mueller. Beverly Hills, CA: Sage.

Bruni, Frank. 2000. "The 2000 Campaign: The Families—Barbara Bush Joins GOP Women on Stump to Bridge Gender Gap." *New York Times,* October 19.

Campbell, Angus, Philip E. Converse, Warren E. Miller, and Donald E. Stokes. 1960. *The American Voter.* New York: John Wiley and Sons.

Carroll, Susan. 1994. *Women as Candidates in American Politics.* 2nd ed. Bloomington: Indiana University Press.

———. 1999. "The Disempowerment of the Gender Gap: Soccer Moms and the 1996 Election." *Political Science* 32(1) (March): 7–11.

Center for American Women and Politics. 1997. "The Gender Gap: Attitudes on Public Policy Issues." (Fact Sheet.) New Brunswick, NJ: Center for American Women and Politics.

Chafe, William H. 1991. *The Paradox of Change: American Women in the 20th Century.* Oxford, UK: Oxford University Press.

Clymer, Adam. 1980. "Displeasure with Carter Turned Many to Reagan." *New York Times,* November 9.

Cox, Elizabeth M. 1996. *Women State and Territorial Legislators, 1895–1995.* Jefferson, NC: McFarland.

Dolan, Kathleen. 2004. *Voting for Women: How the Public Evaluates Women Candidates.* Boulder, CO: Westview Press.

Edsall, Thomas. 1994. "Revolt of the Discontented: The GOP Got the Votes of Key Groups It Can't Expect to Satisfy When It's in Power." *Washington Post,* November 11.

Flexner, Eleanor. 1974. *Century of Struggle: The Women's Rights Movement in the United States.* New York: Atheneum.

Foerstel, Karen, and Herbert N. Foerstel. 1996. *Climbing the Hill: Gender Conflict in Congress.* New York: Praeger.

Foner, Philip S. 1976. *Frederick Douglass on Women's Rights.* Westport, CT: Greenwood.

Frankovic, Kathleen. 1982. "Sex and Politics—New Alignments, Old Issues." *Political Science* 15(3) (Summer): 439–448.

Freeman, Jo. 1993. "Feminism Versus Family Values: Women at the 1992 Democratic and Republican Conventions." *Political Science* 26(1) (March): 21–27.

———. 2000. *A Room at a Time: How Women Entered Party Politics.* Lanham, MD: Rowman and Littlefield.

Gilbert, Craig, and Katherine Skiba. 2000. "Politics: Gender Gap Is Here to Stay—Experts Tie Trend to Views of Government Role." *Milwaukee Journal-Sentinel,* October 30.

Gordon, Ann D. 1995. "Woman Suffrage (Not Universal Suffrage) by Federal Amendment." In *Votes for Women: The Woman Suffrage Movement in Tennessee, the South, and the Nation.* Edited by Marjorie Spruill Wheeler. Knoxville: University of Tennessee Press.

Harris, Louis. 1954. *Is There a Republican Majority?* New York: Harper and Brothers.

Harvey, Anna. 1998. *Votes without Leverage: Women in American Electoral Politics, 1920–1970.* New York: Cambridge University Press.

Jamieson, Kathleen Hall, Erika Falk, and Susan Sherr. 1999. "The Enthymeme Gap in the 1996 Presidential Campaign." *Political Science* 32(1) (March): 12–16.

Kaufmann, Karen M., and John R. Petrocik. 1999. "The Changing Politics of American Men: Understanding the Sources of the Gender Gap." *America Journal of Political Science* 43(3) (July): 864–87.

Kraditor, Aileen. 1965. *Ideas of the Woman Suffrage Movement, 1890–1920.* New York: Columbia University Press.

Ladd, Everett C. 1997. "Media Framing of the Gender Gap." In *Women, Media, and Politics.* Edited by Pippa Norris. New York: Oxford University Press.

Leonard, Mary. 2000. "Gore Gains Upper Hand Among Female Voters." *Boston Globe,* September 9.

Martinez, Gebe, and Mary Agnes Carey. 2004. "Erasing the Gender Gap Tops Republican Playbook." *Congressional Quarterly Weekly* (March 6): 564–570.

Mattei, Laura R. Winsky, and Franco Mattei. 1998. "If Men Stayed Home . . . The Gender Gap in Recent Congressional Elections." *Political Research Quarterly* 51(2): 411–36.

Page, Susan. 2000. "Women Hold the Key: In a Close Race, Female Vote Might Deliver Victory." *USA Today,* March 15.

Peck, M. G. 1944. *Carrie Chapman Catt: A Biography.* New York: H. W. Wilson.

Poole, Barbara, and Melinda Mueller. 2001. "To Kiss or Not to Kiss: The Politics of the Gender Gap in the 2000 Presidential Election." Paper presented at the annual meeting of the American Political Science Association, August 31, San Francisco, CA.

Ranney, Austin. 1975. *Curing the Mischiefs of Factions: Party Reform in America.* Berkeley: University of California Press.

Schroedel, Jean R., and Bruce Snyder. 1994. "The Mom in Tennis Shoes Goes to the Senate." In *The Year of the Woman: Myth and Realities.* Edited by Elizabeth Adell Cook, Sue Thomas, and Clyde Wilcox. Boulder, CO: Westview Press.

Seltzer, Richard A., Jody Newman, and M. Voorhees Leighton. 1997. *Sex as a Political Variable.* Boulder, CO: Lynne Rienner Publishers.

Shapiro, Robert Y., and Harpreet Mahajan. 1986. "Gender Differences in Policy Preferences: A Summary of Trends from the 1960s to the 1980s." *Public Opinion Quarterly* 50 (Spring): 42–61.

Silverberg, Helene. 1988. "Political Organization and the Origin of Political Identity: The Emergence and Containment of Gender in American Politics, 1960–1984." Ph.D. diss., Cornell University.

Smith, Tom W., and Lance A. Selfa. 1992. "When Do Women Vote for Women?" *Public Perspective* 3 (September/October): 30–31.

Toner, Robin. 2000. "Presidential Race Could Turn on Bush's Appeal to Women." *New York Times*, March 26.

Welch, Susan, and John Hibbing. 1992. "Financial Conditions, Gender, and Voting in American National Elections." *Journal of Politics* 54(1) (February): 197–213.

Wilcox, Clyde. 1994. "Why Was 1992 the 'Year of the Woman'? Explaining Women's Gains in 1992." In *The Year of the Woman: Myth and Realities*. Edited by Elizabeth Adell Cook, Sue Thomas, and Clyde Wilcox. Boulder, CO: Westview Press.

Wilkie, Dana. 2000. "Experts Surprised by Bush's Ability to Leap Gender Gap." *San Diego Union-Tribune*, May 29.

Young, Lisa. 2000. *Feminists and Party Politics*. Vancouver: University of British Columbia Press.

5
Women in Public Office

Americans elect thousands of individuals to public office, from local library and park board officials (and in some communities even coroner) to president of the country. In any one year, citizens of an area can go to the polls several times to cast ballots for public officials: in nonpartisan elections for local officials, in partisan primary elections for candidates for state and national office, and in general elections for those offices. Special elections may occur when an incumbent dies or leaves office for some other reason in the middle of a term, and in many communities citizens can be called upon to vote to recall officials before their term of office is up. Of all the people who have sought office and have won elective positions in the United States, exactly how many have been women is not known. It is known that the percentage of female elective officials is much less than their presence in the population. A few women did serve in elective office prior to the adoption of the suffrage amendment in 1920, but it has only been since the second women's rights movement, beginning in the 1960s, that women have been elected to public office in substantial numbers and have been moving into legislative and executive positions, but they still are far from being numerically representative, especially in higher-level offices.

In addition, the fact that women obtained the vote with the passage of the Nineteenth Amendment in 1920 did not automatically mean that they had the right to run for and hold public office. Some states initially tried to prevent women from running for public office. For example, New Hampshire's attorney general issued an official statement saying that under common law a woman could not hold office, but in 1920 New Hampshire voters elected two women to the state legislature anyway. In Arkansas, however, a woman had to withdraw her candidacy because the state had disqualified her. To clarify women's status, women's rights activists lobbied for specific legislation granting the right to hold office. A Detroit circuit judge settled the issue in Michigan. An opponent of women's rights had sued to remove a woman justice of the peace on the grounds that since she was married, she was a chattel and not a person, a "woman by law not being permitted to exercise a judicial office and to discharge the duties thereof, she being sexually unable to do so as a matter of nature and as a matter of law," the attorney argued. The judge cut off his plea and dismissed the case with the remark that the Nineteenth Amendment had settled all that. Elsewhere the issue dragged on for years; Iowa amended its constitution in 1926, Oklahoma in 1942 (Lemons 1973, 68–69). In addition, women have had to sue in court to obtain the right to sit on juries.

During the late-nineteenth and early-twentieth centuries, before the passage of the Nineteenth Amendment, women ran for and won office in both suffrage and nonsuffrage states, though the offices to which they were elected almost uniformly related to the governance of school systems. In the 1860s and 1870s, for example, a few women were elected to Massachusetts school committees even though women could not vote in their own elections, and in 1906 eighteen women were elected county school superintendents (out of fifty-three) in South Dakota (Andersen 1996, 113).

Women in Congress

In the year 2000, seventy-five years after obtaining national suffrage, women held 22.5 percent of the seats in state legislatures and 56 of the 435 seats in the U.S. House of Representatives (13.6 percent). Three of the 100 U.S. senators and 3 of the 50 governors were women. No woman had ever been elected president or vice president of the United States. One woman had received a major party nomination for vice president, Geraldine Ferraro, who was the Democratic

Party's vice presidential candidate in 1984. This means that 77.5 percent of state legislators, 87 percent of U.S. representatives, 97 percent of senators, and 94 percent of governors were men, and all of our presidents and vice presidents have been men, even though women are more than 50 percent of the population.

The first women to serve as representatives in state legislatures were the three who were elected to the Colorado General Assembly in 1894. They were Republicans. The first woman elected to the U.S. Congress was Jeannette Rankin, elected as a Republican from Montana in 1916, four years before women were granted the constitutional right to vote nationally. Montana had already granted women the suffrage. Rankin ran promising "to work for a federal suffrage amendment, an eight-hour day for women, improved health care for mothers and infants, tax law reform, Prohibition, and a stronger national defense" (Freeman 2000, 80). She served one term, during which time she cast one of fifty votes in the House opposing the declaration of war against Germany. She ran for the U.S. Senate in Montana in 1918 but lost. She was again elected to the U.S. House of Representatives in 1940. In that session of Congress, she cast the lone vote opposing the declaration of war against Japan. That vote effectively ended her career in elective office. Writing about women in the twentieth century, Sophonisba Breckinridge (1933) lamented the personage of the next woman to serve office in the U.S. House of Representatives after Jeannette Rankin. "A melancholy fate decreed that the first woman to sit in the House of Representatives after women all over the country were enfranchised should be an antisuffragist, Miss Alice Robertson of Oklahoma, who served only one term, received the nomination of the Republican Party a second time but failed of election in 1922."

The first woman to serve in the U.S. Senate was Rebecca Felton, who was appointed to her seat by the governor of Georgia in 1922 when the incumbent died. "Hers was a token appointment, part of a cynical process manipulated by the political ambitions of the men around her" (Foerstel and Foerstel 1996, 6). She served for only a short period until a new senator would be elected; during her tenure Congress was not in session. Thus, she never even had the opportunity to cast a vote. The first woman to win an election to the U.S. Senate was Hattie Caraway, Democrat of Arkansas. She was first appointed to her husband's seat when he died in office. She then won her own election in 1932 and was reelected in 1938. In 1992, California became the first state to have women as both its U.S. senators. Since then Maine and Washington have joined California with an all-female delegation to the U.S. Senate.

Many of the early women in Congress were tokens. Some were appointed rather than elected, and many came to their office through "special elections" held to complete the term for a seat left vacant by the death or retirement of a spouse or other congressional incumbent. Often, the woman filling out the term had to agree not to seek further office. Terms of only a few months were not unusual (Foerstel and Foerstel 1996, 1). Five of the first eight women in Congress obtained their seats through the death of an incumbent. Some of these women did go on to serve long, distinguished careers in Congress.

Through 1970, women completing the term of a deceased incumbent still represented the majority of all women who had served in Congress. Even today, widowhood remains a path for some members of Congress. In the 108th Congress (2002–2003), three of the fifty-nine female members of the U.S. House of Representatives entered through the "widow" route. Women members of Congress in the twenty-first century, however, are more likely to be strategic politicians than widows or women whose principal resource is the sociopolitical and economic status of their families. Strategic politicians tend to be ambitious, skilled, resourceful, and experienced professional politicians who run for a seat in the national legislature when the political opportunity presents itself for advancement (see Gertzog 2002). Figure 5.1 shows the trends in the percentage of women state legislators and U.S. representatives since 1961.

The first African American woman elected to Congress was Shirley Chisholm, who ran on the slogan "unbought and unbossed" in 1968. She was elected from the Twelfth Congressional District, in Brooklyn, New York, to serve in the U.S. House of Representatives. In 1972, she sought the Democratic nomination for president. Since then, eighteen more Black women have been elected to the House, making up 10 percent of all congresswomen who have served in that body. Through the 1990 election, the Black women elected to the U.S. House tended to represent urban districts outside the South. In 1992, however, five southern Black women were elected to the House. The 1992 election also saw the first Black woman to be elected to the U.S. Senate, Carol Moseley Braun. She beat an incumbent senator in the Democratic primary in Illinois and went on to win 55 percent of the vote in the general election. She was only to serve one term, being defeated for reelection in 1998. In 2003, she entered the Democratic Party's campaign for the 2004 presidential nomination, although she dropped out before any delegates to the party's nomination convention had been selected. As a result of the 2002 election, two Hispanic sisters were serving in the U.S. House of Representatives. With her

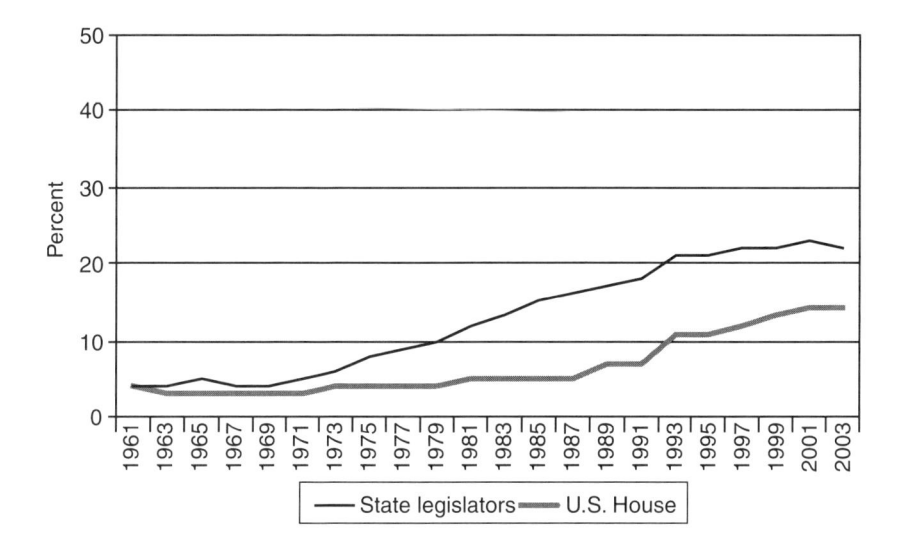

FIGURE 5.1 Women in State Legislatures and the U.S. House of Representatives, 1961–2003

victory in the Thirty-ninth District of California, Democrat Linda Sanchez joined her sister, Loretta Sanchez, in the House.

Case Study: The Sanchez Sisters

Loretta Sanchez was the first woman elected to the U.S. House in 1996 from the Forty-sixth District in Orange County, California. Prior to being elected to Congress, Representative Sanchez was a financial manager at the Orange County Transportation Authority. She had worked at a number of financial agencies and had run her own consulting business in Santa Ana, assisting public agencies and private firms with financial matters, including cost-benefit analysis, strategic planning, and capital acquisition. Her parents were Mexican immigrants who had worked at a local manufacturing plant. She has a masters' degree in business administration from American University. In 1996, she entered the Democratic primary to win the right to challenge incumbent Republican Bob Dornan in the general election. Her victory in the general election was characterized as one of the biggest upsets in the 1996 elections. Representative Dornan was a leader among right-wing conservatives and had raised huge sums of money for his many reelection campaigns. In 1996, he had even campaigned in the Republican primaries for the party's presidential nomination. Sanchez won the election by running a person-to-person grassroots campaign that focused on registering many Hispanic residents and on cable TV advertisement. The demographic makeup of the district had been moving in a more moderate public-policy direction, and Loretta Sanchez took advantage of that change. Congressman Dornan did not know what hit him until it was too late to respond effectively (Burton and Shea 2003).

In the House of Representatives in the 108th Congress, Congresswoman Sanchez was the ranking woman on the House Armed Services Committee. She was also the third-ranking Democrat on the Select Committee for Homeland Security. In the House, she was a member of the Hispanic Caucus, the Blue Dog Democrats, the New Democratic Coalition, the Congressional Human Rights Caucus, the Women's Congressional Caucus, the Older Americans Caucus, the Law Enforcement Caucus, and the Congressional Sportsman's Caucus.

Her sister, Linda Sanchez, joined her as a U.S. representative in 2003, having won an open seat to represent the 39th District of California. Linda Sanchez graduated from the University of California, Berkeley, where she earned a bachelor of arts in Spanish literature, with an emphasis in bilingual education. After working her way through undergraduate school as a bilingual aide and English as a Second Language instructor, she attended law school at the University of California–Los Angeles (UCLA), graduating and passing the bar exam in 1995. During her legal studies at UCLA, Linda Sanchez interned with the Honorable Judge Terry Hatter Jr., chief justice of the Central District Court in California, and spent a summer working for the National Organization for Women Legal Defense and Education Fund (NOW LDEF) in New York City. After law school, she practiced law in the areas of appellate law, civil rights, and employment law. She worked on Loretta's 1996 and 1998 congressional campaigns. She then lectured across the country for the National Association of Elected and Appointed Officials (NALEO) on how to run an effective grassroots political campaign. After the 1998 election, she went to work for the International Brotherhood of Electrical Workers (IBEW) Local 441 and the National Electrical Contractors Association (NECA) as a compliance officer on public works and prevailing wage issues. Prior to her election to Congress, she served as the executive secretary-treasurer for the Orange County Central Labor Council,

AFL-CIO. The Sanchez sisters often campaigned together and appeared with their mother in TV commercials.

Women State Officials

In the last three decades of the twentieth century, women increased their presence as state legislators fourfold, bringing their numbers to over 20 percent of legislative membership nationally. But women have not been equally successful in expanding their numerical representation across the states. In 2003, Washington State had the highest percentage of women among its legislators, with 36.7 percent, followed by Colorado and Maryland with 33 percent each. At the low end were South Carolina, where women were 9.4 percent of the state legislators and Alabama with 10 percent. Only 2 of the 46 state senators and 14 of the 124 state house members were women in South Carolina. Of the 1,648 women state legislators serving nationwide in 2003, 299, or 18.1 percent, were women of color. They included 83 senators and 216 representatives; all but 18 were Democrats. Women of color constituted 4 percent of the total 7,382 state legislators (CAWP 2003).

In 1998, Arizona voters achieved a historical first by electing women to all five of the top state offices, including governor. Executive offices are perhaps the ultimate elective leadership positions. How successful have women been in achieving these positions? Even in recent elections, questions have been raised about women being perceived as effective and tough enough to hold chief executives positions (The White House Project 2003).

Twenty-three women have been governors in the United States. The first three women in the governor's office were elected to replace their husbands. The first, Democrat Nellie Tayloe Ross of Wyoming, was elected in 1924 in a special election to replace her deceased husband. She served as governor from 1925 to 1927. She ran as the Democratic candidate for reelection in 1926 but was defeated in a close race. The next two women governors were elected as surrogates for husbands who could no longer serve as governor. Miriam "Ma" Ferguson was elected governor of Texas from 1925 to 1927. When her husband was impeached in 1917 and wasn't able to run in 1924, she ran and won. She ran for governor four times, winning twice. Lurleen Wallace was the third woman to head a state. She was elected governor of Alabama in 1966 as a consequence of an Alabama law that did not allow her husband, George, to succeed himself. George assured the voters there would be no "petticoat government. If [Lurleen] were elected she would be governor in name only. He would run the state as he always had." Lurleen Wallace died in office in 1968. Ella Grasso, Democrat of Connecticut, was the first woman governor elected in her own right. She became governor in 1974 after serving in the U.S. House of Representatives. She was elected to a second term in 1978. All of the women elected as governors since that time have won the position on their own.

Women Governors

The media dubbed the 2002 election as the "Year of the Woman Governor." "In 2002, Woman's Place May Be in the Statehouse," according to a *New York Times* headline (Clymer 2002). Opportunities for strategic politicians seeking these positions were plentiful in large part because term limitations prohibiting incumbents from running for reelection had opened up governorships for newcomers, and women were in a position to run credible campaigns for that office. Among the women seeking governorships were three lieutenant governors, two state attorneys general, one secretary of state, three state treasurers, one state insurance commissioner, and one former U.S. attorney general. Ten women ended up with their party's nomination for governor, nine Democrats and one Republican. In Hawaii, two women faced each other in the general election.

The media raised gender issues in its commentary on women running for governorships in 2002. Political consultants were quoted in the *New York Times,* for example, speculating that "women face a challenge in demonstrating 'toughness' so as to overcome doubts that they can make the cuts to balance the budget that would put people out of work, or cut day care or pull the switch on a convicted killer." "Running for governor is probably the hardest task because it's seen as a CEO position. A lot of voters are most resistant to voting for a woman for governor, asking, 'Can they be effective? Can they be decisive? Can they get things accomplished?'" (Clymer 2002). Others saw a changed political atmosphere that would play to women's advantage in seeking executive office. A *Chicago Tribune* story on the emerging number of women gubernatorial candidates stressed the idea that as a consequence of the September 2001 terrorist attacks, people have come to "realize that the best public servants can balance passion and emotion with expertise on foreign politics and economics. It plays to the strength of women with a holistic view of politics. Building relationships as well as being tough would be important" (Bierma 2002).

Four women were elected governor in 2002, joining two incumbents not up for reelection, bringing their total to an all-time high of six, four Democrats and two Republicans, 12 percent of the fifty governors. In 2003, two more women became governors when Kathleen Blanco won the governorship of Louisiana and Lieutenant Governor Dian Walker moved up to the governorship of Utah when her predecessor resigned to take a presidential appointment. Governorships are often the route to the White House, and women must run successful campaigns for governor if their chances of winning the presidency are to advance.

In many states elected executive positions, besides governors, include lieutenant governors, attorneys general, secretaries of state, and treasurers. In 2003, 80 women held statewide elective executive offices across the country, 25.3 percent of the 316 available positions. Among these women, 35 were Democrats, 42 were Republicans, and 3 were elected in nonpartisan races (CAWP 2003). These positions vary greatly in terms of their power and in terms of being stepping stones to higher office.

As of June 2002, among the 100 largest cities in the United States, 15 had women mayors. One was African American, Shirley Franklin, mayor of Atlanta, Georgia. And one was Latina, Heather Fargo, mayor of Sacramento, California (CAWP 2003).

The United States in Comparative Perspective

Although the United States may be one of the oldest democracies, it lags behind many other nations in the extent to which women have achieved political leadership status. The Inter-Parliamentary Union, an international organization of parliaments of sovereign states, headquartered in Geneva, Switzerland, was established in 1889. Among other goals, it works with parliaments to improve the status of women, particularly in economic and social fields, and tracks the numerical presence of women in national parliaments. The union classifies 181 countries on the percentage of women in the lower or single house of their national parliaments. Sixty-seven countries have a larger percentage of women legislators in their national parliaments than the United States has (Figure 5.2).

Structural features of electoral systems seem to matter in how well women have done across nations in getting elected to national par-

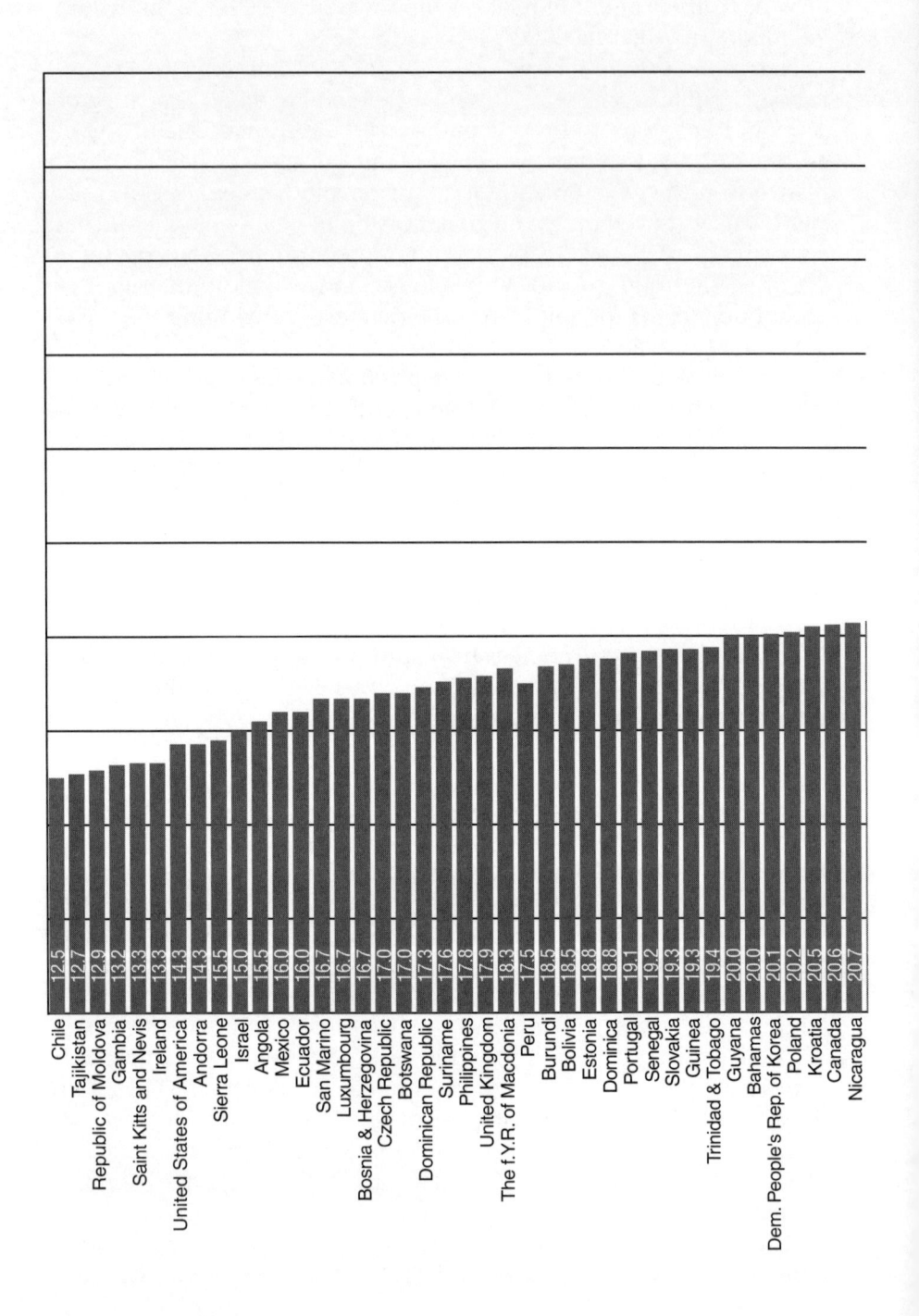

Country	Value
Chile	12.5
Tajikistan	12.7
Republic of Moldova	12.9
Gambia	13.2
Saint Kitts and Nevis	13.3
Ireland	13.3
United States of America	14.3
Andorra	14.3
Sierra Leone	15.5
Israel	15.0
Angola	15.5
Mexico	16.0
Ecuador	16.0
San Marino	16.7
Luxumbourg	16.7
Bosnia & Herzegovina	16.7
Czech Republic	17.0
Botswana	17.0
Dominican Republic	17.3
Suriname	17.6
Philippines	17.8
United Kingdom	17.9
The f.Y.R. of Macdonia	18.3
Peru	17.5
Burundi	18.5
Bolivia	18.5
Estonia	18.8
Dominica	18.8
Portugal	19.1
Senegal	19.2
Slovakia	19.3
Guinea	19.3
Trinidad & Tobago	19.4
Guyana	20.0
Bahamas	20.0
Dem. People's Rep. of Korea	20.1
Poland	20.2
Kroatia	20.5
Canada	20.6
Nicaragua	20.7

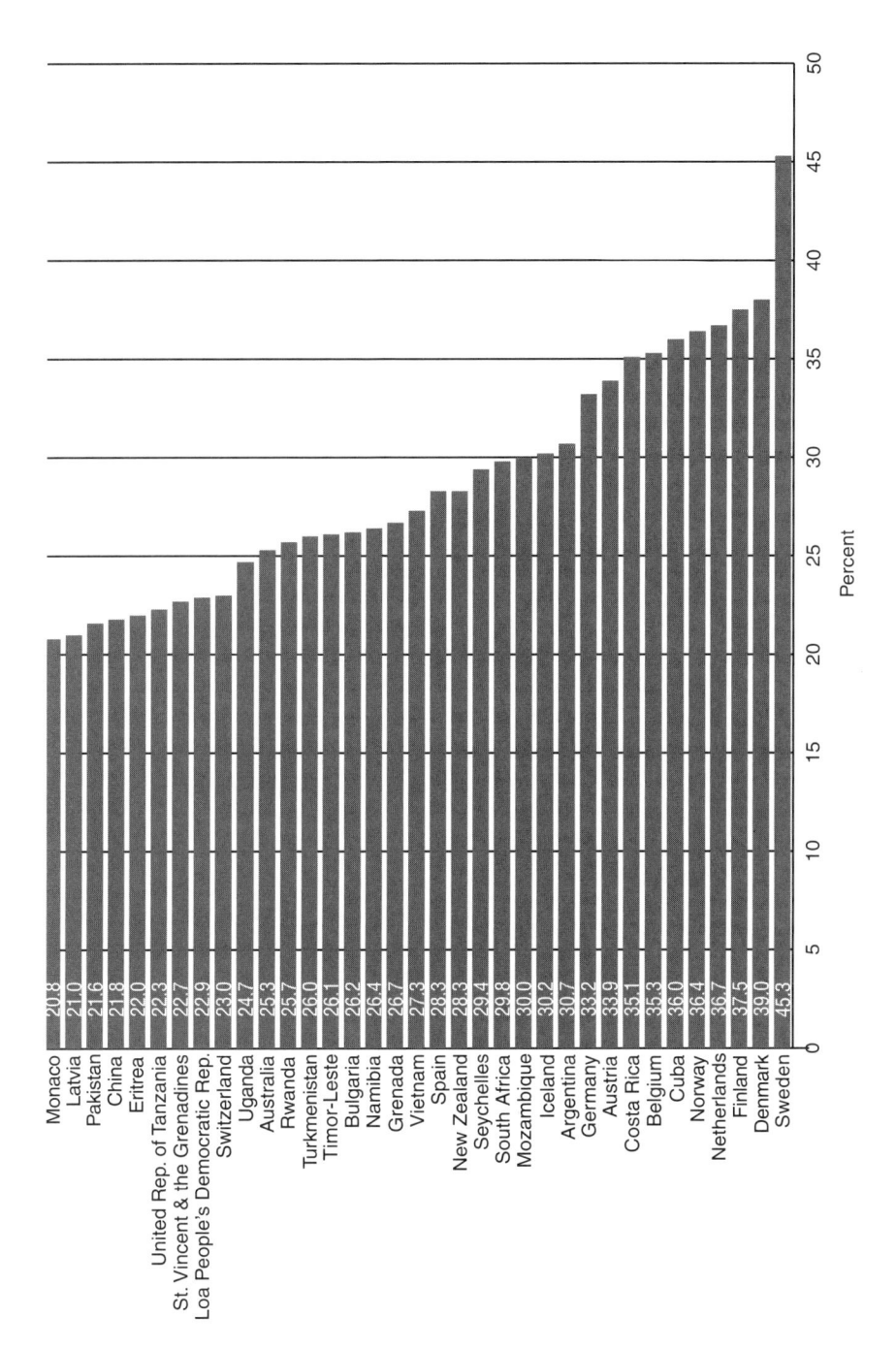

FIGURE 5.2   Women in National Parliaments

liaments. Proportional representation is the most advantageous system for women. In proportional-representation systems, political parties in legislatures are represented in the same proportion as the percentage of the vote they obtain in an election, usually with a percentage threshold. Voters cast ballots for the party, and each party receives seats in the legislature equal to its proportion of the votes. Parties select a list of candidates, often in rank order, to be their representatives in the legislature, and voters select more than one representative when they vote for a party. This system encourages parties to include women in their list of nominees; thus they are part of the slate of candidates. The ten highest-ranking countries in terms of women's representation all use proportional-representation systems. In a single-member-district system, such as that in the United States, voters can choose only one person to represent them. The person who gets the most votes wins the single seat in the legislature. Women have been less likely to be the "one" representative than one or several among a group of proposed representatives.

In addition, gender quotas for candidates have been an effective means of increasing female representation. Political parties in a number of countries, particularly in western Europe, have adopted quotas to ensure that significant numbers of women are included in their candidate lists. Since 1991, twelve Latin American countries have enacted legislation mandating that parties use quotas (Schmidt 2003). "Parity" has become the law in France. According to an amendment to the French Constitution ratified in 1999, "The law favors the equal access of women and men to electoral mandates and elective functions," and political parties are responsible for facilitating equal access. The law created a financial penalty for parties or political groupings that did not respect a balance between the number of women and men among their candidates. The public funding that a party receives from the state will be reduced if the deviation from parity reaches 2 percent among electoral candidates.

The Political Parties and Women Elected Officials

Most elective offices, particularly at the state and national level, are partisan in nature, that is, political parties nominate candidates for the office and their party affiliations are listed on the ballot. The Democratic and Republican Parties have dominated this process. In assessing the participation of women in political leadership positions, it is important to ask how well they have done within each of these two major parties. Determining how "women friendly" the two parties have been in electing female legislators and how supportive voters have been in casting ballots for the female candidates of each party requires that we consider each party's overall share of the body of legislators and the presence of female legislators within each party's cohort of legislators.

In thirty of thirty-three legislative sessions from 1938 to 2002, Democrats have had more state legislators than have Republicans. But between 1938 and 1974, there were more Republican women state legislators than Democratic women state legislators. Elizabeth Cox, who has chronicled the election of women state legislators since 1895 when the first women were elected to these positions, attributes this advantage to Republican women being better educated and having better financial resources than their Democratic counterparts (1996, 26–27). Since 1974, however, Democratic women have become the majority of female state legislators. Republican women continued to be a larger percentage of their party's legislative membership until 1994. In more recent elections Democratic women have become a larger percentage of their party's state legislators than Republican women. In 2002, they were over one-quarter of the state Democratic legislators (27.7 percent), compared with 17.6 percent for Republican women (Figure 5.3).

A different pattern emerges when one looks at the numbers of Republican and Democratic women members of the U.S. House of Representatives. Since 1955, more Democratic women have served in the House in each Congress than Republican women. Prior to that time, the parties fluctuated back and forth in terms of who had the greater number of women, although the number in total never exceeded eleven women, 2 percent of the total membership. Democratic women sharply increased their numerical presence as a result of the 1992 election, the "Year of the Woman" election. Their number went from nineteen to thirty-six, whereas Republican women went from nine to twelve. Democratic women maintained their advantage even after seven members were defeated in the 1994 "Year of the Angry White Male" election. Republican women have made some incremental gains since then, while the number of Democratic women members has been fairly stable. For Republican women, research has shown that the biggest problem appears to be in winning primary elections in open seats (Burrell 1994, King and Matland 2002). They are often viewed as being too liberal for the primary electorate, which tends to be very conservative. Democrats were also advantaged in

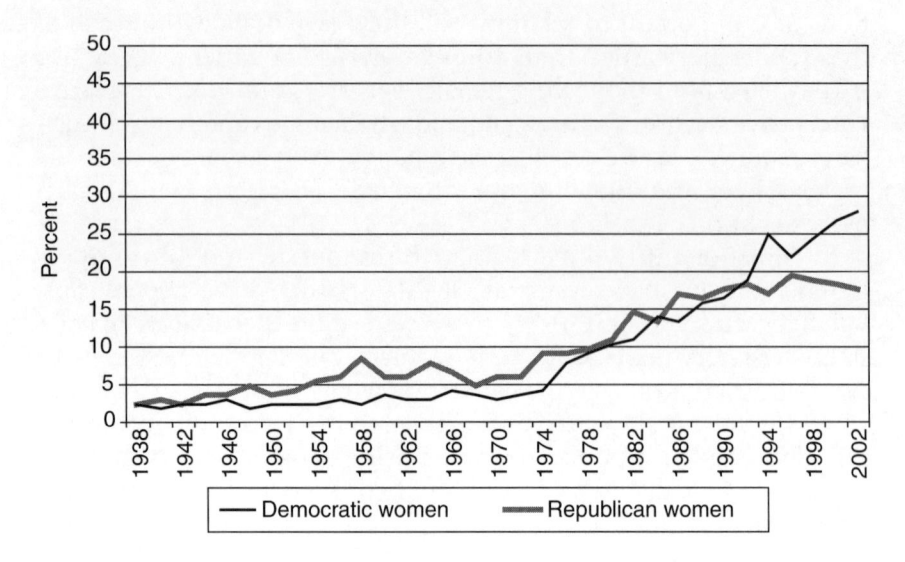

FIGURE 5.3 Percentage of Women Among State Legislators per Party, 1938–2002

having more women contest open-seat primaries (contests without an incumbent running for reelection) in elections at the end of the twentieth century. Women entering House races have been disproportionately Democrats.

Neither party has had much advantage among the few women who have been elected to the U.S. Senate. In the most recent Congresses, Democratic women have had some slight advantage. In the first two Congresses of the twenty-first century, the 107th and 108th, nine Democratic women have served as senators, whereas four Republican women served in the 107th Congress and five served in the 108th. A sixth female Republican became a U.S. Senator when Senator Frank Murkowski was elected governor of Alaska in 2002 and appointed his daughter Lisa, who was a state representative, to take his place in the U.S. Senate.

Both the Democratic and the Republican Parties have considered it to their advantage to establish programs to promote women's candidacies in response to the gender gap in voting and to the paucity of women in public office. Reacting to the perception of the Republican

Party as being "antiwoman" in 1983, the Republican Senatorial Campaign Committee (RSCC) issued a press statement declaring that "a concerted drive by the Republican Party to stamp itself as the party of the woman elected official would serve our nation as well as it served our own political interests.... The full political participation of women is a moral imperative for our society, and intelligent political goal for the Republican Party." Thus, Senator Richard Lugar, chair of the committee, pledged to "commit the RSCC to the maximum legal funding and support for any Republican woman who is nominated next year, regardless of how Democratic the state or apparently formidable the Democratic candidate." He added, "I am prepared to consider direct assistance to women candidates even prior to their nomination, a sharp departure from our usual policy" (Lugar 1983). Female senatorial candidates in 1984 were given $15,000 each to use in their primaries against other GOP contenders.

The National Federation of Republican Women (NFRW) has organized workshops and training sessions for would-be women candidates and campaign managers. The federation states that its mission is to "train women to run campaigns at every level of government."

Campaigning for Public Office

Women candidates for elective office have overcome a long history of discrimination. Given the obstacles in their path, we may be surprised that women have such a long history of service in public office. Over much of this history, women were encouraged by their parties to run for office primarily in "sacrificial lamb" situations, elections where their party was at a distinct disadvantage and had little hope of winning. They were believed to be inadequate fundraisers, without the fortitude to run tough campaigns. It was thought that voters would not support them and that they would be ignored by the media or that when the media did pay attention, they would focus on women candidates' appearance and on asking who was taking care of their children. The media were less likely to highlight the issues women candidates campaign on and more likely to focus on their male opponents' issues (Kahn 1996).

Citizens have tended to apply gender stereotypes when appraising candidates' personality traits and issue competencies. Women candidates have been seen as more warm, compassionate, and people-oriented, and less tough and aggressive than male politicians. Female politicians have been perceived as better able to handle compassion issues, such as education, health care, and poverty, but worse at dealing with big business, the military, and defense issues (Huddy 1994). Women candidates have struggled to overcome these stereotypes. Depending on the electoral context, women candidates may be advantaged because of these stereotypes, such as in the 1992 elections, and sometimes put at a disadvantage, as in the 1994 elections when crime was a major issue.

Women seeking public office have overcome most of those barriers. Contemporary research shows that when women run, they win as often as men. Women obtain the same percentage of the vote, raise equal amounts of money, and receive similar financial support from their national party organizations. Women candidates have also had an effect on the way campaigns are run and perceptions of political leaders. For example, Senator Barbara Mikulski promoted the idea that "you can be a lady and still go out there and give 'em hell" (Robson 2000, 208). "Just a mom in tennis shoes," was a theme that played well in the 2002 Washington State senatorial campaign of Patty Murray and has become infamous in campaign folklore. Running for the governorship of California and for U.S. senator, Dianne Feinstein was "tough but caring."

Yet women lag far behind men in their presence among elected officials at state and national levels. Two factors at opposite ends of the process seem to primarily account for this situation. One factor is incumbency. Incumbents tend to run for reelection, and when they do, they tend to have the advantage and most often win; moreover, because for such a long part of U.S. history, public life was considered to be inappropriate for women, most incumbents tend to be men. Therefore, opportunities to run viable campaigns for elective office at the state and national level are few. At the other end of the spectrum, when opportunities do arise, women are less likely to take advantage of them than men. For example, even in the 1992 elections, the "Year of the Woman" in U.S. politics, of the seventy-five seats in the U.S. House of Representatives that did not have an incumbent seeking reelection, only fifty-five had a Democratic woman seeking her party's nomination for that seat, and twenty-seven had a Republican woman seeking her party's nomination. Women in occupations from which candidates for public office most often come are less likely to become candidates than men in similar occupations because they are less

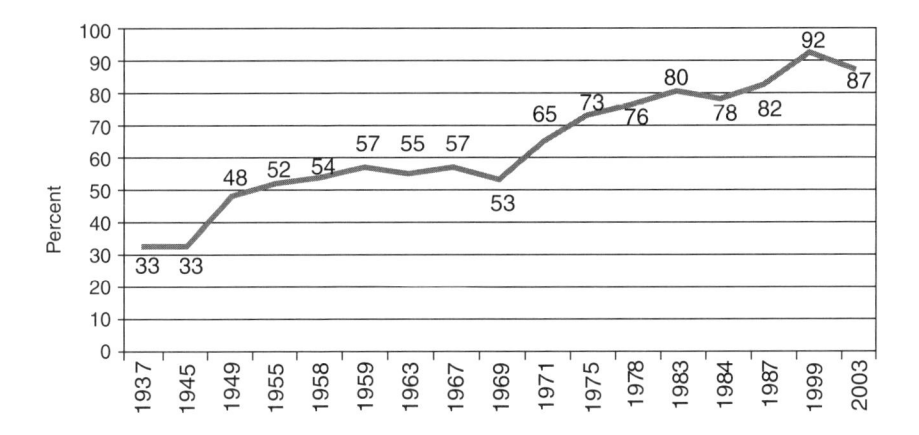

FIGURE 5.4 Willingness to Vote for a Woman Candidate for President, 1937–2003

likely to feel they are qualified to seek public office and because they are less likely to be asked (Fox and Lawless 2004).

A Woman for President?

Citizens of more than thirty-two countries have had a woman as either president or prime minister, but not the United States. Americans have come to support the idea of a woman being president of the United States at least in their response to General Social Survey public opinion polls asking them about whether they would vote for a woman for president (Figure 5.4).

Although no woman has ever been nominated by the Democratic or Republican Party as its presidential candidate, several women have sought their party's nomination. U.S. Senator Margaret Chase Smith (R-ME) was the first such candidate. She sought the nomination of the Republican Party in 1964. Senator Smith announced her candidacy in a speech to the Women's National Press Club in Washington, D.C. She said she considered entering the Republican primaries a test of "how much support will be given a candidate without funds . . . without a professional campaign organization of paid supporters, but instead with nonpaid volunteers, ... a campaign limited to times the Senate is not in session voting on legislation ... how much support will be given to a candidates who will not purchase time on television or radio or political advertisements in newspapers who will campaign on her record rather than on promises" (*Congressional Quarterly* 1964). Although she came in fifth in the New Hampshire primary, the first in the nation, she had her name placed in nomination at the Republican National Convention and received 27 votes out of 1,334. Barry Goldwater won the nomination.

One other woman has had her name placed in nomination for president by one of the two major parties: Shirley Chisholm, in 1972. She received 152 votes in the balloting at the 1972 Democratic National Convention. Representative Pat Schroeder explored a run for the Democratic Party nomination in 1987, and former transportation and labor secretary Elizabeth Dole sought the Republican nomination in 2000. Elizabeth Dole dropped out of the race before any of the primaries, citing her inability to raise adequate funds to continue her quest. Carol Moseley Braun sought the Democratic Party nomination for president in the 2004 election but dropped out before the first caucuses in Iowa. The first woman to seek the presidency was Victoria Woodhull, who ran as the Equal Rights Party nominee in 1872; Belva Lockwood ran as the Equal Rights Party nominee in 1884. Needless to say, they received few votes.

Case Study: Geraldine Ferraro, Vice Presidential Nominee

The "gender gap" in voting behavior was very much on the minds of candidates for the presidency in the 1984 election. Women's groups took advantage of the new status of women as a significant and distinct segment that needed to be appealed to in the electoral process. They held forums for the seekers of the Democratic Party nomination to give them the opportunity to address issues deemed to be of particular importance to women. In October 1983, NOW asked the candidates in one of these forums whether they would pledge to name a women running mate. The candidates who met with NOW all agreed to give serious consideration to a woman nominee. Having a woman named as the vice presidential nominee became a major goal of NOW and other women's organizations in 1984.

In December 1983 NOW endorsed Walter Mondale, the eventual Democratic Party nominee, for president. By the time of the Democratic Party's National Convention in July 1984, President Reagan seemed in a fairly strong position to win reelection, according to public opinion polls. The Democrats needed something to generate enthusiasm for its ticket and attract voters. Party officials as well as feminist activists saw possibilities in nominating a woman for vice president. Geraldine Ferraro, U.S. representative from New York, became the consensus candidate for this position among many groups within the Democratic Party. On July 12, 1984, Walter Mondale named her as his choice to be his running mate.

In the end, the Democratic Party ticket was overwhelmingly defeated. Massive numbers of voters did not turn out in support of Representative Ferraro, as supporters of a woman on the ticket had hoped or expected. Relatively few voters indicated that the vice presidential candidates had an impact on the way they voted. Among those voters who did cite an impact, there was a tiny net gain for the Democrats. As a potential leader of the country, Geraldine Ferraro suffered from traditional stereotypes the public has had of women candidates. Public opinion polls showed that potential voters saw a weakness in her ability to handle a crisis. From the time she won the Democratic nomination for vice president, she was viewed as less capable of handling foreign policy than George H. W. Bush, the incumbent vice president and Republican nominee for reelection (Frankovic 1988). At the same time, the Mondale campaign had not allowed her to appeal distinctively to women voters. She could not speak out strongly on issues that would resonate with certain segments of women voters and potentially generate higher turnout among them.

Case Study: EMILY's List and the WISH List

When women vote, Democrats win.
—Ellen R. Malcolm, President of EMILY's List

EMILY's List, which stands for "Early Money Is Like Yeast—it makes the dough rise," describes itself as a "political network for pro-choice

Democratic women that raises money to make women credible contenders." In 1992, CBS *60 Minutes* host Morley Safer described EMILY's List in a profile as "one of the most effective political action committees in the country." In the 2000 election cycle, EMILY's List was the number-two fundraiser among all the federal political action committees (PACs), according to the Federal Elections Commission, having receipts of over $14.5 million. EMILY's List began informally in 1984 when founder and president Ellen Malcolm and other politically active friends came together and circulated a list of Democratic women senatorial candidates to solicit money for their campaigns. As the need to make the group more formal became apparent, they began hosting across the country what political consultant Jeri Rasmussen has termed "the ultimate Tupperware party, with the grand prize being a U.S. Senate seat." A member might invite thirty to forty other women and tell them to bring their address books, which brought new names into the chain. The women, armed with Rolodexes, wrote letters and made phone calls, with the goal of raising money early for viable Democratic women candidates. They hoped to enlist a thousand members who would donate $100 to $1,000 each to a campaign (Southgate 1986).

EMILY's List became a formal PAC in 1986. But unlike traditional PACs, EMILY's List pioneered the campaign financing strategy of being a donor network, a practice that greatly enhanced its ability to give money to candidates and expand its influence. Usually, a PAC receives funds from members and then its board decides which candidates should receive donations and how much. Under federal election laws, PACs are limited to a $5,000 contribution per candidate in federal races. But as a donor network, EMILY's List has had a much greater impact. The donor network method of campaign contributing involves an individual paying a membership fee to join EMILY's List and choosing a candidate or (candidates) to support. The individual member makes a donation directly to that woman, using EMILY's List as a conduit; that is, rather than sending the check directly to the candidate, the check is sent to EMILY's List to pass on to candidates. In the parlance of the campaign finance literature, this technique is called "bundling." Checks to individual candidates from individual contributors are bundled together and presented to the candidate by EMILY's List. "This difference between the List and a traditional PAC is everything. There is no limit on how much EMILY's List can funnel to endorsed candidates through this process" (Spake 1988).

Candidates selected for EMILY's List support have had to be progressive, pro-choice, pro-ERA women. Viability is also a crucial factor in receiving money from the organization. Its primary strategy has been to raise seed money for the earliest stages of a campaign, when funds are hardest to obtain. Since 1986, EMILY's List has not only given money to candidates, but it has also trained candidates, campaign managers, fundraisers, and field organizers, and developed the Campaign Corps and the WOMEN VOTE! project. The Campaign Corps works to give young people an entry into politics. According to its Web site, "Campaign Corps trains recent college graduates and sends them out to targeted, progressive Democratic campaigns for the critical last three months of the election. After election day, Campaign Corps helps participants find their next political job and begin building a career."

The WOMEN VOTE! project is a long-term program aimed at mobilizing women voters to go to the polls. EMILY's List WOMEN VOTE! strategy is centered on giving resources to Democratic state parties so that they can "reach millions of women with messages that speak straight to them." WOMEN VOTE! was first employed as an election strategy in 1994 in California, where the state Democratic Party, with EMILY's List's support, targeted more than 900,000 women voters who had no history of voting in nonpresidential elections. The women received several get-out-the-vote messages delivered by mail and telephone. In May 1995, EMILY's List launched a national multimillion-dollar effort to help mobilize women voters nationwide.

EMILY's List promotes the WOMEN VOTE! project as educating women on the issues they care about—health care, education, and Social Security, for example. It conducts a WOMEN VOTE! Monitor poll to determine which issues are at the top of the agenda for women voters and which demographic groups of women voters are the best targets for Democratic candidates.

The results of this research are used to create mailing pieces and telephone scripts to motivate women voters targeted by EMILY's List. Political activists are trained to lead grassroots campaigns to increase voter turnout for Democratic candidates. In the 2000 election, EMILY's List raised and contributed $10.8 million for WOMEN VOTE! projects, with the aim of reaching many women by mail, by telephone, and in person to bring them to the polls.

In December 1991, EMILY's List was joined on the Republican side by the WISH List. WISH is an acronym for "Women in the Senate and House." The WISH List describes itself as a forward-thinking group of Republicans determined to transform the U.S. political landscape. The WISH List has adopted EMILY's List's strategy of soliciting members and then bundling checks together for endorsed candidates. Indeed,

Ellen Malcolm trained Glenda Greenwald, WISH List founder, in techniques to organize a counterpart structure within the Republican Party.

In its first campaign, the WISH List helped elect three women to the U.S. House of Representatives. In the 2000 election cycle (1999–2000), the WISH List had receipts of over $986,000. Like EMILY's List "Tupperware parties," the WISH List "Living Room groups" gain members and contributors. The WISH List also conducts campaign-training sessions. It supports Republican women for governor as well as U.S. representative and senator.

Although the WISH List supports only pro-choice female candidates, it also emphasizes on its Web site a belief in core Republican principles of individual freedoms and responsibilities, a sound economy, limited government, healthy communities, an educated citizenry, and a strong and secure nation. EMILY's List and the WISH List have even gone up against each other, supporting opposing candidates in general elections.

Women in Legislative Leadership Positions

Getting elected to public office is the first step toward parity in political leadership for women. The second step is gaining leadership positions within elective bodies. These positions include such offices as president or majority leader of senates, speaker or minority leader in assemblies, and powerful committee chairs or leading policy-making, campaign, or other organizational positions within a party caucus in the legislative body. Women have made some progress at this second stage in the state and national legislatures, but leadership positions are still more likely to be held by men than by women. The election of Nancy Pelosi as House minority leader in the 108th Congress (2003–2004) was a historic event. That was the highest leadership position a woman had achieved in Congress. If the Democrats were to become the majority party in the U.S. House of Representatives, she would become Speaker, third in line for the presidency, and the only constitutional officer of the House.

On the Republican side, Deborah Pryce, of Ohio, rose to the fourth position in the party hierarchy when she became chair of the Republican Conference in the 108th Congress. Conference chair is responsible for shaping and delivering the party's message.

In the U.S. Senate, women have chosen by their fellow party members to serve in party leadership positions, although no woman had ever been elected to the top positions within the party caucuses. In the 108th Congress five female senators held party leadership positions, four Democrats and one Republican: Barbara Boxer (D-CA), chief deputy for strategic outreach; Hillary Rodham Clinton (D-NY), chair, Democratic Senate Steering and Coordination Committee; Kay Bailey Hutchison (R-TX), vice chair, Senate Republican Conference; Barbara Mikulski (D-MD), secretary, Senate Democratic Conference; and Deborah Stabenow (D-MI), vice chair, Democratic Senate Campaign Committee.

Committees are the "central structural components" of the U.S. Congress (Smith and Deering 1990, vii) as it is in the committees that public policy is primarily developed and constructed. Committees differ in their importance in the legislative body. Appropriations, Finance, and Foreign Policy are the prestige committees in the Senate, along with the Rules Committee in the House. Few women in the U.S. Senate have risen to being chairs of committees, let alone the leaders of these prestige committees. In the 108th Congress, two women chaired committees—Susan Collins and Olympia Snowe, both Republicans from the state of Maine. Senator Collins chaired the Committee on Governmental Affairs, and Senator Snowe chaired the Committee on Small Business and Entrepreneurship. Only two other women have ever chaired Senate committees.

Very few women have chaired committees in the U.S. House of Representatives. Committees are particularly important in the U.S. House, and they vary in importance. The only woman to be a committee chair since 1977 has been Representative Jan Meyers, Republican of Kansas, who chaired the Committee on Small Business in the 104th Congress (1995–1996). According to Center for the American Woman and Politics (CAWP) fact sheets, only six women have achieved this status in the U.S. House. For most of the history of the House in the twentieth century, the selection of chairs of committees was determined by seniority, and since so few women held House seats and kept them long enough to rise to senior status, few had the opportunity to chair a committee.

In terms of power and influence in the legislative bodies, it is important to serve on the prestige committees. During World War II, Margaret Chase Smith, then a member of the House of Representatives, gained an assignment to the House Naval Affairs Committee, and Republican Clare Boothe Luce was appointed to the Military Affairs Committee. In making the appointments Minority Leader Joe Martin stated, "In singling out the women members for these assignments, the committee was guided by the realization that the women of the country take an important part in the war effort" (Sherman 2001).

Case Study: Nancy Pelosi, House Minority Leader

Nancy Pelosi became a U.S. representative after winning a special election on June 2, 1987, to fill the vacancy left by the death of Sala Burton (D-CA). Pelosi was born in Baltimore on March 26, 1940, the daughter of Thomas D'Alesandro Jr., who served in the House of Representatives from 1939 to 1947 and later was mayor of Baltimore. Pelosi's brother also served as mayor of Baltimore. Representative Pelosi received her undergraduate degree in 1962 from Trinity College in Washington, D.C., where she met her future husband, Paul F. Pelosi, son of another political American Catholic family, when they both took a class at Georgetown University. In 1969, they moved to California, where her husband's brother served on the San Francisco Board of Supervisors. There Nancy Pelosi began to do volunteer work for the Democratic Party. She did not consider running for office when her children were small. She had five children—four daughters and one son—in six years. "It would have been impossible," she recalled. "But I was always a hardworking volunteer."

Her baptism in national politics came in 1976, when Jerry Brown, governor of California, ran for president. Pelosi, with her connections in Baltimore, helped him pull off a surprise win in Maryland's Democratic primary. "That's the episode that took me out of the kitchen and put me into official party responsibilities," she said. Within a few years, she became party chairwoman for Northern California, joining forces with the political dynasty of Phillip Burton, who served in Congress for twenty years. She served as chair of the California State Democratic Party from 1981 to 1983, during which time she helped secure San Francisco as the site of the national convention in 1984. She also served as finance chair of the Democratic Senatorial Campaign Committee in 1986, when the party regained a majority in the U.S. Senate.

When Philip Burton died in 1983, his widow, Sala, won a special election to fill the seat and was twice reelected. When she was dying of cancer in 1987, she urged Pelosi to run for her seat. With the support of Burton's backers and her knowledge of the state party organization, Pelosi won a close race in the special primary and easily won the runoff election. "I only had seven weeks to campaign," Pelosi recalled. "We had 100 house parties and we got 4,000 volunteers to go door-to-door and to man phone banks. I raised $1 million in seven weeks." In that first election, she won 35 percent against

Supervisor Harry Britt, a gay man, who garnered 31 percent of the vote. She never looked back, routinely coasting to reelection in a district the *Almanac of American Politics* (Barone, Cohen, and Cook 2002, 182) calls "among the two dozen most Democratic and liberal in the nation." In January 2002 Pelosi broke one glass ceiling by being elected as minority whip, the number-two position within the party organization in the U.S. House. She then went on to win the minority leader's post when incumbent Richard Gephardt relinquished it after the Democrats failed to pick up seats in the 2002 congressional election. She obtained the leadership position in a traditional way, raising large sums of money during the 2002 campaign and contributing it to House candidates in the expectation that her generosity would be rewarded. According to the Center for Responsive Politics, campaign reports through September 2002 showed that Pelosi had donated more than $1 million from her personal campaign account and leadership committee to various candidates, making her number one in that category, just ahead of Representative Tom DeLay, Republican of Texas, who was elected House majority leader after the 2002 election.

Women's Leadership in State Legislatures

The CAWP at Rutgers University has reported that in 2003, of the 337 state legislators holding leadership positions nationwide, 46, or 13.6 percent, were women. Women held 21, or 12.6 percent, of the 167 leadership positions in state senates and 25, or 14.7 percent, of the 170 leadership positions in state houses. Women held leadership positions in fifteen state senates and in eighteen state houses; in twenty-five states, women did not hold leadership positions in either chamber. Leadership positions included senate presidents, senate presidents pro tempore, speakers of the house, and speakers pro tempore.

At the second level of leadership are the chairs of committees. In 2003, the CAWP reports, of the 1,826 state legislators nationwide chairing standing committees, 346, or 18.9 percent, were women. Women held 148, or 18.1 percent, of the 816 committee chair positions in state senates and 198, or 19.6 percent, of the 1,008 committee chair positions in state houses. Women chaired committees in forty-five state senates and in all but one state house, Pennsylvania (CAWP 2003).

Do Women in Public Office Make a Difference?

In what ways does it matter whether women run for and are elected to public office? The importance of electing more women to public office grows out of a belief that representative democracy demands that all citizens, regardless of gender, have an equal opportunity to participate in politics. Women's rights activists claim that increased representation of women in elective and appointive positions of power is a matter of justice and equity. Furthermore, women politicians serve as role models for other women and for girls, encouraging them to overcome traditional sex roles. For these symbolic reasons, then, the numerical presence of women in the corridors of power is important. For example, most studies have found women to be less politically knowledgeable than men. But one study has shown that in states where there is a woman candidate or incumbent for U.S. Senate, women were more likely than men to know a senator's name (Burns, Schlozman, and Verba 2001, 342).

But does it matter in terms of the policies that are enacted and how public-policy-making organizations work whether women are present as members? Research on women elected officials at the local, state, and national levels has found them affecting the way institutions work, bringing different issues to the policy-making agendas of these bodies, looking at solutions to problems in distinct ways, framing them in distinctive fashion, and voting distinctively. Women have exhibited different leadership styles than men.

In a 2003 White House Project report on *Why Women Matter,* Karen O'Connor chronicled the results of three decades of research on the difference women make. At state and local levels key findings were that women conceptualize problems differently from men and are more likely to offer new solutions. Nonfeminist women are more likely than nonfeminist male colleagues to work on legislation affecting women. Women legislators of both parties are more likely than men to advance "women's issues," define women's issues more broadly, put them at the top of their legislative agendas, and to take a leadership role in those issue areas. Their presence results in bills dealing with children, education, and health care becoming legislative priorities. Women are more likely to view crime as a societal, rather than an individual, problem. Women legislators are more likely to make certain that their policy positions are translated into new programs to help women. Women legislators receive more constituent casework requests than their male colleagues and are three times more likely to agree that they would do more if they had more staff. Women not only are more responsive to constituent requests, they are more likely to be persistent in their follow-through to get a favorable resolution for their constituents. Women legislators believe that they need to help other women transcend barriers to success.

Women view themselves as more prepared, more diligent, and more organized than men. Women emphasize a "hands on" approach, employing collegiality and collaboration, instead of a hierarchical "command" approach. Compared to men, women rely on a wider range of individuals in formulating policy, creating more sensitive and thoughtful policy. Women who meet as a caucus are more likely to work on bills dealing with women's rights. First-term women sponsor less legislation than their male counterparts, whereas more-senior women sponsor more than their male counterparts. Female committee chairs use their positions to facilitate interaction among committee members rather than to control and direct the debate. This affects the behavior of witnesses and other committee members. In general, women-sponsored legislation has a slightly higher rate of passage. Particularly, women's priority bills on women's issues become law at a higher pass rate than men's priority bills. When women make up less than 15 percent of the legislative body, their minority status constrains their behavior. States with the lowest percentage of women in their legislatures pass the lowest number of women's bills. Men believe that women in the legislative body help sensitize them to women's issues.

O'Connor reports that women members of Congress get women's issues on the agenda; widen the range of policy solutions proposed and frame the policy debate in different terms; give more attention and support to women's issues than men, regardless of their party affiliation or ideology; introduce most women's legislation; are more likely than men to cosponsor legislation dealing with women's issues; use the Congressional Caucus for Women's Issues (CCWI) to champion women's issues; use their strategic positions to make the difference in drafting legislation and on the floor; use their positions on committees to advance legislation benefiting women; and use conference committee assignments to advance and protect women's policy issues.

Case Study: The Congressional Caucus for Women's Issues

Fifteen representatives formed the Women's Congressional Caucus in 1977. Initially, the caucus focused on sponsoring executive briefings, introducing minor pieces of legislation, writing letters to the administration urging more female appointees, and building camaraderie among the female members. It expanded into the CCWI in 1981, opening its membership to men, although its executive committee would consist only of women members. The change allowed the caucus to "transform itself into a large and effective body dedicated to legislative achievement" (Thompson 1984, 16). The CCWI aspired to enact major legislation. It sought to "perform legislative leadership functions, linking members to outside groups, forming legislative proposals, planning strategy, and mobilizing like-minded members for floor debates, amendments, or votes" (Thompson 1985). According to Thompson, "the Congresswomen's Caucus filled a gap in the representative structures of Congress by dealing with an issue which was of public concern but for which no formal congressional structure could formulate a response" (1984, 2).

Each Congress, the CCWI has adopted a set of legislative priorities and set up a formal process for endorsing legislation introduced by its members. The caucus developed an omnibus legislative package called the Economic Equity Act to help women "balance their work and family roles," which was its focus in the 1980s. The "feminization of poverty," as highlighted by the U.S. Civil Rights Commission 1982 report, *A Growing Crisis: Disadvantaged Women and Their Children,* which showed that women were a disproportionate number of America's poor in the early 1980s, served as an incentive for pushing the Economic Equity Act. Early legislation stressed pensions (both for employees and homemakers), benefits in divorce, child support, and inheritance taxes, all measures seeking equality in resources.

A second major legislative set of bills championed by the CCWI was the Women's Health Equity Act (WHEA). In 1990, the General Accounting Office issued a report that the caucus had requested that showed that women had been systematically excluded or underrepresented in many clinical health studies in which subjects ranged from heart disease to the overuse of prescription drugs. A month after the release of this report, the caucus introduced more than a dozen bills aggregated under the general heading of the WHEA. In 1991, the caucus endorsed a package of twenty bills under an expanded, more ambitious WHEA. Among the measures that became law was a bill to increase low-income women's access to mammography and Pap smears, authorization of more than $200 million for breast cancer research at the National Cancer Institute, and a bill to create an Office of Women's Health Research in the National Institutes of Health (NIH). In June 1993, Congress passed the National Institutes of Health Revitalization Act, which responded to unresolved issues addressed by the 1991 set of bills. The act authorized development of infertility and contraceptive research centers and encouraged health professionals to enter these fields; provided for significant increases in research on breast, ovarian, and other cancers of women's reproductive systems; and gave permanent status to the NIH Office of Research on Women's Health (Gertzog 1995.)

During the caucus's first fifteen years, abortion was kept off its agenda out of deference to several caucus members who opposed abortion. However, in 1992, after most of those members had left Congress, the caucus voted to become pro-choice. Abortion issues then became a priority of the caucus, especially during the 104th Congress (1995–1996). Its pro-choice stance kept some women members of Congress, particularly a number of Republicans, from joining the caucus. Therefore, in the 105th Congress (1997–1998), caucus co-chairs, Nancy Johnson (R-CT) and Eleanor Holmes Norton (D-DC), removed the abortion issue from the caucus agenda to make it more inclusive and bipartisan. As a result, its membership grew to include almost every women member of Congress.

In the 1994 elections, the Republicans won a majority of the seats in the U.S. House of Representatives, and among their early moves they disbanded all legislative service organizations (LSOs), which included such groups as the Black, Hispanic, and women's caucuses. A reorganized women's caucus incorporated its staff into a separate nonprofit research arm, Women's Policy, that works to provide the same information services that were available from the caucus in its earlier structure. The privatization of the caucus's communication and information function in Women's Policy, Inc., made it possible for it to accept subscription fees from corporations, universities, nonprofit agencies, women's groups, and other private organizations. As an LSO, a public entity, this option had been closed to the caucus. One can receive electronic updates on women's issues in Congress by subscribing to the Women's Policy, Inc., newsletter, *The Source*.

The caucus also reformed itself into a members' organization but kept its name, the CCWI. This change meant that male members could no longer belong to the caucus. In the 107th Congress (2001–2002), caucus members divided themselves into five legislative teams, each co-chaired by a Republican and a Democrat. The issues of the five teams, respectively, were education and children, health and older women, violence against women, women in business and the workplace, and economic empowerment.

Congressional caucus scholar Irwin Gertzog believes that the CCWI's efficacy and visibility have been attenuated since its elimination as an LSO and transformation into a membership organization. He attributes the decline of the CCWI as a central organization in the lives of female representatives in part to the greater access congresswomen have to become members of consequential committee and leadership positions. The strategic women politicians in the ranks of contemporary U.S. representatives believe they can be more effective promoting issues of special concern to women in legislative settings that are integral to House decision making. Gertzog concludes, "They are as ardently feminist as the solid core of caucus activists, but as modern-day strategic politicians, they have less of an incentive to manifest the cooperative, sisterly spirit evidence by the women who created and sustained the caucus in years past. They are more likely to be entrepreneurs exerting influence directly on house colleagues than agents of a marginal women's collective whose resources have been cut back drastically, whose influences had been largely indirect, and whose track record is mixed" (2002, 114–15). This change reflects positive movement to the extent that it represents expanded political leadership on the part of women and the opportunity to affect policies that impact distinctively on women.

Presidential Appointments and Presidential Staff

In addition to winning elective office, women exercise political leadership in appointive positions in the executive and judicial branches. Through 2003, a total of twenty-nine women have held cabinet or cabinet-level appointments in presidential administrations. Of the twenty-nine, twenty-one had cabinet posts, including two women who headed two different departments and two who had both a cabinet post and a position defined as cabinet-level. Democratic presidents appointed sixteen of these women, and Republican presidents appointed thirteen. Frances Perkins was the first woman appointed to the cabinet when Franklin Roosevelt selected her in 1933 to head the Department of Labor. The second woman was not appointed until 1953, when President Eisenhower appointed Oveta Culp Hobby to be secretary of health, education, and welfare. Women of color have been appointed to cabinet positions. Patricia Roberts Harris, who was appointed by President Jimmy Carter to serve as secretary of housing and urban development and later to serve as secretary of health and human services, was the first Black woman to hold a cabinet position. Aida Alvarez was the first Hispanic woman to hold a cabinet-level position. Elaine Chao became the first Asian American woman to hold a cabinet position when President George W. Bush appointed her secretary of labor. Three cabinet positions are considered to be the inner cabinet, or the most important cabinet offices: state, defense, and treasury. Only one woman has been appointed to any of these positions, Madeleine Albright, appointed by President Clinton to be secretary of state.

In 1883, Congress passed the Civil Service Act, also known as the Pendleton Act, making both men and women eligible to compete for federal civil service appointments. It created a merit system. The salaries for women, however, were usually lower than the salaries for men, and the service remained job-segregated, like employment in general, for nearly ninety years. In addition, administrators hiring federal workers were able to restrict a position to only men or only women applicants. In 1919, all competitive civil service examinations were opened to women. In 1923, the Classification Act banned sex discrimination in civil service pay scales by the enactment of a requirement for equal pay for equal work. Job segregation, however, diluted the effect of this measure.

The depression of the 1930s further hurt women's status in the federal sector through actions taken by the president and Congress. Congress, for example, in responding to the nation's needs at that time, passed Section 213 of the 1932 National Economy Act, which prohibited husbands and wives from working in the federal civil service at the same time. This action forced some women to leave government. In 1933 all women working in the federal government had to take their husband's names. With Section 213 in place, some women were forced to lead double lives, keeping marriages secret if they wanted to keep their federal jobs. Section 213 was repealed in 1937 following an intensive lobbying campaign by the National Woman's Party (NWP) and the Women's Bureau.

A concerted effort to have women appointed to executive branch positions began during the 1940 and 1950s when a number of women's organizations came together in Washington, D.C., to discuss the role of women in postwar policy making. The National Federation of Business and Professional Women's Clubs (BPW) formed a talent bank of potential women appointees.

In addition to presidential appointments, a position on the White House staff is an important route to political influence and a measure of political equality. Women have made a great deal of progress in terms of their numbers and seniority in the White House staff. White House staff became an organizational entity during the Franklin Roosevelt administrations. By the time of the George W. Bush administration, the White House staff included nearly a thousand individuals. Women on the White House staff have constituted from 6 percent during the Eisenhower administration to 39 percent in the Clinton presidency. Seven women served as assistants to the president in the first year of the Clinton administration (Tenpas 1997). With the appointment of Condoleezza Rice as national security adviser and Karen Hughes as counselor to the president in 2001 at the beginning of the George W. Bush administration, women finally achieved a presence in the inner circle of White House staff.

Prior to joining the Bush presidential campaign as a primary foreign policy adviser, Condoleezza Rice had been provost of Stanford University and a professor in its Political Science Department. From 1989 through March 1991, the period of German reunification and the final days of the Soviet Union, she served in the prior Bush administration as director, and then senior director, of Soviet and East European Affairs in the National Security Council, and as special assistant to the president for national security affairs. In 1986, while an international affairs fellow of the Council on Foreign Relations, she served as special assistant to the director of the Joint Chiefs of Staff. In 1997, she served on the Federal Advisory Committee on Gender-Integrated Training in the Military. Born on November 14, 1954, in Birmingham, Alabama, she earned her bachelor's degree in political science, cum laude and Phi Beta Kappa, from the University of Denver in 1974, her master's from the University of Notre Dame in 1975, and her Ph.D. from the Graduate School of International Studies at the University of Denver in 1981. She is a fellow of the American Academy of Arts and Sciences and has been awarded honorary doctorates from Morehouse College in 1991, the University of Alabama in 1994, and the University of Notre Dame in 1995 (http://usinfo.state.gov/topic/po/crbio.htm).

Karen Hughes has been described in the media as "the most powerful woman ever to serve in the White House" (*Dallas Morning News*) and President George W. Bush's "most essential adviser" (ABC News). She served as director of communications for both of President Bush's gubernatorial campaigns, in 1994 and 1998, and was one of the "Iron Triangle" of Texans who led his campaign for the presidency. She also served as director of communications in Bush's state office during his tenure as governor. Hughes is a former executive director of the Republican Party of Texas and a former television news reporter for KXAS-TV, the NBC affiliate in Dallas/Fort Worth. She is a Phi Beta Kappa and summa cum laude graduate of Southern Methodist University, where she earned a bachelor of arts degree in English and bachelor of fine arts degree in journalism (http://www.harrywalker.com/speakers).

Women in the Judiciary

In 2001, more than a quarter of the judges on state courts of last resort, the highest jurisdiction in the state judicial systems, were women, and all but two states had at least one women judge at this level. In the courts of last resort, the chief justices were female in fifteen states and the District of Columbia.

The federal judiciary system consists of district courts, appeals courts, and the Supreme Court. The president of the United States appoints these judges, and they are confirmed by the U.S. Senate. The first woman was appointed to a federal court in 1934 when President Franklin Roosevelt nominated Judge Florence Ellinwood Allen, from the Ohio Supreme Court, to the Sixth Circuit Court of Appeals. She served until her retirement in 1959. Women's groups lobbied for her to be nominated to fill vacancies on the Supreme Court during the Roosevelt and Truman presidential administrations, but to no avail.

In 1978, Congress enacted the Omnibus Judgeship Act, which created 152 judgeships, 117 at the district court level and 35 appellate seats. This act allowed President Jimmy Carter to have a substantial impact on the federal courts in terms of appointments. By the time his term ended, he had appointed a majority of the appellate judges on five of the circuits. He appointed an unprecedented number of women and minorities: 93 women, African Americans, and Hispanics out of a total 258 appointments (Mezey 2000). In fiscal year 2000, 24 percent of federal appellate courts justices and 17 percent of district court justices were women.

Table 5.6, in the appendix to this chapter, gives the percentages of district court and appeals court appointments who were women for presidential administrations from 1963 through 2002. The Clinton administration (1993–2001) stands out in terms of female appointments to federal district courts and to U.S. appeals courts (Mezey 2000; Goldman et al. 2003).

Does it matter in terms of the outcomes of court cases and jurisprudence whether women serve on the federal courts? The scholarly studies that have been conducted have found little systematic evidence to suggest that gender makes a difference in judicial decision making. "Contrary to popular belief, and in some cases their own expectations, employing a variety of methodologies, the studies showed that women did not always vote in a more liberal, more civil libertarian manner than men, nor were they always more sensitive to issues of sex or race discrimination. Indeed, in some studies, women judges were reported to be even less supportive of women's rights issues than men" (Mezey 2000, 222–23).

One hundred eight individuals have served on the U.S. Supreme Court. Two of them have been women, Sandra Day O'Connor, appointed by President Ronald Reagan in 1981, and Ruth Bader Ginsburg, appointed by Bill Clinton in 1993. When O'Connor was nominated to sit on the U.S. Supreme Court, she had been a judge on the Arizona State Court of Appeals since 1979. Prior to holding that position, she had been a judge on the Superior Court of Arizona for Maricopa County and had been a state senator in the Arizona legislature, serving as majority leader in the 1973–1974 session. She received her law degree from Stanford Law School. When she graduated, she was unable to obtain a position with a private law firm other than as a legal secretary, even though she ranked third in her class at Stanford.

Ruth Bader Ginsburg served on the U.S. Court of Appeals for the District of Columbia Circuit prior to her nomination to the Supreme Court. She received her law degree from Columbia Law School, and was a professor there from 1972 to 1980. Justice Ginsburg had also served as the first director of the American Civil Liberties Union Women's Rights Law Project. As had Justice O'Connor, Justice Ginsburg had been refused a job by the private law firms to which she applied after graduation from law school despite her position at the head of her class at both Harvard and Columbia law schools.

Conclusion

References to women's participation in American politics reveal a rich history of efforts to achieve equality with men and to influence the political process as women. Moreover, the second women's rights movement was one of the dominant political phenomena of the latter half of the twentieth century. At the beginning of the twenty-first century, there exists a rich organizational life centering on women in the political process and policy making on issues of particular concern to women. At the same time, commentators have talked about a postfeminist era, suggesting either that women have achieved equity or that new generations of women do not view themselves as disadvantaged. Some people argue that feminism is alive and well and that young women approach issues of equity in new and wider ways. Others have organized to oppose a broader role for women in the political leadership of the nation.

Women have organized to transform the political system. Some have sought to achieve equality with men within the established system of economics and politics. Others have pursued a larger transformation of the political system, seeking major changes in the capitalist system and in personal relationships. Women of color have challenged the dominant system to understand how race, sex, and class intersect to exclude them from having their voices heard and issues of particular concern to them addressed in policy-making forums.

Women have also organized to maintain traditional values and family systems. Some women have seen equality being achieved through government actions mandating equality, and others have advocated for less government action so that women would be free to achieve in a merit-based system. Women have utilized a host of political persuasion techniques available in a free society to influence policy making. They have formed social movements, grassroots organizations, and national associations. They have marched, protested, boycotted, lobbied, filed lawsuits, and run for political leadership positions. Women have been especially active in their local communities, leading organizations to make their communities safer places for their children and improving educational systems.

Some now focus on achieving the "crown jewel" in political leadership positions, electing a woman as president of the United States. Women have been elected president and prime minister of other countries; therefore it is natural to ask why, since the United States views itself as the leading democracy of the world, no woman been elected to the highest office and why that is still an issue of discussion and debate.

Appendix: Women Elected and Appointed to Political Office

TABLE 5.1 Women in the U.S. House of Representatives

Name	State	Party	Dates Served
Rankin, Jeanette	Montana	Republican	1917–1919, 1941–1943
Robertson, Alice M.	Oklahoma	Republican	1921–1923
Huck, Wonnifred S. M.	Illinois	Republican	1922–1923
Nolan, Mae E.	California	Republican	1923–1925
Kahn, Florence P.	California	Republican	1925–1927
Norton, Mary T.	New Jersey	Democrat	1925–1951
Rogers, Edith N.	Massachusetts	Republican	1925–1960
Langley, Katherine G.	Kentucky	Republican	1927–1931
McCormick, Ruth H.	Illinois	Republican	1929–1931
Oldfield, Pearl P.	Arkansas	Democrat	1929–1931
Owen, Ruth B.	Florida	Democrat	1929–1933
Pratt, Ruth S. B.	New York	Republican	1929–1933
Wingo, Effiegene	Arkansas	Democrat	1930–1933
Eslick, Willa M. B.	Tennessee	Democrat	1932–1933
Clarke, Marian W.	New York	Republican	1933–1935
Greenway, Isabella S.	Arizona	Democrat	1933–1937
Jenckes, Virginia E.	Indiana	Democrat	1933–1939
McCarthy, Kathryn O'Laughlin	Kansas	Democrat	1933–1935
O'Day, Caroline L. G.	New York	Democrat	1935–1943
Honeyman, Nan W.	Oregon	Democrat	1937–1939
Gasque, Elizabeth H.	South Carolina	Democrat	1938–1939
McMillan, Clara G.	South Carolina	Democrat	1939–1941
Sumner, Jessie	Illinois	Republican	1939–1947
Bolton, Frances P.	Ohio	Republican	1940–1969
Gibbs, Florence R.	Georgia	Democrat	1940–1941
Smith, Margaret Chase	Maine	Republican	1940–1949
Byron, Katherine E.	Maryland	Democrat	1941–1943
Boland, Veronica G.	Pennsylvania	Democrat	1942–1943
Luce, Clare Boothe	Connecticut	Republican	1943–1947
Stanley, Winifred C.	New York	Republican	1943–1945
Fulmer, Willa L.	South Carolina	Democrat	1944–1945
Douglas, Emily T.	Illinois	Democrat	1945–1947
Douglas, Helen G.	California	Democrat	1945–1951
Woodhouse, Chase G.	Connecticut	Democrat	1945–1947, 1949–1951
Mankin, Helen D.	Georgia	Democrat	1946–1947
Pratt, Eliza J.	North Carolina	Democrat	1946–1947
Lusk, Georgia L.	New Mexico	Democrat	1947–1949
St. George, Katherine P. C.	New York	Republican	1947–1965
Bosone, Reva Z.B.	Utah	Democrat	1949–1953
Harden, Cecil M.	Indiana	Republican	1949–1959
Kelly, Edna F.	New York	Democrat	1949–1969
Buchanan, Vera D.	Pennsylvania	Democrat	1951–1955

TABLE 5.1 *(continued)*

Name	State	Party	Dates Served
Church, Marguerite S.	Illinois	Republican	1951–1963
Kee, Maude E.	West Virginia	Democrat	1951–1965
Thompson, Ruth	Michigan	Republican	1951–1957
Pfost, Gracie B.	Idaho	Democrat	1953–1963
Sullivan, Leonore K.	Missouri	Democrat	1953–1977
Farrington, Mary E. (Del.)	Hawaii	Republican	1954–1957
Blitch, Iris F.	Georgia	Democrat	1955–1963
Green, Edith	Oregon	Democrat	1955–1975
Griffiths, Martha W.	Michigan	Democrat	1955–1974
Knutson, Cova G.	Minnesota	Democrat	1955–1959
Granahan, Kathryn E.	Pennsylvania	Democrat	1956–1963
Dwyer, Florence P.	New Jersey	Republican	1957–1973
May, Catherine D.	Washington	Republican	1959–1971
Simpson, Edna O.	Illinois	Republican	1959–1961
Weis, Jessica McCullough	New York	Republican	1959–1963
Hansen, Julia B.	Washington	Democrat	1960–1974
Norrell, Catherine D.	Arkansas	Democrat	1961–1963
Reece, Louise G.	Tennessee	Republican	1961–1963
Riley, Corinne B.	South Carolina	Democrat	1962–1963
Reid, Charlotte T.	Illinois	Republican	1963–1971
Baker, Irene B.	Tennessee	Republican	1964–1965
Mink, Patsy T.	Hawaii	Democrat	1965–1977, 1990–2002
Thomas, Lera M.	Texas	Democrat	1966–1967
Heckler, Margaret M.	Massachusetts	Republican	1967–1983
Chisholm, Shirley	New York	Democrat	1969–1983
Abzug, Bella S.	New York	Democrat	1971–1977
Grasso, Ella T.	Connecticut	Democrat	1971–1975
Hicks, Louise Day	Massachusetts	Democrat	1971–1973
Andrews, Elizabeth B.	Alabama	Democrat	1972–1973
Boggs, Corinne C.	Louisiana	Democrat	1973–1991
Burke, Yvonne B.	California	Democrat	1973–1979
Collins, Cardiss R.	Illinois	Democrat	1973–1997
Holt, Marjorie S.	Maryland	Republican	1973–1987
Holtzman, Elizabeth	New York	Democrat	1973–1981
Jordan, Barbara C.	Texas	Democrat	1973–1979
Schroeder, Patricia	Colorado	Democrat	1973–1997
Fenwick, Millicent	New Jersey	Republican	1975–1983
Keys, Martha E.	Kansas	Democrat	1975–1979
Lloyd, Marilyn	Tennessee	Democrat	1975–1995
Meyner, Helen S.	New Jersey	Democrat	1975–1979
Pettis, Shirley N.	California	Republican	1975–1979
Smith, Virginia	Nebraska	Republican	1975–1991
Spellman, Gladys Noon	Maryland	Democrat	1975–1981

(continues)

TABLE 5.1 *(continued)*

Name	State	Party	Dates Served
Mikulski, Barbara A.	Maryland	Democrat	1977–1987
Oakar, Mary Rose	Ohio	Democrat	1977–1995
Byron, Beverly	Maryland	Democrat	1979–1995
Ferraro, Geraldine	New York	Democrat	1979–1985
Snowe, Olympia	Maine	Republican	1979–1995
Fiedler, Bobbi	California	Republican	1981–1987
Martin, Lynn M.	Illinois	Republican	1981–1991
Roukema, Marge	New Jersey	Republican	1981–2003
Schneider, Claudine	Rhode Island	Republican	1981–1991
Ashbrook, Jean	Ohio	Republican	1982–1983
Hall, Katie	Indiana	Democrat	1982–1985
Kennelly, Barbara B.	Connecticut	Democrat	1982–2001
Boxer, Barbara	California	Democrat	1983–1993
Burton, Sala	California	Democrat	1983–1987
Johnson, Nancy L.	Connecticut	Republican	1983–2003
Kaptur, Marcy	Ohio	Democrat	1983–present
Vucanovich, Barbara	Nevada	Republican	1983–1997
Bentley, Helen Dedich	Maryland	Republican	1985–1995
Long, Cathy	Louisiana	Democrat	1985–1987
Meyers, Jan	Kansas	Republican	1985–1997
Morella, Constance A.	Maryland	Republican	1987–2003
Patterson, Elizabeth J.	South Carolina	Democrat	1987–1993
Saiki, Patricia	Hawaii	Republican	1987–1991
Slaughter, Louise M.	New York	Democrat	1987–present
Long, Jill	Indiana	Democrat	1989–1993
Lowey, Nita M.	New York	Democrat	1989–present
Pelosi, Nancy	California	Democrat	1989–present
Ros-Lehtinen, Ileana	Florida	Republican	1989–present
Unsoeld, Jolene	Washington	Democrat	1989–1993
Molinari, Susan	New York	Republican	1990–1997
Collins, Barbara-Rose	Michigan	Democrat	1991–1997
DeLauro, Rosa	Connecticut	Democrat	1991–present
Horn, Joan Kelly	Missouri	Democrat	1991–1993
Norton, Eleanor Holmes (Del.)	District of Columbia	Democrat	1991–present
Waters, Maxine	California	Democrat	1991–present
Thurman, Karen	Florida	Democrat	1993–2003
Brown, Corrine	Florida	Democrat	1993–present
Byrne, Leslie L.	Virginia	Democrat	1993–1995
Cartwell, Maria	Washington	Democrat	1993–1995
Clayton, Eva M.	North Carolina	Democrat	1993–present
Danner, Pat	Missouri	Democrat	1993–present
Dunn, Jennifer	Washington	Republican	1993–present
English, Karen	Arizona	Democrat	1993–1995

TABLE 5.1 *(continued)*

Name	State	Party	Dates Served
Eshoo, Anna G.	California	Democrat	1993–present
Fowler, Tillie K.	Florida	Republican	1993–present
Furse, Elizabeth	Oregon	Democrat	1993–present
Harman, Jane	California	Democrat	1993–present
Johnson, Eddie Bernice	Texas	Democrat	1993–present
Lincoln, Blanch Lambert	Arkansas	Democrat	1993–1997
Maloney, Carolyn B.	New York	Democrat	1993–present
Margolies-Mezvinsky, Marjorie	Pennsylvania	Democrat	1993–1995
McKinney, Cynthia A.	Georgia	Democrat	1993–2003
Meek, Carrie P.	Florida	Democrat	1993–2001
Pryce, Deborah	Ohio	Republican	1993–present
Roybal-Allard, Lucille	California	Democrat	1993–present
Schenk, Lynn	California	Democrat	1993–1995
Velazquez, Nydia M.	New York	Democrat	1993–present
Woolsey, Lynn C.	California	Democrat	1993–present
Chenoweth, Helen	Idaho	Republican	1995–2001
Cubin, Barbara	Wyoming	Republican	1995–present
Kelly, Sue W.	New York	Republican	1995–present
Lee, Sheila Jackson	Texas	Democrat	1995–present
Lofgren, Zoe	California	Democrat	1995–present
McCarthy, Karen	Missouri	Democrat	1995–present
Myrick, Sue	North Carolina	Republican	1995–present
Rivers, Lynn N.	Michigan	Democrat	1995–2003
Seastrand, Andrea H.	California	Republican	1995–1997
Smith, Linda	Washington	Republican	1995–present
Waldholtz, Enid	Utah	Republican	1995–1997
Millender-McDonald, Juanita	California	Democrat	1996–present
Carson, Julia	Indiana	Democrat	1997–present
Degette, Diana L.	Colorado	Democrat	1997–present
Emerson, Jo Ann	Missouri	Republican	1997–present
Granger, Kay	Texas	Republican	1997–present
Hooley, Darlene	Oregon	Democrat	1997–present
Kilpatrick, Carolyn C.	Michigan	Democrat	1997–present
McCarthy, Carolyn	New York	Democrat	1997–present
Northrup, Anne Meagher	Kentucky	Republican	1997–present
Sanchez, Loretta	California	Democrat	1997–present
Stabenow, Deborah	Michigan	Democrat	1997–2003
Tausher, Ellen	California	Democrat	1997–present
Heather Wilson	New Mexico	Republican	1998–present
Bono, Mary	California	Republican	1999–present
Capps, Lois	California	Democrat	1999–present
Lee, Barbara	California	Democrat	1999–present
Grace Napolitano	California	Democrat	1999–present
Janice Schakowsky	Illinois	Democrat	1999–present

(continues)

TABLE 5.1 *(continued)*

Name	State	Party	Dates Served
Judy Biggert	Illinois	Republican	1999–present
Shelley Berkley	Nevada	Democrat	1999–present
Stephanie Tubbs Jones	Ohio	Democrat	1999
Tammy Baldwin	Wisconsin	Democrat	1999–present
Hilda Solis	California	Democrat	2001–present
Susan Davis	California	Democrat	2001–present
Betty McCollum	Minnesota	Democrat	2001–present
Melissa Hart	Pennsylvania	Republican	2001–present
Jo Ann Davis	Virginia	Republican	2001–present
Shelley Moore Capito	West Virginia	Republican	2001–present
Linda Sanchez	California	Democrat	2003–present
Diane Watson	California	Democrat	2003–present
Marilyn Musgrave	Colorado	Republican	2003–present
Ginny Brown-Waite	Florida	Republican	2003–present
Katherine Harris	Florida	Republican	2003–present
Denise Majette	Georgia	Democrat	2003–present
Candice Miller	Michigan	Republican	2003–present
Marsha Blackburn	Tennessee	Republican	2003–present

TABLE 5.2 Women in the U.S. Senate

Name	State	Party	Dates Served
Rebecca Latimer Felton	Georgia	Democrat	11/21/22–11/22/22
Hattie Wyatt Caraway	Arkansas	Democrat	12/8/31–1/2/45
Rose McConnell Long	Louisiana	Democrat	2/10/36–1/2/37
Dixie Bibb Graves	Alabama	Democrat	8/20/37–1/10/38
Gladys Pyle	South Dakota	Republican	11/9/38–1/3/39
Vera Cahalan Bushfield	South Dakota	Republican	10/6/48–12/27/48
Margaret Chase Smith	Maine	Republican	1/3/49–1/3/73
Eva Kelly Bowring	Nebraska	Republican	4/26/54–11/7/54
Hazel Hempel Abel	Nebraska	Republican	11/8/54–12/31/54
Maurine Brown Neuberger	Oregon	Democrat	11/8/60–1/3/67
Elaine Schwartzenburg Edwards	Louisiana	Democrat	8/7/72–11/13/72
Muriel Buck Humphrey	Minnesota	Democrat	2/6/78–11/7/78
Maryon Pittman Allen	Alabama	Democrat	6/12/78–11/7/78
Nancy Landon Kassebaum	Kansas	Republican	12/23/78–1/7/97
Paula Hawkins	Florida	Republican	1/1/81–1/3/87
Barbara Mikulski	Maryland	Democrat	1/3/87–present
Jocelyn Birch Burdick	North Dakota	Democrat	9/16/92–12/14/92
Dianne Feinstein	California	Democrat	11/10/92–present
Barbara Boxer	California	Democrat	1/5/93–present
Carol Moseley-Braun	Illinois	Democrat	1/5/93–1/6/99
Patty Murray	Washington	Democrat	1/5/93–present
Kay Bailey Hutchison	Texas	Republican	6/14/93–present
Olympia Snowe	Maine	Republican	1/4/95–present
Sheila Frahm	Kansas	Republican	6/11/96–11/8/96
Susan Collins	Maine	Republican	1/7/97–present
Mary Landrieu	Louisiana	Democrat	1/7/97–present
Blanche Lincoln	Arkansas	Democrat	1/6/99–present
Maria Cantwell	Washington	Democrat	1/3/01–present
Jean Carnahan	Missouri	Democrat	1/3/01–11/23/02
Hillary Rodham Clinton	New York	Democrat	1/3/01–present
Debbie Stabenow	Michigan	Democrat	1/3/01–present
Lisa Murkowski	Alaska	Republican	12/20/02–present
Elizabeth Dole	North Carolina	Republican	1/7/03–present

TABLE 5.3 Women Governors

Name	State	Party	Dates Served
Nellie Tayloe Ross	Wyoming	Democrat	1925–1927
Miriam "Ma" Ferguson	Texas	Democrat	1925–1927, 1933–1935
Lurleen Wallace	Alabama	Democrat	1967–1968
Ella Grasso	Connecticut	Democrat	1975–1980
Dixy Lee Ray	Washington	Democrat	1977–1981
Vesta Roy	New Hampshire	Republican	1982–1983
Martha Layne Collins	Kentucky	Democrat	1984–1987
Madeleine Kunin	Vermont	Democrat	1985–1991
Kay Orr	Nebraska	Republican	1987–1991
Rose Mofford	Arizona	Democrat	1988–1991
Joan Finney	Kansas	Democrat	1991–1995
Ann Richards	Texas	Democrat	1991–1995
Barbara Roberts	Oregon	Democrat	1991–1995
Christine Todd Whitman	New Jersey	Republican	1994–2001
Jeanne Shaheen	New Hampshire	Democrat	1997–2003
Jane Dee Hull	Arizona	Republican	1997–2003
Nancy Hollister	Ohio	Republican	1998–1999
Jane Swift	Massachusetts	Republican	2001–2003
Judy Martz	Montana	Republican	2001–present
Ruth Ann Minner	Delaware	Democrat	2001–present
Jennifer M. Granholm	Michigan	Democrat	2003–present
Linda Lingle	Hawaii	Republican	2003–present
Janet Napolitano	Arizona	Democrat	2003–present
Kathleen Sebelius	Kansas	Democrat	2003–present
Olene Walker	Utah	Republican	2003–present
Sila Calderon	Puerto Rico	Popular Democratic Party	2001–present
Kathleen Blanco	Louisiana	Democrat	2004–present

TABLE 5.4 Women in Congressional Leadership Roles

U.S. Senate—Leadership Roles

108th Congress (2003–2005)
Sen. Barbara Boxer (D-CA)	Chief Deputy for Strategic Outreach
Sen. Hilary Rodham Clinton (D-NY)	Chair, Democratic Senate Steering and Coordination Committee
Sen. Kay Bailey Hutchison (R-TX)	Vice Chair, Senate Republican Conference
Sen. Barbara Mikulski (D-MD)	Secretary, Senate Democratic Conference
Sen. Debbie Stabenow (D-MI)	Vice Chair, Democratic Senate Campaign Committee

107th Congress (2001–2003)
Sen. Barbara Boxer (D-CA)	Chief Deputy for Strategic Outreach
Sen. Susan Collins (R-ME)	Senate Deputy Minority Whip
Sen. Kay Bailey Hutchison (R-TX)	Vice Chair, Republican Conference
Sen. Barbara Mikulski (D-MD)	Secretary, Senate Democratic Conference
Sen. Patty Murray (D-WA)	Chair, Democratic Senate Campaign Committee

106th Congress (1999–2001)
Sen. Barbara Boxer (D-CA)	Senate Deputy Minority Whip
Sen. Kay Bailey Hutchison (R-TX)	Senate Deputy Majority Whip
Sen. Barbara Mikulski (D-MD)	Secretary, Senate Democratic Conference
Sen. Olympia Snowe (R-ME)	Secretary, Senate Republican Conference

105th Congress (1997–1999)
Sen. Kay Bailey Hutchison (R-TX)	Senate Deputy Majority Whip
Sen. Barbara Mikulski (D-MD)	Secretary, Senate Democratic Conference
Sen. Olympia Snowe (R-ME)	Secretary, Senate Republican Conference

104th Congress (1995–1997)
Sen. Kay Bailey Hutchison (R-TX)	Senate Deputy Whip
Sen. Barbara Mikulski (D-MD)	Secretary, Senate Democratic Conference

103rd Congress (1993–1995)
Sen. Barbara Boxer (D-CA)	Senate Deputy Majority Whip
Sen. Barbara Mikulski (D-MD)	Assistant Senate Democratic Floor Leader

(continues)

TABLE 5.4 *(continued)*

U.S. Senate—Leadership Roles

90th and 91st Congress (1967–1972)
Sen. Margaret Chase Smith (R-ME) — Chair, Senate Republican Conference

U.S. Senate—Committee Chairs

108th Congress (2003–2005)
Sen. Susan Collins (R-ME) — Committee on Governmental Affairs
Sen. Olympia J. Snowe (R-ME) — Committee on Small Business and Entrepreneurship

104th Congress (1995–1997)
Sen. Nancy Landon Kassebaum (R-KS) — Committee on Labor and Human Resources

73rd through 78th Congress (1933–1945)
Sen. Hattie Wyatt Caraway (D-AR) — Committee on Enrolled Bills

U.S. House of Representatives—Leadership Roles

108th Congress (2003–2005)
Rep. Nancy Pelosi (D-CA) — House Minority Leader
Rep. Barbara Cubin (R-WY) — Secretary, House Republican Conference
Rep. Rosa De Lauro (D-CT) — Co-Chair of the House Democratic Steering Committee
Rep. Deborah Pryce (R-OH) — Chair, House Republican Conference
Rep. Jan Schakowsky (D-IL) — Chief Deputy Whip
Rep. Maxine Waters (D-CA) — Chief Deputy Whip

107th Congress (2001–2003)
Rep. Barbara Cubin (R-WY) — House Republican Conference Secretary
Rep. Rose De Lauro (D-CT) — Assistant to the House Democratic Leader
Rep. Nita Lowey (D-NY) — Chair, Democratic Congressional Campaign Committee
Rep. Nancy Pelosi (D-CA) — House Democratic Whip
Rep. Deborah Pryce (R-OH) — Vice Chair, House Republican Conference
Rep. Maxine Waters (D-CA) — Chief Deputy Whip

106th Congress (1999–2001)
Rep. Barbara Cubin (R-WY) — House Deputy Majority Whip
Rep. Diana DeGette (D-CO) — House Deputy Minority Whip
Rep. Rosa De Lauro (D-CT) — Assistant to the House Democratic Leader

TABLE 5.4 *(continued)*

Rep. Tillie Fowler (R-FL)	Vice Chair, House Republican Conference
Rep. Kay Granger (R-TX)	House Assistant Majority Whip
Rep. Eddie Bernice Johnson (D-TX)	House Democratic Deputy Whip
Rep. Nita Lowey (D-NY)	House Minority Whip At-Large
Rep. Deborah Pryce (R-OH)	House Republican Conference Secretary
Rep. Louise Slaughter (D-NY)	House Minority Whip At-Large
Rep. Lynn Woolsey (D-CA)	House Deputy Minority Whip

105th Congress (1997–1999)

Rep. Eva Clayton (D-NC)	Co-Chair, House Democratic Policy Committee
Rep. Barbara Cubin (R-WY)	House Deputy Majority Whip
Rep. Rosa De Lauro (D-CT)	House Chief Deputy Minority Whip
Rep. Jennifer Dunn (R-WA)	Vice Chair, House Republican Conference
Rep. Tillie Fowler (R-FL)	House Deputy Majority Whip
Rep. Kay Granger (R-TX)	House Assistant Majority Whip
Rep. Barbara Kennelly (D-CT)	Vice Chair, House Democratic Caucus
Rep. Nita Lowey (D-NY)	House Minority Whip At-Large
Rep. Susan Molinari (R-NY)	Vice Chair, House Republican Conference

104th Congress (1995–1997)

Rep. Eva Clayton (D-NC)	Co-Chair, House Democratic Policy Committee
Rep. Barbara Cubin (R-WY)	House Deputy Majority Whip
Rep. Rosa De Lauro (D-CT)	House Chief Deputy Minority Whip
Rep. Tillie Fowler (R-FL)	House Deputy Majority Whip
Rep. Barbara Kennelly (D-CT)	Vice Chair, House Democratic Caucus
Rep. Nita Lowey (D-NY)	House Minority Whip At-Large
Rep. Susan Molinari (R-NY)	Vice Chair, House Republican Conference
Rep. Barbara Vucanovich (R-NV)	Secretary, House Republican Conference

103rd Congress (1993–1995)

Rep. Nancy L. Johnson (R-CT)	Secretary, House Republican Conference
Rep. Barbara Kennelly (D-CT)	House Democratic Chief Deputy Whip

102nd Congress (1991–1993)

Rep. Barbara Kennelly (D-CT)	House Democratic Chief Deputy Whip

(continues)

TABLE 5.4   (continued)

100th Congress (1987–1989)	
Rep. Lynn Martin (R-IL)	Vice Chair, House Republican Conference
Rep. Mary Rose Oakar (D-OH)	Vice Chair, House Democratic Caucus
99th Congress (1985–1987)	
Rep. Lynn Martin (R-IL)	Vice Chair, House Republican Conference
Rep. Mary Rose Oakar (D-OH)	Secretary, House Democratic Caucus
98th Congress (1983–1985)	
Rep. Geraldine Ferraro (D-NY)	Secretary, House Democratic Caucus
97th Congress (1981–1983)	
Rep. Shirley Chisholm (D-NY)	Secretary, House Democratic Caucus
86th to 93rd Congress (1959–1975)	
Rep. Leonor K. Sullivan (D-MO)	Secretary, House Democratic Caucus
83rd, 84th, and 88th Congress (1955–1957), (1963–1965)	
Rep. Edna F. Kelly (D-NY)	Secretary, House Democratic Caucus
81st Congress (1949–1951)	
Rep. Chase G. Woodhouse (D-CT)	Secretary, House Democratic Caucus

U.S. House of Representatives—Committee Chairs

104th Congress (1995–1997)	
Rep. Jan Meyers (R-KS)	Committee on Small Business
93rd and 94th Congress (1973–1977)	
Rep. Leonor Sullivan (D-MO)	Committee on Merchant Marine and Fisheries
83rd Congress (1949–1951)	
Rep. Edith Nourse Rogers (R-MA)	Committee on Veterans' Affairs
81st Congress (1949–1951)	
Rep. Mary Teresa Norton (D-NJ)	Committee on House Administration
80th Congress (1947–1949)	
Rep. Edith Nourse Rogers (R-MA)	Committee on Veterans' Affairs
78th and 79th Congress (1943–1947)	
Rep. Mary Teresa Norton (D-NJ)	Committee on Labor
77th Congress (1941–1943)	
Rep. Mary Teresa Norton (D-NJ)	Committee on Memorials and Committee on Labor
Rep. Caroline O'Day (D-NY)	Committee on Election of President, Vice President, and Representatives
76th Congress (1943–1945)	
Rep. Mary Teresa Norton (D-NJ)	Committee on Labor

TABLE 5.4   (continued)

Rep. Caroline O'Day (D-NY)	Committee on Election of President, Vice President, and Representatives
75th Congress (1937–1943)	
Rep. Mary Teresa Norton (D-NJ)	Committee on District of Columbia and Committee on Labor
Rep. Caroline O'Day (D-NY)	Committee on Election of President, Vice President, and Representatives
72nd to 74th Congress (1931–1937)	
Rep. Mary Teresa Norton (D-NJ)	Committee on District of Columbia
68th Congress (1923–1925)	
Rep. Mae Ella Nolan (R-CA)	Committee on Expenditures in the Post Office Department

176 ■ Women and Political Participation

TABLE 5.5   Women in the U.S. Cabinet

Appointee	Position	Appointed by	Years Served
Frances Perkins	Secretary of Labor	F. Roosevelt (D)	1933–1945
Oveta Culp Hobby	Secretary of Health, Education and Welfare	Eisenhower (R)	1953–1955
Carla Anderson Hills	Secretary of Housing and Urban Development	Ford (R)	1975–1977
Juanita A. Kreps	Secretary of Commerce	Carter (D)	1977–1979
Patricia R. Harris	Secretary of Housing and Urban Development	Carter (D)	1977–1979
Patricia R. Harris	Secretary of Health and Human Services	Carter (D)	1979–1981
Shirley M. Hufdtedler	Secretary of Education	Carter (D)	1979–1981
Jeane J. Kirkpatrick	U.N. Ambassador	Reagan (R)	1981–1985
Margaret M. Heckler	Secretary of Health and Human Services	Reagan (R)	1983–1985
Elizabeth Hanford Dole	Secretary of Transportation	Reagan (R)	1983–1987
Ann Dore McLaughlin	Secretary of Labor	Reagan (R)	1987–1989
Elizabeth Hanford Dole	Secretary of Labor	Bush (R)	1989–1991
Carla Anderson Hills	Special Trade Representative	Bush (R)	1989–1993
Lyn Morley Martin	Secretary of Labor	Bush (R)	1991–1993
Barbara H. Franklin	Secretary of Commerce	Bush (R)	1992–1993
Madeleine K. Albright	U.N. Ambassador	Clinton (D)	1993–1997
Hazel R. O'Leary	Secretary of Energy	Clinton (D)	1993–1997
Alice M. Rivlin	Director, Office of Management and Budget	Clinton (D)	1994–1996
Laura D'Andrea Tyson	Chair, National Economic Council	Clinton (D)	1995–1997
Janet L. Yellen	Chair, Council of Economic Advisors	Clinton (D)	1997–1999

TABLE 5.5 *(continued)*

Appointee	Position	Appointed by	Years Served
Carol M. Browner	Administrator, Environmental Protection Agency	Clinton (D)	1993–2001
Janet Reno	Attorney General	Clinton (D)	1993–2001
Donna E. Shalala	Secretary of Health and Human Services	Clinton (D)	1993–2001
Madeleine K. Albright	Secretary of State	Clinton (D)	1997–2001
Aida Alvarez	Administrator, Small Business Administration	Clinton (D)	1997–2001
Charlene Barshefsky	U.S. Trade Representative	Clinton (D)	1997–2001
Alexis Herman	Secretary of Labor	Clinton (D)	1997–2001
Janice R. Lachance	Director, Office of Personnel Management	Clinton (D)	1997–2001
Christine Todd Whitman	Administrator, Environmental Protection Agency	G. W. Bush (R)	2001–2003
Elaine Chao	Secretary of Labor	G. W. Bush (R)	2001–present
Gale Norton	Secretary of Interior	G. W. Bush (R)	2001–present
Condoleezza Rice	National Security Advisor	G. W. Bush (R)	2001–present
Ann Veneman	Secretary of Agriculture	G. W. Bush (R)	2001–present

TABLE 5.6 Appointment of Women to the Federal Courts

President	District Courts %	Appeals Courts %
Lyndon Johnson (1963–1969)	1.9 (3)	
Richard Nixon (1969–1974)	4.0 (1)	
Gerald Ford (1974–1977)	1.6 (1)	
Jimmy Carter (1977–1981)	14.4 (29)	19.6 (11)
Ronald Reagan (1981–1989)	8.3 (24)	5.1 (4)
George H. W. Bush (1989–1993)	19.6 (29)	18.9 (7)
William Clinton (1993–2001)	28.5 (87)	32.8 (20)
George W. Bush (2001–2002)	20.5 (17)	18.8 (3)

References

Andersen, Kristi. 1996. *After Suffrage: Women in Partisan and Electoral Politics Before the New Deal.* Chicago: University of Chicago Press.

Barone, Michael, and Richard Cohen, with Charles Cook. 2002. *Almanac of American Politics* Washington, DC: National Journal.

Bierma, Nathan. 2002. "Up the Political Ladder, One Rung at a Time." *Chicago Tribune,* September 25.

Breckinridge, Sophonisba. 1933. *Women in the Twentieth Century.* New York: McGraw-Hill.

Burns, Nancy, Kay Lehman Schlozman, and Sidney Verba. 2001. *The Private Roots of Public Action.* Cambridge, MA: Harvard University Press.

Burrell, Barbara. 1994. *A Woman's Place Is in the House: Campaigning for Congress in the Feminist Era.* Ann Arbor: University of Michigan Press.

Burton, Michael John, and Daniel M. Shea. 2003. "Defying Conventional Wisdom: Loretta Sanchez, Forty-Sixth District of California." In *Campaign Mode: Strategic Vision in Congressional Elections.* Lanham, MD: Rowman and Littlefield.

CAWP (Center for the American Woman and Politics). 2003. "Fact Sheet: Women in State Legislatures: 1975–2003." New Brunswick, NJ: Rutgers University.

Clymer, Adam. 2002. "In 2002, Woman's Place May Be the Statehouse." *New York Times,* April 14.

Congressional Quarterly. 1964. "Political Notes." *Congressional Quarterly Weekly Report,* January 31, 223.

Cox, Elizabeth. 1996. *Women State and Territorial Legislators, 1895–1995.* Jefferson, NC: McFarland.

Costello, Cynthia B., and Anne J. Stone. 2001. *The American Woman, 2001–2002: Getting to the Top.* New York: W. W. Norton.

Diedrich, John. 2004. "A Woman Warrior's Role." *Milwaukee Journal Sentinel,* April 18.

Foerstel, Karen, and Herbert N. Foerstel. 1996. *Climbing the Hill: Gender Conflict in Congress.* New York: Praeger.

Fox, Richard, and Jennifer Lawless. 2004. "Entering the Arena? Gender and the Decision to Run for Office." *American Journal of Political Science* 48(2): 264–280.

Frankovic, Kathleen. 1988. "The Ferraro Factor: The Women's Movement, the Polls, and the Press." In *The Politics of the Gender Gap: The Social Construction of Political Influence.* Edited by Carol M. Mueller. Newbury Park, CA: Sage.

Freeman, Jo. 2000. *A Room at a Time: How Women Entered Party Politics.* Lanham, MD: Rowman and Littlefield.

Gertzog, Irwin. 1995. *Congressional Women: Their Recruitment, Integration, and Behavior.* New York: Praeger.

———. 2002. "Changing Pathways to the U.S. House." In *Women Transforming Congress.* Edited by Cindy Simon Rosenthal. Norman: University of Oklahoma Press.

Goldman, Sheldon, Elliot Slotnick, Gerard Gryski, Gary Zuk, and Sara Schiavoni. 2003. "W. Bush Remaking the Judiciary: Like Father, Like Son? *Judicature* 86(6) (May–June): 282–309.

Huddy, Leonie. 1994. "The Political Significance of Voters' Gender Stereotypes." *Research in Micropolitics* 4: 169–93.

Kahn, Kim Fridkin. 1996. *The Political Consequences of Being a Woman: How Stereotypes Influence the Conduct and Consequences of Political Campaigns.* New York: Columbia University Press.

King, David, and Richard Matland. 2002. "Women as Candidates in Congressional Elections." In *Women Transforming Congress.* Edited by Cindy Simon Rosenthal. Norman: University of Oklahoma Press.

Lemons, J. Stanley. 1973. *The Woman Citizen: Social Feminism in the 1920s.* Urbana: University of Illinois Press.

Lugar, Richard. 1983. "A Plan to Elect More GOP Women." *Washington Post*, August 21.

Mezey, Susan. 2000. "Gender and the Federal Judiciary." In *Gender and American Politics: Women, Men, and the Political Process.* Edited by Sue Tolleson-Rinehart and Jyl J. Josephson. Armonk, NY: M. E. Sharpe.

Robson, Deborah Carol. 2000. "Stereotypes and the Female Politicians: A Case Study of Senator Barbara Mikulski." *Communication Quarterly* 48(3): 205–22.

Schmidt, Gregory. 2003. "Unanticipated Success: Lessons from Peru's Experiences with Gender Quotas in Majoritarian Closed List and Open List PR Systems." In *The Implementation of Quotas: Latin American Experiences.* Stockholm, Sweden: International Institute for Democracy and Electoral Assistance.

Sherman, Janann. 2001. "'Senator-at-Large for America's Women': Margaret Chase Smith and the Paradox of Gender." In *The Impact of Women in Public Office.* Edited by Susan Carroll. Bloomington: Indiana University Press.

Smith, Steven, and Christopher J. Deering. 1990. *Committees in Congress.* Washington, DC: Congressional Quarterly Press.

Southgate, Martha. 1986. "EMILY's List: Political Money Where It Counts." *Ms.* 15, September 27.

Spake, Amanda. 1988. "Women Can Be Power Brokers, Too." *Washington Post Magazine,* June 5, 32.

Tenpas, Kathryn Dunn. 1997. "Women on the White House Staff: A Longitudinal Analysis, 1939–1994." In *The Other Elites.* Edited by MaryAnne Borrelli and Janet Martin. Boulder, CO: Lynne Rienner.

Thompson, Joan Hulse. 1984. "The Congressional Caucus for Women's Issues: One-Hundred and Thirty Feminists in the House." Paper presented at the annual meeting of the Midwest Political Science Association, Chicago, April 19.

———. 1985. "Lobbying in the House: The Congressional Caucus for Women's Issues Versus the Insurance Industry." Paper presented at the annual meeting of the Midwest Political Science Association, Chicago, April 15.

The White House Project. 2003. "Barriers and Opportunities: Results and Strategic Recommendations from Dial Groups." New York: Ms. Foundation.

Documents

The Declaration of Sentiments and Resolutions (1848)

When, in the course of human events, it becomes necessary for one portion of the family of man to assume among the people of the earth a position different from that which they have hitherto occupied, but one to which the laws of nature and of nature's God entitle them, a decent respect to the opinions of mankind requires that they should declare the causes that impel them to such a course.

We hold these truths to be self-evident: that all men and women are created equal; that they are endowed by their Creator with certain inalienable rights; that among these are life, liberty, and the pursuit of happiness; that to secure these rights governments are instituted, deriving their just powers from the consent of the governed. Whenever any form of government becomes destructive of these ends, it is the right of those who suffer from it to refuse allegiance to it, and to insist upon the institution of a new government, laying its foundation on such principles, and organizing its powers in such form, as to them shall seem most likely to effect their safety and happiness. Prudence, indeed, will dictate that governments long established should not be changed for light and transient causes; and accordingly all experience hath shown that mankind are more disposed to suffer while evils are sufferable, than to right themselves by abolishing the forms to which they are accustomed. But when a long train of abuses and usurpations, pursuing invariably the same object, evinces a design to reduce them under absolute despotism, it is their duty to throw off such government, and to provide new guards for their future security. Such has been the patient sufferance of the women under this government, and such is now the necessity which constrains them to demand the equal station to which they are entitled.

The history of mankind is a history of repeated injuries and usurpations on the part of man toward woman, having in direct object the establishment of an absolute tyranny over her. To prove this, let facts be submitted to a candid world.

He has never permitted her to exercise her inalienable right to the elective franchise.

He has compelled her to submit to laws, in the formation of which she had no voice.

He has withheld from her rights which are given to the most ignorant and degraded men—both natives and foreigners.

Having deprived her of this first right of a citizen, the elective franchise, thereby leaving her without representation in the halls of legislation, he has oppressed her on all sides.

He has made her, if married, in the eye of the law, civilly dead.

He has taken from her all right in property, even to the wages she earns.

He has made her, morally, an irresponsible being, as she can commit many crimes with impunity, provided they be done in the presence of her husband. In the covenant of marriage, she is compelled to promise obedience to her husband, he becoming, to all intents and purposes, her master—the law giving him power to deprive her of her liberty, and to administer chastisement.

He has so framed the laws of divorce, as to what shall be the proper causes, and in case of separation, to whom the guardianship of the children shall be given, as to be wholly regardless of the happiness of women—the law, in all cases, going upon a flagrant supposition of the supremacy of man, and giving all power into his hands.

After depriving her of all rights as a married woman, if single, and the owner of property, he has taxed her to support a government which recognizes her only when her property can be made profitable to it.

He has monopolized nearly all the profitable employments, and from those she is permitted to follow, she receives but a scanty remuneration. He closes against her all the avenues to wealth and distinction which he considers most honorable to himself. As a teacher of theology, medicine, or law, she is not known.

He has denied her the facilities for obtaining a thorough education, all colleges being closed against her.

He allows her in church, as well as state, but a subordinate position, claiming apostolic authority for her exclusion from the ministry, and, with some exceptions, from any public participation in the affairs of the church.

He has created a false public sentiment by giving to the world a different code of morals for men and women, by which moral delinquencies that exclude women from society are not only tolerated, but deemed of little account in man.

He has usurped the prerogative of Jehovah himself, claiming it as his right to assign for her a sphere of action, when that belongs to her conscience and to her God.

He has endeavored, in every way that he could, to destroy her confidence in her own powers, to lessen her self-respect, and to make her willing to lead a dependent and abject life.

Now, in view of this entire disfranchisement of one-half the people of this country, their social and religious degradation—in view of the unjust laws above mentioned, and because women do feel themselves aggrieved, oppressed, and fraudulently deprived of their most sacred rights, we insist that they have immediate admission to all the rights and privileges which belong to them as citizens of the United States.

In entering upon the great work before us, we anticipate no small amount of misconception, misrepresentation, and ridicule; but we shall use every instrumentality within our power to effect our object. We shall employ agents, circulate tracts, petition the State and National legislatures, and endeavor to enlist the pulpit and the press in our behalf. We hope this Convention will be followed by a series of Conventions embracing every part of the country.

Resolutions

Whereas, The great precept of nature is conceded to be, that "man shall pursue his own true and substantial happiness." Blackstone in his Commentaries remarks, that this law of Nature being coeval with mankind, and dictated by God himself, is of course superior in obligation to any other. It is binding over all the globe, in all countries and at all times; no human laws are of any validity if contrary to this, and such of them as are valid, derive all their force, and all their validity, and all their authority, mediately and immediately, from this original; therefore,

Resolved, That such laws as conflict, in any way, with the true and substantial happiness of women, are contrary to the great precept of nature and of no validity, for this is "superior in obligation to any other."

Resolved, That all laws which prevent woman from occupying such a station in society as her conscience shall dictate, or which place her in a position inferior to that of man, are contrary to the great precept of nature, and therefore of no force or authority.

Resolved, That women is man's equal was intended to be so by the Creator, and the highest good of the race demands that she should be recognized as such.

Resolved, That the women of this country ought to be enlightened in regard to the laws under which they live, that they may no longer publish their degradation by declaring themselves satisfied with their present position, nor their ignorance, by asserting that they have all the rights they want.

Resolved, That inasmuch as man, while claiming for himself intellectual superiority, does accord to woman moral superiority, it is preeminently his duty to encourage her to speak and teach, as she has an opportunity, in all religious assemblies.

Resolved, That the same amount of virtue, delicacy, and refinement of behavior that is required of woman in the social state, should also be required of man, and the same transgressions should be visited with equal severity on both man and woman.

Resolved, That the objection of indelicacy and impropriety, which is so often brought against woman when she addresses a public audience, comes with a very ill-grace from those who encourage, by their attendance, her appearance on the stage, in the concert, or in feats of the circus.

Resolved, That woman has too long rested satisfied in the circumscribed limits which corrupt customs and a perverted application of the Scriptures have marked out for her, and that it is time she should move in the enlarged sphere which her great Creator has assigned her.

Resolved, That it is the duty of the women of this country to secure to themselves their sacred right to the elective franchise.

Resolved, That the equality of human rights results necessarily from the fact of the identity of the race in capabilities and responsibilities.

Resolved, therefore, That, being invested by the Creator with the same capabilities, and the same consciousness of responsibility for their exercise, it is demonstrably the right and duty of women, equally with man, to promote every righteous cause by every righteous means; and especially in regard to the great subjects of morals and religion, it is self-evidently her right to participate with her brother in teaching them, both in private and in public, by writing and by speaking, by any instrumentalities proper to be used, and in any assemblies proper to be held; and this being a self-evident truth growing out of the divinely implanted principles of human nature, any custom or authority adverse to it, whether modern or wearing the hoary sanction of antiquity, is to be regarded as a self-evident falsehood, and at war with mankind.

At the last session Lucretia Mott offered and spoke to the following resolution:

Resolved, That the speedy success of our cause depends upon the zealous and untiring efforts of both men and women, for the overthrow of the monopoly of the pulpit, and for the securing to woman an equal participation with men in the various trades, professions, and commerce.

Source: Elizabeth Cady Stanton, *A History of Woman Suffrage,* vol. 1 (Rochester, NY: Fowler and Wells, 1889), pp. 70–71.

"Ain't I a Woman?"
Sojourner Truth (1851)

Well, children, where there is so much racket there must be something out of kilter. I think that 'twixt the negroes of the South and the women at the North, all talking about rights, the white men will be in a fix pretty soon. But what's all this here talking about?

That man over there says that women need to be helped into carriages, and lifted over ditches, and to have the best place everywhere. Nobody ever helps me into carriages, or over mud-puddles, or gives me any best place! And ain't I a woman? Look at me! Look at my arm! I have ploughed and planted, and gathered into barns, and no man could head me! And ain't I a woman? I could work as much and eat as much as a man—when I could get it—and bear the lash as well! And ain't I a woman? I have borne thirteen children, and seen them most all sold off to slavery, and when I cried out with my mother's grief, none but Jesus heard me! And ain't I a woman?

Then they talk about this thing in the head; what's this they call it? [Intellect, someone whispers.] That's it, honey. What's that got to do with a women's rights or negro's rights? If my cup won't hold but a pint, and yours holds a quart, wouldn't you be mean not to let me have my little half-measure full?

Then that little man in black there, he says women can't have as much rights as men, 'cause Christ wasn't a woman! Where did your Christ come from? From God and a woman! Man had nothing to do with Him.

If the first woman God ever made was strong enough to turn the world upside down all alone, three women together ought to be able to turn it back, and get it right side up again! And now they is asking to do it, the men better let them.

Obliged to you for hearing me, and now old Sojourner ain't got nothing more to say.

Source: Miriam Schneir, ed., *Feminism: The Essential Historical Writings* (New York: Vintage Books, 1972).

United States v. Susan B. Anthony (1872)

MISS ANTHONY: Of all my prosecutors, from the corner grocery politician who entered the complaint, to the United States marshal, commissioner, district-attorney, district-judge, your honor on the bench—not one is my peer, but each and all are my political sovereigns; and had your honor submitted my case to the jury, as was clearly your duty, even then I should have had just cause of protest, for not one of those men was my peer; but, native or foreign born, white or black, rich or poor, educated or ignorant, sober or drunk, each and every man of them was my political superior; hence, in no sense, my peer. Under such circumstances a commoner of England, tried before a jury of lords, would have far less cause to complain than have I, a woman, tried before a jury of men. Even my counsel, Hon. Henry R. Selden, who has argued my cause so ably, so earnestly, so unanswerably before your honor, is my political sovereign. Precisely as no disfranchised person is entitled to sit upon a jury, and no woman is entitled to the franchise, so none but a regularly admitted lawyer is allowed to practice in the courts, and no woman can gain admission to the bar—hence, jury, judge, counsel, all must be of the superior class.

JUDGE HUNT: The Court must insist—the prisoner has been tried according to the established forms of law.

MISS ANTHONY: Yes, your honor, but by forms of law all made by men, interpreted by men, administered by men, in favor of men and against women; and hence your honor's ordered verdict of guilty, against a United States citizen for the exercise of the "citizen's right to vote," simply because that citizen was a woman and not a man. But yesterday, the same man-made forms of law declared it a crime punishable with $1,000 fine and six months' imprisonment to give a cup of cold water, a crust of bread or a night's shelter to a panting fugitive tracking his way to Canada; and every man or woman in whose veins coursed a drop of human sympathy violated that wicked law, reckless of consequences, and was justified in so doing. As then the slaves who got their freedom had to take it over or under or through the unjust forms of law, precisely so now must women take it to get their right to a voice in this government; and I have taken mine, and mean to take it at every opportunity.

JUDGE HUNT: The Court orders the prisoner to sit down. It will not allow another word.

MISS ANTHONY: When I was brought before your honor for trial, I hoped for a broad and liberal interpretation of the Constitution and its recent amendments, which should declare all United States citizens under its protecting aegis—which should declare equality of rights the national guarantee to all persons born or naturalized in the United States. But failing to get this justice—failing, even, to get a trial by a jury *not* of my peers—I ask not leniency at your hands but rather the full rigor of the law.

Bradwell v. Illinois (1873)

Justice Bradley delivered the opinion:

The civil law, as well as nature herself, has always recognized a wide difference in the respective spheres and destinies of man and woman. Man is, or should be, women's protector and defender. The natural and proper timidity and delicacy which belongs to the female sex evidently unfits it for many of the occupations of civil life. The constitution of the family organization, which is founded in the divine ordinance, as well as in the nature of things, indicates the domestic sphere as that which properly belongs to the domain and functions of womanhood. The harmony, not to say identity of interest and views which belong, or should belong to the family institution is repugnant to the idea of a woman adopting a distinct and independent career from that of her husband. So firmly fixed was this sentiment in the founders of the common law that it became a maxim of that system of jurisprudence that a woman had no legal existence separate from her husband, who was regarded as her head and representative in the social state; and, notwithstanding some recent modifications of this civil status, many of the special rules of law flowing from and dependent up this cardinal principle still exist in full force in most States. One of these is, that a married woman is incapable, without her husband's consent, of making contracts which shall be binding on her or him. This very incapacity was one circumstance which the Supreme Court of Illinois deemed important in rendering a married woman incompetent fully to perform the duties and trusts that belong to the office of an attorney and counsellor.

It is true that many women are unmarried and not affected by any of the duties, complications, and incapacities arising out of the married state, but these are exceptions to the general rule. The paramount destiny and mission of woman are to fulfill the noble and benign offices of wife and mother. This is the law of the Creator. And the rule of civil society must be adapted to the general constitution of things, and cannot be based upon the exceptional cases.

Proposed Equal Rights Amendment (1923)

This proposed amendment has been introduced in Congress every year since 1923:

Section 1. Equality of rights under the law shall not be denied or abridged by the United States or by any State on account of sex.

Section 2. The Congress shall have the power to enforce, by appropriate legislation, the provisions of this article.

Section 3. This amendment shall take effect two years after the date of ratification.

Executive Order 10980, President's Commission on the Status of Women (1961)

Whereas prejudices and outmoded customs act as barriers to the full realization of women's rights which should be respected and fostered as part of our nation's commitment to human dignity, freedom, and democracy; and

Whereas measures that contribute to family security and strengthen home life will advance the general welfare; and

Whereas it is in the national interest to promote the economy, security, and national defense through the most efficient utilization of the skills of all persons; and

Whereas in every period of national emergency women have served with distinction in widely varied capacities but thereafter have been subject to treatment as a marginal group whose skills have been inadequately utilized; and

Whereas women should be assured the opportunity to develop their capacities and fulfill their aspirations on a continuing basis irrespective of national exigencies; and

Whereas a governmental commission should be charged with the responsibility for developing recommendations for overcoming discriminations in government and private employment on the basis of sex and for developing recommendations for services which will enable women to continue their role as wives and mothers while making a maximum contribution to the world around them:

Now, therefore, by virtue of the authority vested in me as President of the United States by the Constitution and statutes of the United States, it is ordered as follows:

Part I—Establishment of the President's Commission on the Status of Women

Sec. 101. There is hereby established the President's Commission on the Status of Women, referred to herein as the "Commission." The Commission shall terminate not later than October 1, 1963.

Sec. 102. The Commission shall be composed of twenty members appointed by the President from among persons with a competency in the area of public affairs and women's activities. In addition, the Secretary of Labor, the Attorney General, the Secretary of Health, Education, and Welfare, the Secretary of Commerce, the Secretary of Agriculture, and the Chairman of the Civil Service Commission shall also serve as members of the Commission. The President shall designate from among the membership a Chairman, a Vice-Chairman, and an Executive Vice-Chairman.

Sec. 103. In conformity with the Act of May 3, 1945 (59 Stat. 134, 31 U.S.C. 691), necessary facilitating assistance, including the provision of suitable office space by the Department of Labor, shall be furnished the Commission by the federal agencies whose chief officials are members thereof. An Executive Secretary shall be detailed by the Secretary of Labor to serve the Commission.

Sec. 104. The Commission shall meet at the call of the Chairman.

Sec. 105. The Commission is authorized to use the services of consultants and experts as may be found necessary and as may be otherwise authorized by law.

Part II—Duties of the President's Commission on the Status of Women

Sec. 201. The Commission shall review progress and make recommendations as needed for constructive action in the following areas:

(a) Employment policies and practices, including those on wages, under federal contracts.

(b) Federal social insurance and tax laws as they affect the net earnings and other income of women.

(c) Federal and state labor laws dealing with such matters as hours, night work, and wages, to determine whether they are accomplishing the purposes for which they were established and whether they should be adapted to changing technological, economic, and social conditions.

(d) Differences in legal treatment of men and women in regard to political and civil rights, property rights, and family relations.

(e) New and expanded services that may be required for women as wives, mothers, and workers, including education, counseling, training, home services, and arrangements for care of children during the working day.

(f) The employment policies and practices of the government of the United States, with reference to additional affirmative steps which should be taken through legislation, executive or administrative action to assure nondiscrimination on the basis of sex and to enhance constructive employment opportunities for women.

Sec. 202. The Commission shall submit a final report of its recommendations to the President by October 1, 1963.

Sec. 203. All executive departments and agencies of the federal government are directed to cooperate with the Commission in the performance of its duties.

Part III—Remuneration and Expenses

Sec. 301. Members of the Commission, except those receiving other compensation from the United States, shall receive such compensation as the President shall hereafter fix in a manner to be hereafter determined.

John F. Kennedy
The White House, December 14, 1961

National Organization for Women (NOW) Statement of Purpose (1966)

We, men and women, who hereby constitute ourselves as the National Organization for Women, believe that the time has come for a new movement toward true equality for all women in America, and toward a fully equal partnership of the sexes, as part of the worldwide evolution of human rights now taking place within and beyond our national borders.

The purpose of NOW is to take action to bring women into full participation in the mainstream of American society now, exercising all the privileges and responsibilities thereof in truly equal partnership with men.

We believe the time has come to move beyond the abstract argument, discussion and symposia over the status and special nature of women which has raged in America in recent years; the time has come to confront, with concrete action, the conditions that now prevent women from enjoying the equality of opportunity and freedom of which is their right, as individual Americans, and as human beings.

NOW is dedicated to the proposition that women, first and foremost, are human beings, who, like all other people in our society, must have the chance to develop their fullest human potential. We believe that women can achieve such equality only by accepting to the full the challenges and responsibilities they share with all other people in our society, as part of the decision-making mainstream of American political, economic and social life.

Roe v. Wade (1973)

The Constitution does not explicitly mention any right of privacy. In a line of decisions, however . . . the Court has recognized that a right of personal privacy, or a guarantee of certain areas or zones of privacy, does exist under the Constitution. . . . The right of privacy whether it is founded in the Fourteenth Amendment's reservation of rights to the people, is broad enough to encompass a woman's decision whether or not to terminate her pregnancy. . . . We . . . conclude that the right of personal privacy includes the abortion decision, but that this right is not unqualified and must be considered against important state interests in regulation . . . the State does have an important and legitimate interest in preserving and protecting the health of the pregnant woman . . . and . . . it has still another important and legitimate interest in protecting the potentiality of human life. These interests are separate and distinct. Each grows substantially as the woman approaches term, and at a point during pregnancy, each becomes "compelling."

With respect to the State's important and legitimate interest in the health of the mother, the "compelling" point, in the light of present medical knowledge, is at approximately the end of the first trimester. This is so because of the now-established medical fact . . . that until the end of the first trimester mortality in abortion may be less than mortality in normal childbirth. It follows that . . . for the period of pregnancy prior to this "compelling" point, the attending physician, in consultation with his patient, is free to determine without regulation by the State, that in his medical judgment, the patient's pregnancy should be terminated.

For the state subsequent to approximately the end of the first trimester, the State, in promoting its interest in the health of the mother, may, if it chooses, regulate the abortion procedure in ways that are reasonably related to maternal health. For the state subsequent to viability, the State in promoting its interest in the potentiality of human life may, if it chooses, regulate, and even proscribe, abortion except where it is necessary, in appropriate medical judgment, for the preservation of the life or health of the mother.

The Combahee River Collective Statement (1977)

The most general statement of our politics at the present time would be that we are actively committed to struggling against racial, sexual, heterosexual, and class oppression, and see as our particular task the development of integrated analysis and practice based upon the fact that the major systems of oppression are interlocking. The synthesis of these oppressions creates the conditions of our lives. As Black women we see Black feminism as the logical political movement to combat the manifold and simultaneous oppression that all women of color face.

Third-Wave Manifesta: A Thirteen-Point Agenda (2000)

1. To out unacknowledged feminists, specifically those who are younger, so that Generation X can become a visible movement and, further, a voting block of eighteen- to forty-year-olds.

2. To safeguard a woman's right to bear or not to bear a child, regardless of circumstances, including women who are younger than eighteen or impoverished. To preserve this right throughout her life and support the choice to be childless.

3. To make explicit that the fight for reproductive rights must include birth control; the right for poor women and lesbians to have children; partner adoption for gay couples; subsidized fertility treatments for all women who choose them; and freedom from sterilization abuse. Furthermore, to support the idea that sex can be—and usually is—for pleasure, not procreation.

4. To bring down the double standard in sex and sexual health, and foster male responsibility and assertiveness in the following areas: achieving freedom from STDs; more fairly dividing the burden of family planning as well as responsibilities such as child care; and eliminating violence against women.

5. To tap into and raise awareness of our revolutionary history, and the fact that almost all movements began as youth movements. To have access to our intellectual feminist legacy and women's history; for the classics of radical feminism, womanism, mujeristas, women's liberation, and all our roots to remain in print; and to have women's history taught to men as well as women as part of all curricula.

6. To support and increase the visibility and power of lesbians and bisexual women in the feminist movement, in high schools, colleges, and the workplace. To recognize that queer women have always been at the forefront of the feminist movement, and that there is nothing to be gained—and much to be lost—by downplaying their history, whether inadvertently or actively.

7. To practice "autokeonony" ("self in community"): to see activism not as a choice between self and community but as a link between them that creates balance.

8. To have equal access to health care, regardless of income, which includes coverage equivalent to men's and keeping in mind that women use the system more often than men do because of our reproductive capacity.

9. For women who so desire to participate in all reaches of the military, including combat, and to enjoy all the benefits (loans, health care, pensions) offered to its members for as long as we continue to have an active military. The largest expenditure of our national budget goes toward maintaining this welfare system, and feminists have a duty to make sure women have access to every echelon.

10. To liberate adolescents from slut-bashing, listless educators, sexual harassment, and bullying at school, as well as violence in all walks of life, and the silence that hangs over adolescents' heads, often keeping them isolated, lonely, and indifferent to the world.

11. To make the workplace responsive to an individual's wants, needs, and talents. This includes valuing (monetarily) stay-at-home

parents, aiding employees who want to spend more time with family and continue to work, equalizing pay for jobs of comparable worth, enacting a minimum wage that would bring full-time workers with two children over the poverty line, and providing employee benefits for freelance and part-time workers.

12. To acknowledge that, although feminists may have disparate values, we share the same goal of equality, and of supporting one another in our efforts to gain the power to make our own choices.

13. To pass the Equal Rights Amendment so that we can have constitutional foundation of righteousness and equality upon which future women's rights conventions will stand.

Source: Jennifer Baumgardner and Amy Richards, *Manifesta: Young Women, Feminism, and the Future* (New York: Farrar, Straus and Giroux, 2000).

Key People, Laws, and Terms

Abzug, Bella (1920–1998): Bella Abzug was elected to the U.S. House of Representatives from New York's Nineteenth Congressional District in 1970 and served until 1976, when she unsuccessfully sought a seat in the U.S. Senate. She introduced legislation calling for an end to the Vietnam War, banning discrimination against women seeking credit, gay rights, and reproductive freedom. She was a champion of women's rights and was considered one of the leaders of the second women's rights movement. She was a founder of the National Women's Political Caucus and worked as an attorney in civil rights and labor law.

Adams, Abigail (1744–1818): Abigail Adams was the wife of the second U.S. president, John Adams, and mother of President John Quincy Adams. She spoke out for women's rights and for their education in the new nation and was a close adviser to her husband. In her famous "Remember the Ladies" letter, Abigail Adams proposed that women should claim their share of liberty.

Afghan Women and Children Act (2001): Authorized health care and educational assistance to Afghan women and children refugees.

Anthony, Susan B. (1820–1906): Along with Elizabeth Cady Stanton, Anthony was leader of the suffrage movement. She traveled extensively across the country advocating votes for women. From 1868 to 1870 she edited *The Revolution*, a radical journal demanding suffrage, equal education, equal employment opportunities, and trade unions for women. In 1869 she and Stanton formed the National

Woman Suffrage Association, and in 1880 she convened the founding meeting of the International Council of Women. In 1892 she became president of the National American Woman Suffrage Association. In 1904 Anthony and Carrie Chapman Catt founded the International Woman Suffrage Alliance in Berlin. She also coedited the four-volume *History of Woman Suffrage, 1881–1902.*

Catt, Carrie Chapman (1859–1947): Catt was a suffrage leader and founder of the League of Women Voters. She is credited with turning the National American Woman Suffrage Association into a strong organization as its president from 1900 to 1904 and 1915 to 1920. She also served as president of the International Woman Suffrage Alliance from 1904 to 1923. After suffrage was won in 1920, Catt became active in the peace movement and founded the National Committee on the Cause and Cure of War.

Chisholm, Shirley (1924–): Shirley Chisholm was elected to the U.S. House of Representatives to represent the Brooklyn district of New York State in 1968. She was the first African American woman elected to Congress and served until 1983. She was also the first African American to actively seek the presidential nomination of a major U.S. political party when she ran for president in 1972. She served as secretary to the Democratic Caucus, a leadership position in the 97th Congress (1981–1983). She founded the National Political Congress of Black Women.

Civil Rights Act of 1964, Title VII: Title VII of the Civil Rights Act of 1964 bans discrimination in employment on the basis of gender, race, and age. The Civil Rights Act created the Equal Employment Opportunity Commission (EEOC) and granted it power to investigate discrimination complaints if efforts at conciliation fail.

Commission on the Advancement of Women and Minorities in Science, Engineering, and Technology Development (1998): The Commission on the Advancement of Women and Minorities in Science, Engineering, and Technology Development was established to examine ways to encourage more women and minorities to pursue careers in science, engineering, and technology and explore ways to increase female and minority participation in undergraduate and graduate programs in engineering, physics, and computer science.

Concerned Women for America (CWA): CWA is a fundamentalist religious antifeminist women's organization founded by Beverly LaHaye in 1979. The group has approximately 2,500 local chapters and a mailing list of more than 600,000 names. The CWA actively opposes abortion, secular humanism in the schools, and homosexuality and often uses litigation as a tactic to achieve its goals.

Contraceptive Coverage Act (1998): The Contraceptive Coverage Act requires health plans participating in the federal government's health-benefits program to cover contraceptives for federal workers and their dependents if they also cover other prescription drugs.

Coverture: Coverture is the doctrine that the husband and wife are one person in law. The being or legal existence of a woman was suspended during marriage. As a basic principle of English common law, its result was that a woman upon marriage lost all the rights she possessed when single. Her property became her husband's and she fell under his complete control. The practice of this doctrine in the United States was a catalyst for the first women's rights movement.

Displaced Homemaker Self-Sufficiency Assistance Act (1990): The Displaced Homemaker Self-Sufficiency Assistance Act authorizes funding to expand and coordinate existing training and support services at the state and local levels. Under the statute, states are required to give special consideration to women age forty and older, as well as to minority displaced homemakers.

Eagle Forum: The Eagle Forum is an antifeminism organization founded by Phyllis Schlafly. This organization opposes abortion, day care, comparable worth, family leave, and domestic violence shelters. It champions women as homemakers.

Education Amendments, Title IX (1972): Title IX of the Educational Amendments prohibited discrimination on grounds of gender in federally assisted education programs and activities, including athletic activities.

Equal Credit Opportunity Act (1974): The Equal Credit Opportunity Act prohibits discrimination based on gender or marital status in any credit transaction.

Equal Pay Act (1963): The Equal Pay Act requires employers to pay equal wages for equal work regardless of the gender of the workers. However, it has not been enforced, and four decades later, women and minorities still make less than white men at the same jobs.

Equal Rights Amendment (ERA): The ERA to the Constitution was first introduced by the National Woman's Party in 1923. It provides that "equality of rights shall not be denied or abridged by the United States or by any State on account of sex." The amendment received the required two-thirds vote in both the U.S. House of Representatives and the U.S. Senate but did not receive approval by three-quarters of the states' legislatures by the congressionally imposed 1982 deadline.

Family and Medical Leave Act (1993): The Family and Medical Leave Act entitles employees in companies with fifty or more employees to twelve weeks during any twelve-month period of combined parental leave and temporary medial leave in cases involving the birth, adoption, or serious illness of a child, the serious health condition of a parent, or the inability to work due to a serious health condition. It provides that such leave might be leave without pay.

Feminization of Poverty: This term describes the growing proportion of the poor in the United States that is composed of women and their children. This increase is attributed to the instability of marriage and the lack of economic support for women and their children.

Freedom of Access to Clinic Entrances Act (1993): The Freedom of Access to Clinic Entrances Act amends the federal criminal code to impose civil or criminal penalties on persons who intentionally prevent others from entering or exiting a medical facility.

Friedan, Betty (1921–): Betty Friedan is the author of *The Feminine Mystique,* published in 1963, which analyzed the role of women, indicting the ideology that forced women into the role of full-time housewife, and described the psychological costs of such a limited life. The book became an immediate best seller and led to Friedan's becoming a leader of the second women's rights movement. She was a founder of the National Organization of Women, the National Women's Political Caucus, and the National Abortion Rights Action League. She is also the author of *It Changed My Life* (1976), *Second Stage* (1981), and *The Fountain of Age* (1993).

Gender Gap: The gender gap is the difference between men's and women's political opinions and voting behavior. The gender gap was first recorded in the 1980 election of President Ronald Reagan and has grown in every election since, except for the 2000 election of President George W. Bush. (Because the major polling agencies were accused of inaccuracy that year, no gender gap statistics were released.)

Glass Ceiling: This term refers to the discriminatory barriers that affect women in midmanagement positions, preventing them from advancing to higher ranks. Although women are advancing to middle-level managerial positions in substantial numbers, few are found in top-level positions and directorships. "Breaking the glass ceiling" refers to efforts to increase women's presence at the highest leadership levels.

Homemaker Individual Retirement Account Act (1996): The Homemaker Individual Retirement Account Act allows a single-income married couple to deduct IRA contributions at the same amount as two-earner couples.

International Women's Year (1975): The UN Conference in 1972 designated 1975 as International Women's Year and directed the Commission on the Observance of International Women's Year to organize and convene a National Women's Conference in 1977. The purpose of the conference was to recognize historic contributions for women in national development, to set goals for eliminating discrimination based on gender, and to recognize the contributions of women toward world peace.

Jordan, Barbara (1936–1996): When Barbara Jordan was elected to the Texas Senate, she was the first African American woman to serve in the Texas legislature. She was then elected to the U.S. House of Representatives in 1972, where she served until 1979. She was a member of the House Judiciary Committee, which deliberated on the impeachment of President Richard Nixon in 1974, and was remembered for delivering one of the most powerful speeches in U.S. history about the Constitution. She also gave the keynote speech at the Democratic National Convention in 1976.

League of Women Voters: The League of Women Voters was formally organized in 1920 as the postsuffrage successor to the National American Woman Suffrage Association; its goal was to integrate women into the political system. The league worked within the early social feminist coalition, the Women's Joint Congressional Committee, but withdrew from it in the 1950s and avoided feminist issues until its endorsement of the ERA in 1972. The league has since become a major force within state and national women's rights lobbies. It does not consider itself to be a "women's" group but rather a "public interest" group. It has been a training ground for many women who have sought public office.

Mammography Quality Standards Act (1992): The Mammography Quality Standards Act is designed to help make screening for breast cancer safer and more accurate by establishing a set of national standards.

Mankiller, Wilma (1945–): Wilma Mankiller was the first female chief of a major Indian tribe. She served as chief of the Cherokee Nation from 1985 to 1995. In 1969, she became active in the Native American rights movement when a group of Native Americans took over the former Alcatraz prison to protest federal government treatment, and continues to serve as a role model in both the Native American and women's movements today.

NARAL Pro-Choice America: NARAL Pro-Choice America was formed in 1969 as the National Association for the Repeal of Abortion Laws. After abortion was legalized in 1973 with the Supreme Court decision in *Roe v. Wade,* the organization changed its name to the National Abortion Rights Action League. It became NARAL Pro-Choice America in 2003. NARAL Pro-Choice America has more than 400,000 individual and organizational members within affiliates in almost all states. The group has a well-staffed Washington, D.C., headquarters, a political action committee, and a foundation.

National American Woman Suffrage Association (NAWSA): NAWSA was formed in 1890 when the National Woman Suffrage Association and the American Women Suffrage Association merged. They were two competing advocates for suffrage. After suffrage was won, the NAWSA became the League of Women Voters.

NAWSA has a dues-paying membership of around 280,000 in almost 700 local chapters in all 50 states.

National Woman's Party (NWP): The NWP grew out of the Congressional Union (CU), which Alice Paul founded in 1913 to promote women suffrage. Considered the militant wing of the suffrage movement, the CU changed its name to the National Woman's Party in 1916. After suffrage was won, the NWP worked to advance equality feminism and, in 1923, proposed the equal rights amendment, which became its sole domestic issue for many years. The NWP maintained a feminist presence in Washington, D.C., until 1960, even during the time when the feminist movement was largely in the doldrums.

Parks, Rosa (1913–): Rosa Parks was instrumental in launching the civil rights movement in the 1950s when she refused to relinquish her seat on a Montgomery, Alabama, bus to a white man and move to the back of the bus. Her refusal to comply with the city's bus segregation laws provide the catalyst for a 381-day bus boycott and a U.S. Supreme Court decision that bus segregation was illegal. She has been called "the first lady of civil rights" and "the mother of the freedom movement."

Pregnancy Discrimination Act (1978): The Pregnancy Discrimination Act prohibits discrimination against pregnant women in any area of employment, including hiring, promotion, seniority rights, and job security. The act requires public and private employers who offer health insurance and temporary disability plans to provide coverage for pregnancy, childbirth, and related medical conditions.

President's Commission on the Status of Women (PCSW): The PCSW was established in 1961 by President John F. Kennedy to appease female supporters and deflect demands for the equal rights amendment (ERA). Eleanor Roosevelt was appointed honorary chair and Esther Peterson, head of the Women's Bureau, served as executive vice chair. It was the first government body to study the status of women in the United States. The commission released its report, *American Woman,* in 1963, which recommended: equal pay and equal employment opportunities for women, paid maternity leave, marital property reforms, child care, and a legal campaign, using the Fifth and Fourteenth Amendments, against sex discrimination. More than 64,000 copies of the report were sold in less than a year.

Protective Labor Laws: Protective labor laws were enacted in the late-nineteenth and early-twentieth centuries in a number of states to protect women working in factories from hardships such as long workdays, low pay, and heavy lifting. First applied to all workers, male and female, these laws were invalidated under federal constitutional doctrines that held up personal liberties and freedom to contract above state legislative efforts to regulate the workplace. In 1908 the Supreme Court in *Mueller v. Oregon* upheld one of these protective laws that applied only to women. Although seen at first as protecting women, protective labor laws later came to be seen by feminists as limiting women's economic opportunities.

Redstockings: Shulamith Firestone and Ellen Willis founded the Redstockings, a radical feminist group, in New York in 1969. It only functioned for less than two years but became nationally known when its members disrupted a state legislative hearing on abortion law reform to demand repeal. The group is also credited with developing the theory of consciousness-raising, voicing the pro-woman line, and inventing the speak-out. In 1969, it circulated the "Redstockings Manifesto" and other literature that helped to spread the messages of feminism.

Republican Motherhood: Republican Motherhood was an ideology prominent in the years after the Revolutionary War. It saw women's role in the public life of the nation as involving the education of sons to be active and interested in public involvement. Mothers would educate their children and guide them in the paths of morality and virtue. It was argued that the best contribution that a woman could make to the republican cause was to instill republican values in her children and to support her spouse in the performance of his civic duties. Although this concept did not give women a direct political role, it did encourage the education of women and legitimated women's charitable work.

Schlafly, Phyllis (1924–): Phyllis Schlafly is the leading spokesperson of the conservative movement opposing the women's liberation movement. She was the chief spokesperson against passage of the ERA and is widely credited with preventing its ratification. She was the founder of the Stop ERA movement in 1972 and the Eagle Forum in 1975. Since 1967, she has published a monthly newsletter, the *Phyllis Schlafly Report*.

Second-Wave Feminism: Second-wave feminism represents the revival of the organized women's rights movement, beginning in the late 1960s. It emerged from the protest politics of the time and from the anger of women involved in state commissions on the status of women.

Sexual Harassment and Violence in the Military Act (2003): The Sexual Harassment and Violence in the Military Act requires the secretary of defense to establish a civilian and military task force to address sexual harassment and violence at the U.S. Military and Naval Academies as part of the Defense Authorization bill. The legislation also includes a provision requiring travel and transportation allowances to be made for military dependents who are victims of domestic violence and are relocating for personal safety, a provision requiring that transitional compensation be made available to victims for three years after the sentencing of a domestic-violence offender, and a mandatory review by the secretary of defense of each act of domestic violence or child fatality.

Sheppard-Towner Maternity and Infancy Act (1921): The Sheppard-Towner Maternity and Infancy Act extended federal aid to state programs to promote the welfare and hygiene of maternity and infancy.

Smeal, Eleanor (1939–): A leader of the second women's rights movement, Eleanor Smeal is known as a political analyst, strategist, and grassroots organizer. The first to identify the "gender gap"—the difference in the way women and men vote—she popularized its usage in election and polling analyses to enhance women's voting clout. Smeal is the author of *How and Why Women Will Elect the Next President* (1984), which predicted that women's votes would be decisive in presidential politics. As president of the National Organization for Women (NOW), she led the drive to ratify the ERA. She founded the Feminist Majority Foundation in 1987 and shifted women's organizations' strategies on electing women from carefully targeting a few races to recruiting record numbers of feminists to run for political office. Among other activities, the Feminist Majority Foundation developed the National Clinic Access Project, which defends abortion clinics. The foundation has trained over 45,000 clinic defenders in twenty-six states in nonviolent clinic defense techniques. Smeal was also the chief architect of the Feminist Majority Foundation's landmark 1994 U.S. Supreme Court case upholding the use of buffer zones to protect clinics, *Madsen v. Women's Health Center*. In 1997 Smeal launched the international Campaign to Stop Gender Apartheid in Afghanistan to counter the Taliban's abuse of women. Since the fall of the Taliban, Smeal has been leading efforts to increase reconstruction and humanitarian aid to Afghanistan and expand peacekeeping troops. A Phi Beta Kappa graduate of Duke University, Smeal holds an M.A. in political science from the University of Florida and an honorary doctor of law degree from Duke University.

Stanton, Elizabeth Cady (1815–1902): Stanton drafted the Declaration of Sentiments at the first women's rights convention in Seneca Falls. The founding theorist of the women's rights movement, she was considered brilliant, insightful, and eloquent. Stanton ranged widely on areas of women's rights, including the *Women's Bible,* in addition to her work on suffrage with Susan B. Anthony. When her seven children were no longer small, she toured the country repeatedly, calling for voting rights, coeducation, dress reform, and other advances.

Steinem, Gloria, (1934–): Gloria Steinem became a major feminist leader in the late 1960s. In 1971 she cofounded *MS* magazine, where she continues as a contributing editor. In 1971 she was a coconvener of the National Women's Political Caucus (NWPC) and in 1972 helped found the Ms. Foundation for Women, which raises funds to assist underprivileged girls and women. She is a founding member of the Coalition of Labor Union Women, and her books, *Outrageous Acts and Everyday Rebellions* (1983) and *Revolution from Within: A Book of Self-Esteem* (1992), are best sellers. She is perhaps the best known of the leaders of the second women's rights movement in the United States.

Suffrage Movement: The suffrage movement lasted more than seventy years, from 1848 to 1920, when the Nineteenth Amendment was added to the Constitution. Several organizations lobbied, demonstrated, petitioned, and lectured around the country to obtain the right to vote for women. The movement began in 1848 with the Seneca Falls, New York, Women's Rights Convention and grew into the National American Woman Suffrage Association.

Third-Wave Feminism: Third-wave feminism, which emerged in the 1990s, represents a resurgent involvement of young women in the United States with feminist activism. Several new groups work to include women of color and poor women and to use direct action in order to spread feminist ideas. The best-known of the new groups, the Women's Action Coalition (WAC), has been termed the "the National Organization for Women of the 1990s." The coalition was formed in 1992; its motto as "WAC is watching. We will take action."

Unborn Victims of Violence Act (2004): The Unborn Victims of Violence Act confers legal status to fetuses injured by crimes against pregnant women.

Victims of Trafficking and Violence Protection Act (2000): The Victims of Trafficking and Violence Protection Act provides money for grant programs to help police investigate violence against women and provide victims' services. It expands the investigation and prosecution of crimes of violence against women and continues to fund the National Domestic Violence hotline. It also provides new protections for mistreated immigrants, expands assistance to programs targeting dating violence, and gives money to American Indians who are victims of domestic violence.

Violence Against Women Act I (1994): The purpose of the Violence Against Women Act of 1994 was to prevent and punish rape, domestic violence, sexual assault, hate crimes based on gender, and other violent acts against women. It increased federal penalties for sex or gender crimes, provided restitution for victims, encouraged states to increase their arrest and prosecution rates, extended civil rights protection to all gender-motivated crimes, provided grants to combat violent crimes against women, funded programs for state and federal judges and other court personnel to overcome attitudinal barriers, and created a National Commission on Violence Against Women.

Violence Against Women Act II (2002): The 2002 Violence Against Women Act establishes a Violence Against Women's Office, with a director appointed by the president and confirmed by the Senate. The director is authorized to award all grants and contracts under the office and is responsible for generally carrying out the responsibilities of the Violence Against Women Act.

Women in Apprenticeship and Nontraditional Occupations Act (1992): The Women in Apprenticeship and Nontraditional Occupations Act created a program under which the Department of Labor serves as a liaison between employers and workers to assist businesses in providing women with apprenticeships in nontraditional occupations.

Women's Bureau, Department of Labor (1920): Created as a temporary agency during World War I, the Women's Bureau developed the first U.S. standards for the employment of women workers. After the war, women's organizations successfully lobbied Congress to establish the bureau permanently.

The bureau was authorized to "formulate standards and policies which shall promote the welfare of wage-earning women, improve their working conditions, increase their efficiency and advance their opportunities for profitable employment."

Women's Business Ownership Act (1988): The Women's Business Ownership Act authorized a demonstration project making available $10 million to private organizations to provide management assistance and other types of help to women-owned firms. The act also created a nine-member national Women's Business Council to monitor the progress of federal, state, and local governments in assisting women-owned firms.

Women's Educational Equity Act (1974): The Women's Educational Equity Act authorized grants to conduct special education programs and activities designed to achieve educational equity at all levels of education.

Resources

International Groups

The Inter-Parliamentary Union (IPU)
5, chemin du Pommier
Case postale 330
CH-1218 Le Grand Saconnex
Geneva, Switzerland
Web site: http://www.ipu.org

The IPU, founded in 1889, is the international organization of parliaments of sovereign states. The union is the focal point for worldwide parliamentary dialogue and works for peace and cooperation among peoples and for the firm establishment of representative democracy. It tracks the number of women in national parliaments.

Political Advocacy Organizations

Democratic National Committee Women's Vote Center
430 South Capitol Street SE
Washington, DC 20003
Phone: (202) 863-7179
Web site: http://www.democrats.org/wvc

Founded in 2001 under the leadership of Democratic National Committee Chairman Terry McAuliffe and led by National Chair Ann Lewis, the DNC Women's Vote Center is dedicated to educating, engaging, and mobilizing women voters across the nation to help elect more Democrats to office at all levels of government.

EMILY's List
1120 Connecticut Avenue NW, Suite 1100
Washington, DC 20036
Web site: http://www.emilyslist.org

EMILY's List, the nation's largest grassroots political network, is dedicated to taking back the country from the radical Right by electing pro-choice Democratic women to federal, state, and local office. It is a network of nearly 85,000 Americans—from all across the country and all walks of life—committed to recruiting and funding viable women candidates, helping them build and run effective campaign organizations, and mobilizing women voters to help elect progressive candidates across the nation.

Feminist Majority Foundation (FMF)
1600 Wilson Boulevard, Suite 801
Arlington, VA 22209
Phone: (703) 522-2214
Web site: http://www.feminist.org

The FMF, founded in 1987 by Eleanor Smeal, is dedicated to women's equality, reproductive health, and nonviolence, and to empowering women economically, socially, and politically. The focus of its research and action programs is on advancing the legal, social, and political equality of women with men, countering the backlash to women's advancement, and recruiting and training young feminists to encourage future leadership for the feminist movement in the United States. To carry out these aims, the FMF engages in research and public-policy development, public-education programs, grassroots organizing projects, and leadership training and development programs, and participates in and organizes forums on issues of women's equality and empowerment. The FMF's sister organization, the Feminist Majority, engages in lobbying and other direct political action, pursuing equality between women and men through legislative avenues.

Feminists for Life of America
733 15th Street NW, Suite 1100
Washington, DC 20005
Web site: http://www.feministsforlife.org

Feminists for Life argues that abortion is a reflection that our society has failed to meet the needs of women. They are dedicated to systematically eliminating the root causes that drive women to abortion—primarily lack of practical resources and support—through holistic, women-centered solutions.

Hispanics Organized for Political Equality (HOPE)
634 S. Spring Street, Suite 920
Los Angeles, CA 90014
Phone: (213) 622-0606
Web site: http://www.latinas.org

HOPE is a nonprofit, nonpartisan organization committed to ensuring political and economic parity for Latinas through leadership, advocacy, and education to benefit all communities and the status of women. HOPE also has a political action committee.

League of Women Voters
1730 M Street NW, Suite 1000
Washington, DC 20036-4508
Web site: http://www.lwv.org

The League of Women Voters, a nonpartisan political organization, encourages the informed and active participation of citizens in government, works to increase understanding of major public policy issues, and influences public policy through education and advocacy. The League of Women Voters grew out of the suffrage movement.

MANA
1725 K Street NW, Suite 501
Washington, DC 20006
Phone: (202) 833-0060 / Fax: (202) 496-0588

MANA, a national Latina organization, was founded in 1974 as the Mexican-American Women's National Association. MANA's original intent was to provide a voice for Mexican-American women at the national, state, and local levels. Since then, the organization has expanded into a diverse group of Latinas in all areas of political, social and professional fields. MANA is unique since this makes MANA the single largest pan-Latina organization in the United States.

National Association of Commissions for Women (NACW)
8630 Fenton Street, Suite 934
Silver Spring, MD 20910

Phone: (301) 585-8101 / Fax: (301) 585-3445
Web site: http://www.nacw.org

The NACW serves as a national network for state and local commissions on the status of women. The mission of the NACW is to serve as the national voice for state, county, and local commissions for women; to develop, conduct, and promote research and training; to facilitate communication and cooperation on issues affecting women and their families; and to provide support, technical assistance, and expertise to impact public policy.

National Council of Women's Organizations (NCWO)
733 15th Street NW, Suite 1011
Washington, DC 20005
Phone: (202) 393-7122
Web site: http://www.womensorganizations.org

The NCWO is a nonpartisan, nonprofit umbrella organization of almost two hundred groups that collectively represent more than 10 million women across the United States. The only national coalition of its kind, the NCWO has more than twenty years' experience uniting American women's groups. The NCWO members collaborate through substantive policy work and grassroots activism to address issues of concern to women, including workplace and economic equity, education and job training, affirmative action, Social Security, child care, reproductive freedom, health, and global progress for women's equality.

National Federation of Republican Women (NFRW)
1600 Wilson Boulevard, Suite 801
Arlington, VA 22209
Phone: (703) 522-2214
Web site: http://www.nfrw.org

The NFRW is one of the largest women's political organizations in the country, with a grassroots membership of 100,000 women and 1,800 local units nationwide. Its mission is to positively impact the nation by advocating crucial issues; to strengthen the Republican Party through recruiting and training candidates; and to empower women of all ages, ethnicities, and backgrounds in the political process.

National Organization for Women (NOW)
733 15th Street NW, 2nd Floor

Washington, DC 20005
Phone: (202) 628-8669 (628-8NOW)
Fax: (202) 785-8576
Web site: http://www.now.org

NOW is the largest organization of feminist activists in the United States. It has about 250,000 contributing members and 400 chapters in all fifty states and the District of Columbia. Since the organization was founded in 1966 by Betty Friedan and others, NOW's goal has been to take action to bring about equality for all women. NOW works to eliminate discrimination and harassment in the workplace, schools, the justice system, and all other sectors of society; secure abortion, birth control, and reproductive rights for all women; end all forms of violence against women; eradicate racism, sexism, and homophobia; and promote equality and justice in society.

National Women's Alliance (NWA)
1807 18th Street NW, 2nd Floor
Washington, DC 20009
Phone: (202) 518-5411
Web site: http://www.nwaforchange.org

The NWA is a multi-issue human rights and social justice organization devoted to addressing the intersections of race, class, gender, ethnicity, nationality, sexual orientation, and other markers of difference. Using a multilevel approach, the NWA works at the local, state, and national levels to influence public policy outcomes, increase political participation and action among women/girls of color and low-income women, and bring diverse communities and organizations together to work toward a multi-issue agenda for social and political change. Through training, technical assistance, coalition building, public education campaigns, community organizing, and resource leveraging/sharing, the NWA strives to help end all forms of oppression and promote initiatives led by women of color.

National Women's Political Caucus (NWPC)
1634 Eye Street NW, Suite 310
Washington, DC 20006
Phone: (202) 785-3605
Web site: http://www.nwpc.org

The NWPC is a multicultural, intergenerational, and multi-issue grassroots organization dedicated to increasing women's participation in the political process and creating a true women's political power base to achieve equality for all women. It recruits, trains, and supports pro-choice women candidates for elected and appointed offices at all levels of government regardless of party affiliation. In addition to financial donations, the caucus offers campaign training for candidates and campaign managers as well as technical assistance and advice. State and local chapters provide support to candidates running for all levels of office by helping raise money and providing crucial hands-on volunteer assistance.

Third Wave Foundation
511 W 25th Street, Suite 301
New York, NY 10001
Phone: (212) 675-0700 / Fax: (212) 255-6653
Web site: http://www.thirdwavefoundation.org

Through grants and scholarships, the Third Wave Foundation gives direct financial support to young women activists and the organizations they lead, helping ensure that their cutting-edge strategies get the resources needed to help change our communities. Through public education campaigns, Third Wave highlights issues that concern young women and their allies. It amplifies the voices and concerns of young women to decision makers, the media, and other institutions that should be responsive to their ideas and issues.

The White House Project
110 Wall Street, 2nd Floor
New York, NY 10005
Phone: (212) 785-6001
Web site: http://www.thewhitehouseproject.org

The White House Project is a nonprofit, nonpartisan public awareness campaign to change the political climate so that women can launch successful campaigns for the U.S. presidency and other key positions. The project is committed to raising awareness of women's leadership in American politics and mobilizing Americans of all ages to participate in civic life.

WISH List
499 S. Capitol Street SW, Suite 408
Washington, DC 20003

Phone: (202) 479-1230 or (800) 756-9474
Web site: http://www.thewishlist.org

The WISH List raises funds to identify, train and elect pro-choice Republican women at all levels of government—local, state, and national.

Women's Campaign Fund
734 15th Street NW, Suite 500
Washington, DC 20005
Phone (202) 393-8164 or (800) 446-8170 / Fax (202) 393-0649
Web site: http://www.wcfonline.org

Women's Campaign Fund (WCF) was founded in 1974 after *Roe v. Wade*. It is the oldest nonpartisan political action committee dedicated to electing pro-choice women running for office at all levels. Since 1974 it has contributed to over 2,000 campaigns for local, state, and federal office; to Republicans, Democrats, and Independents; to fledgling candidates and veteran politicians. Its mission is to provide pro-choice women of all parties with the resources they need to win—not just money, but strategic consulting, fundraising, networking, field campaigning, and get-out-the-vote assistance.

The Women's Campaign School
Yale University
P.O. Box 3307
New Haven, CT 06515-0407
Phone: (203) 734-7385 or (800) 353-2878
Web site: http://www.wcsyale.org

The Women's Campaign School (WCS) at Yale University teaches women the required skills, strategies, and tactics to run a winning campaign. The WCS is jointly sponsored by the Yale Law School and Women's Studies. It is a nonprofit corporation offering a unique nonpartisan, non–issue based campaign training program and inclusive of women from the entire spectrum of political interests. Most training sessions are held on the Yale campus. The mission of the WCS is to prepare women to be candidates for public office and/or senior-level campaign staff members. The WCS strives to impart knowledge of contemporary political campaigning and to teach women the skills required to implement a successful political campaign.

Research Institutions

Center for American Women and Politics
Eagleton Institute of Politics
Rutgers, The State University of New Jersey
191 Ryders Lane
New Brunswick, NJ 08901-8557
Phone: (732) 932-9384
Web site: http://www.cawp.rutgers.edu

The Center for American Women and Politics (CAWP) is a university-based research, education, and public service center. Its mission is to promote greater knowledge and understanding about women's participation in politics and government and to enhance women's influence and leadership in public life.

Center for Women in Politics and Public Policy
John W. McCormack Institute of Public Affairs
University of Massachusetts
100 Morrissey Boulevard
Boston, MA 02125-3393
Phone: (617) 287-5541
Web site: http://www.mccormack.umb.edu/cwppp

The Center for Women in Politics and Public Policy provides education, research, and on-line resources to advance women's participation in the public life of Massachusetts, the New England region, and the nation.

Center for Women Policy Studies
1211 Connecticut Avenue NW, Suite 312
Washington, DC 20036
Phone: (202) 872-1770 / Fax: (202) 296-8962
Web site: http://www.centerwomenpolicy.org

Since its founding in 1972 as the nation's first feminist policy research organization, the Center for Women Policy Studies has been on the front line of efforts to promote justice and equality for women.

Clare Boothe Luce Policy Institute
112 Elden Street, Suite P
Herndon, VA 20170
Phone: (703) 318-0730
Web site: http://www.cblpolicyinstitute.org

The Clare Boothe Luce Policy Institute's dual missions are to prepare young women for effective conservative leadership and to promote school choice opportunities for all K–12 children in the United States.

Institute for Women's Policy Research (IWPR)
1707 L Street NW, Suite 750
Washington, DC 20036
Phone: (202) 785-5100
Web site: http://www.iwpr.org

The IWPR is a public policy research organization dedicated to informing and stimulating the debate on public policy issues of critical importance to women and their families. The institute focuses on issues of poverty and welfare, employment and earnings, work and family issues, health and safety, and women's civic and political participation.

Ms. Foundation for Women
120 Wall Street, 33rd Floor
New York, NY 10005
Phone: (212) 742-2300 / Fax: (212) 742-1653
Web site: http://www.ms.foundation.org

The Ms. Foundation supports the efforts of women and girls to govern their own lives and influence the world around them. The foundation champions an equitable society by effecting change in public consciousness, law, philanthropy, and social policy. The Ms. Foundation is a leading advocate for the issues that touch women's lives, from reproductive rights and violence in communities to gaining access to resources to care for families' well-being. The foundation actively seek solutions for these issues, supporting cutting-edge initiatives and organizations to ensure that women and girls have the tools to lead safe, healthy lives; gain economic self-sufficiency; and hone their leadership skills. To meet these goals, the Ms. Foundation awards grants, conducts public education, and provides training and assistance in three main areas: economic security; health and safety; and girls, young women, and leadership.

National Women's Law Center
11 DuPont Circle NW, Suite 800
Washington, DC 20036
Phone: (202) 588-5180
Web site: http://www.nwlc.org

The National Women's Law Center uses the law in all its forms: getting new laws on the books and enforced, litigating groundbreaking cases in state and federal courts all the way to the Supreme Court, and educating the public about ways to make the law and public policies work for women and their families. The staff of nearly fifty takes on women's and girls' issues in education, employment, family economic security, and health—with special attention given to the needs of low-income women and their families.

Women and Public Policy Program
John F. Kennedy School of Government
79 JFK Street
Cambridge, MA 02138
Phone: (617) 496-6973
Web site: http://www.ksg.harvard.edu/wappp

The Women and Public Policy Program of Harvard's John F. Kennedy School of Government was founded with the internal goal of incorporating an understanding of gender perspectives on public policy into the education of future and current leaders trained at the school and the external goal of contributing to the canon of scholarship on women and public policy. The mission of the Women and Public Policy Program is to address public policies that have an impact on women and to inform and learn from women who shape public policies, with the ultimate goal of creating a world more balanced in opportunity and more secure.

Women Impacting Public Policy
2709 W. I-44 Service Road
Oklahoma City, OK 73112
Phone: (888) 368-5759
Web site: http://www.wipp.org

Women Impacting Public Policy is a national bipartisan public policy organization that advocates for and on behalf of women in business, strengthening their sphere of influence in the legislative process of the nation, creating economic opportunities, and building bridges and alliances to other small business organizations.

Women in Politics Institute
American University
4400 Massachusetts Ave NW
Washington, DC 20016

Web site: http://www.american.edu/oconnor/wandp

Located within the School of Public Affairs at American University, the Women and Politics Institute is dedicated to advancing the study and discussion of women and politics, promoting opportunities for women in politics, and training young women to become political leaders. The institute's strategic location in Washington, D.C., allows students and faculty alike easy access to the resources of the nation's capital. The institute offers undergraduate and graduate students the opportunity to take courses taught by nationally recognized experts within their fields, to work in career-building internships with women's organizations and in the offices of women members of Congress, and to attend leadership workshops and lectures featuring distinguished women leaders. Also the Women and Politics Institute offers one of the few professional development certificates in the subject of women, policy, and political leadership.

WomenMatter
8511 Navajo Street
Philadelphia, PA 19118
Phone: (215) 242-8959
Web site: http://www.womenmatter.com

WomenMatter helps American women to educate themselves on key issues so they can assume a stronger role in the nation's political life. It is a nonpartisan, web-centric, nonprofit organization whose goal is to empower women by helping them become part of the political process. WomenMatter seeks to increase the number of well-informed, politically active women so that the concerns and perspectives of women will be better represented. WomenMatter serves as a political mentor site, offering a comfortable place for women to access important information and to think through the issues so that they might change the face of politics in the United States.

Women's eNews
135 W. 29th Street, Suite 1005
New York, NY 10001
Web site: http://www.womensenews.org

Women's eNews is the definitive source of substantive news—unavailable anywhere else—covering issues of particular concern to women and providing women's perspectives on public policy. It enhances women's ability to define their own lives and to participate fully in every sector of human endeavor. Women's eNews editors seek out freelance writers from around the world to write on every topic—politics, religion, economics, health, science, education, sports, legislation—and commission them to write 800-word news articles for distribution each day to subscribers and for posting on the Web site.

Women's Policy
409 12th Street SW, Suite 310
Washington, DC 20024
Phone: (202) 554-2323
Web site: http://www.womenspolicy.org

Women's Policy is a nonprofit, nonpartisan organization whose sole focus is to help ensure that the most-informed decisions on key women's issues are made by policy makers at the federal, state, and local levels. Audiences include elected officials, regulators, women's groups, labor groups, academia, the business community, the media, and the general public. The institute was created when the Congressional Caucus for Women's Issues had to disband its offices within the U.S. House of Representatives in 1995. It publishes a newsletter called *The Source*.

State-Level Women's Organizations

Alabama

Alabama Solution
P.O. Box 370821
Birmingham, AL 35237

Alabama Women's Initiative and the Greenbook
P.O. Box 59323
Birmingham, AL 35259-9323

California

California List
253 26th Street, Suite 150
Santa Monica, CA 90402
Web site: http://www.californialist.org

California Women's Political Summit
1531 Purdue Avenue
Los Angeles, CA 90025
Phone: (310) 477-8081

Democratic Activists for Women Now (DAWN)
P.O. Box 6614
San Jose, CA 95150
Phone: (408) 738-4807
Web site: http://www.sccdawn.org

Los Angeles African American Women's Political Action Committee
4102 Olympiad Drive
Los Angeles, CA 90043

Seneca Network
980 9th Street, Suite 1600
Sacramento, CA 95814-2736
Web site: http://www.SenecaNetwork.com

Florida

Project "W"
P.O. Box 531198
Miami, FL 33153
Phone: (305) 576-6105
Web site: http://www.withoutboundaries.com/FLWProject.html

Women's Political Caucus of Broward County
161 South East 13th Street
Pompano Beach, FL 33060

Georgia

Georgia's WIN List
1266 West Paces Ferry Road, #2002
Atlanta, GA 30327-2306

Illinois

Illinois Lincoln Excellence in Public Service Series
P.O. Box 414

Winfield, IL 60190
Web site: http://www.lincolnseries.com

Illinois Women's Institute for Leadership (IWIL)
P.O. Box 1149
Springfield, IL 62705
Web site: http://www.il-democrats.org/IWIL

Iowa

Iowa Women and Public Policy Group (WIPP)
P.O. Box 71142
Des Moines, IA 50325
Phone: (515) 440-2623
Web site: http://www.iowawipp.com

Louisiana

Women of Louisiana
P.O. Box 44091
Baton Rouge, LA 70804

Maryland

Harriet's List
P.O. Box 16361
Baltimore, MD 21210

Massachusetts

Massachusetts Women's Political Caucus PAC
59 Temple Place, Suite 449
Boston, MA 02110

Minnesota

Women's Campaign Fund
P.O. Box 582944
Minneapolis, MN 55548
Phone: (612) 331-2366
Web site: http://www.mnwomenscampaignfund.org

Missouri

Greater Kansas City Women's Political Caucus
P.O. Box 10095
Kansas City, MO 64171

Win With Women
155 Hanley Road, #202
St. Louis, MO 63105

New Jersey

GROW—Republican Women
28 W. State Street, Suite 319
Trenton, NJ 08054
PAC: c/o Linda Bowker
376 Inverness Court
Mount Laurel, NJ 08054

PAM's List (Power and Money for Choice and Change)
160 W. State Street
Trenton, NJ 08608

New York

Eleanor Roosevelt Legacy Committee
P.O. Box 20293
Greeley Square Station
New York, NY 10001-0003
Phone: (212) 725-8825, ext 237
Web site: http://www.eleanorslegacy.com

Empire Women
New York Republican State Committee
315 State Street
Albany, NY 12210
Phone: (518) 462-2601
Web site: http://www.empirewomen.com

Women's Taking Action in Politics (TAP) Fund
P.O. Box 54
Buffalo, NY 14201-0054

North Carolina

Lillian's List
P.O. Box 2473
Chapel Hill, NC 27515

Ohio

Hope Chest
P.O. Box 09956
Columbus, OH 43209

Oregon

Women's Investment Network (WIN-PAC)
P.O. Box 8432
Portland, OR 97207

Pennsylvania

Pennsylvania Women's Campaign Fund
P.O. Box 621
Lewisburg, PA 17837
Phone: 866-956-9254
Web site: http://www.pawcf.com

South Carolina

B-List
1202 Main Street, Suite 200
Columbia, SC 29201

Tennessee

Women in the Nineties (WIN)
P.O. Box 150928
Nashville, TN 37215

Texas

Women Initiative PAC (WIN-PAC) (formerly Task Force 2000 PAC)
5115 Park Avenue
Dickinson, TX 77539

Virginia

Sojourner 21 PAC
P.O. Box 533
Richmond, VA 23218-0533

Wisconsin

Wisconsin Women's Network (WWN)
122 State Street, Room 404
Madison, WI 53703
Web site: http://www.wiwomensnetwork.org

State Commissions on the Status of Women

Alabama

Alabama Women's Commission
200 S. Franklin Drive
Troy, AL 36081-4508
205-566-8744
Jeane Boutwell, elected Sec'y

California

California Commission on the Status of Women
1303 J Street, Suite 400
Sacramento, CA 95814-2900
916-445-3173 / fax 916-322-9466
Mary M. Wiberg, Exec. Director
Dodie Orndorf, Administration

Connecticut

CT Permanent Commission on the Status of Women
18-20 Trinity Street
Hartford, CT 06106
860-240-8300 / fax 860-240-8314
Leslie J. Brett, Exec. Director
Web site: http://www.cga.state.ct.us/PCSW

Delaware

Delaware Commission for Women
4425 N. Market Street, 4th Floor
Wilmington, DE 19802
302-761-8005 / fax 302-761-6652
Romona S. Fullman, Esq., Director
Web site: http://www.delawareworks.com/divisions/dcw/welcome.htm
E-mail: cgomez@state.de.us

Florida

Florida Commission on the Status of Women
Office of the Attorney General
The Capitol
Tallahassee, FL 32399-1050
850-414-3300 / fax 850-921-4131
Kelly Sciba, Exec. Asst. II
Michelle Manning, Admin. Asst. III
Web site: http://www.fcsw.net

Georgia

Georgia State Commission on Women
151 Ellis Street, Suite 207
Atlanta, GA 30303
404-657-9260 / fax 404-657-2963
Jessica Jones, Exec. Director
Web site: www.gawomen.com
E-mail: gawomen20003@yahoo.com

Hawaii

Hawaii State Commission on the Status of Women
235 S. Beretania Street, Rm. 407
Honolulu, HI 96813
808-586-5757 / fax 808-586-5756
Allicyn Hikida Tasaka, Exec. Director
Web site: http://www.hawaii.gov/hscsw
E-mail: hscsw@pixi.net

Idaho

Idaho Commission on the Women's Program
P.O. Box 83720
Boise, ID 83720-0036
208-334-4673 / fax 208-334-4646
Linda Hurlbutt, Director
Web site: http://www.state.id.us/women

Illinois

Governor's Commission on the Status of Women
James R. Thompson Center
100 W. Randolph Street, Ste. 16-100
Chicago, IL 60601
312-814-5743 / fax 312-814-3823
Alice Smedstad, Exec. Director

Indiana

Indiana Commission for Women
Indiana Government Center South
100 N. Senate Ave., Rm. N103
Indianapolis, IN 46204
317-233-6303 / fax 317-232-6580
Kimberly Thacker, Adm. Asst.

Iowa

Iowa Commission on the Status of Women
Lucas State Office Building
Des Moines, IA 50319
515-281-4461 / fax 515-242-6119
Charlotte B. Nelson, Exec. Director
Web site: http://www.state.ia.us/government/dhr/sw

Kentucky

Kentucky Commission on Women
312 West Main Street
Frankfort, KY 40601
502-564-6643 / fax 502-564-2315

Betsy Nowland-Curry, Exec. Director
Web site: http://women.state.ky.us
E-mail: betsy.curry@mail.state.ky.us

Louisiana

Louisiana Office of Women's Services
1885 Wooddale Blvd.
P.O. Box 94095
Baton Rouge, LA 70804-9095
504-922-0960 / fax 504-922-0959
Vera Clay, Exec. Director
E-mail: vera@ows.state.la.us

Maryland

Maryland Commission for Women
45 Calvert Street
Annapolis, MD 21401
410-260-6047 / fax 410-974-2307
Dory Stacks, Exec. Director
Web site: http://www.marylandwomen.org
E-mail: mcw@dhr.state.md.us

Massachusetts

MA Governor's Advisory Committee on Women's Issues
Governor's Office
State House, Room 111
Boston, MA 02133
617-973-8646 / fax 617-973-8637
Web site: www.state.ma.us/womenissues

MA Commission on the Status of Women
The Charles F. Hurley Building
19 Stanford Street, 6th Floor
Boston, MA 02114
617-626-6520 / fax 617-626-6530
Linda Brantley, Exec. Director
E-mail: LindaBrantley@state.ma.us
Web site: http://www.mass.gov/women

Michigan

Michigan Women's Commission
110 West Michigan Ave., Suite 800
Lansing, MI 48933
517-373-2884 / fax 517-335-1649
Judy Karandjeff, Exec. Director
LuAnne Maurerla, staff
Web site: www.michigan.gov/mdcr
E-mail: karandjeff@mighigan.gov

Minnesota

Minnesota Commission on the Economic Status of Women
85 State Office Building
St. Paul, MN 55155
612-296-8590
Aviva Breen, Exec. Director

Mississippi

Mississippi Commission on the Status of Women
P.O. Box 5711
Brandon, MS 39047
601-829-3864 / fax: 601-829-9957
Betty Ward-Fletcher, Chair

Missouri

Missouri Council on Women's Economic Development and Training
421 E. Dunklin
P.O. Box 1684
Jefferson City, MO 65102
573-751-0810 / fax 573-751-8835
Gale Kessler, Exec. Director

Nebraska

Nebraska Commission on the Status of Women
301 Centennial Mall South
P.O. Box 94985

Lincoln, NE 68509-4985
402-471-2039 / fax 402-471-5655
Lisa J. Good, Exec. Director
Web site: http://www.women.state.ne.us
E-mail: ncswmail@mail.state.ne.us

Nevada

Nevada Commission for Women
c/o Denise Dumenie
8615 Channell Way
Reno, NV 89506
702-972-1413

New Hampshire

New Hampshire Commission on the Status of Women
State House Annex, Room 334
Concord, NH 03301
603-271-2660 / fax: 603-271-4032
Theresa deLangis, Ph.D., Exec. Director
Web site: http://www.state.nh.us/csw
E-mail: tdelangis@admin.state.nh.us

New Jersey

New Jersey Advisory Commission on the Status of Women
c/o Division on Women
Department of Community Affairs
101 South Broad Street, Box 801
Trenton, NJ 08625-0801
609-292-8840 / fax 609-633-6821
Theresa Daniels, Legislative Coordinator
Web site: http://www.nj.gov/dca/dow/adviscom.htm
E-mail: T.daniels@dca.state.nj.us

New Mexico

New Mexico Commission on the Status of Women
4001 Indian School Rd., Suite 300
Albuquerque, NM 87110
800-432-9168; 505-841-8902 / fax 505-841-8926

Rebecca Jo Dakota, Exec. Director
Web site: http://www.state.nm.us/womenscommission
E-mail: rebecca.dakota@state.nm.us

New York

New York State Division for Women
State of New York Executive Chambers
633 3rd Avenue, 38th Floor
New York, NY 10017
212-681-4547 / fax 212-681-7626
Elaine Wingate Conway, Director
Web site: http://www.women.state.ny.us
E-mail: elaine.conway@chamber.state.ny.us

North Carolina

North Carolina Council for Women
1320 Mail Service Center
Raleigh, NC 27699-1320
919-733-2455 / fax 919-733-2464
Leslie Starsomeck, Exec. Director
Web site: http://www.doa.state.nc.us/doa/cfw/cfw.htm
E-mail: Leslie.Starsomeck@ncmail.net

North Dakota

North Dakota Governor's Commission on the Status of Women
P.O. Box 1913
Bismarck, ND 58502-1913
701-530-2059 / fax 701-530-2111
Carol Reed, Chair
Web site:
http://governor.state.nd.us/boards/boardsquery.asp?Board_ID=114

Oklahoma

Oklahoma Commission on the Status of Women
c/o Office of Personnel Management
2101 N. Lincoln Blvd.
Oklahoma City, OK 73105-4904
Attn: Debbe Leftwich, Chair

405-522-6897 / fax 405-524-6942
E-mail: d_leftwich@ocmeokc.state.ok.us

Oregon

Oregon Governor's Commission for Women
P.O. Box 751-CW
Portland, OR 97207
503-725-5889 / fax 503-725-8152
Jennifer Webber, Exec. Director

Pennsylvania

Pennsylvania Commission for Women
205 Finance Bldg.
Harrisburg, PA 17120
717-787-8128 / fax: 717-772-0653
Leslie S. Stiles, Executive Director
Web site: http://www.pcw.state.pa.us
E-mail: lstiles@state.pa.us

Puerto Rico

Puerto Rico Commission for Women's Affairs
Office of the Governor
Commonwealth of Puerto Rico
P.O. Box 11382, Fernandez Juncos Station
Santruce, PR 00910
787-721-0606; 787-724-7404 / fax 787-723-3611

Rhode Island

Rhode Island Commission for Women
One Capitol Hill, 2nd Floor
Providence, RI 02908-5816
401-222-6105 / fax 401-222-5638
Toby Ayers, Ph.D., Exec. Director

South Carolina

Governor's Office Commission on Women
Edgar A. Brown Building

1205 Pendleton Street, #366
Columbia, SC 29201
803-734-1609 / fax 803-734-0241
Rebecca Collier, Exec. Director
Web site: http://www.govoepp.state.sc.us/gcw.htm
E-mail: rcollier@govoepp.state.sc.us

Tennessee

Tennessee Economic Council on Women
Snodgrass Tennessee Tower, 3rd fl.
312 8th Avenue North
Nashville, TN 37243
615-253-4264 / fax 615-253-4263
Barbara Devaney, Exec. Director

Texas

Texas Governor's Commission for Women
P.O. Box 12428
Austin, TX 78711
512-475-2615 / fax 512-463-1832
Lesley Guthrie, Director
Web site: http://www.governor.state.tx.us/women/index.htm

Utah

Utah Governor's Commission for Women and Families
111 State Capitol
Salt Lake City, UT 84114
801-538-1533 / fax 801-538-1304
Melanie Reese, Exec. Director

Vermont

Vermont Commission on Women
126 State Street
Montpelier, VT 05633-6801
802-828-2851; 800-881-1561
fax 802-828-2930
Wendy Love, Exec. Director
Web site: http://www.women.state.vt.us
E-mail: info@women.state.vt.us

Virginia

Virginia Council on the Status of Women
7805 Kahlua Drive
Richmond, VA 23227
804-786-7765

West Virginia

West Virginia Women's Commission
Capitol Complex
Building 6, Room 850
Charleston, WV 25305
304-558-0070 / fax 304-558-5167
Cinda Kindsey, Exec. Director
Web site: http://www.wvdhhr.org/women
E-mail: cindakindsey@wvdhhr.org

Wisconsin

Wisconsin Women's Council
c/o T. Herman
P.O. Box 7864
Madison, WI 53707-7863
608-266-2219
Kathy Manuck, Exec. Director

Wyoming

Wyoming Council for Women's Issues
c/o Wyoming Business Council
214 West 15th Street
Cheyenne, WY 82002
307-332-9402

Chronology

1776	New Jersey grants women the right to vote in its state constitution.

Abigail Adams writes her famous letter to John Adams advocating that the declarers of independence "remember the ladies." |
1807	The New Jersey legislature disenfranchises women.
1839	Mississippi passes the first married women's property law in the nation.
1848	First women's rights convention is held in Seneca Falls, New York.
1850	The first national women's rights convention is held in Worcester, Massachusetts.
1851	Sojourner Truth addresses a women's rights convention in Akron, Ohio, making what becomes known as her "Ain't I a Woman" speech.
1866	Congress passes the Fourteenth Amendment, introducing the word *male* into the Constitution for the first time in defining voting rights.

The American Equal Rights Association is founded. It is the first organization in the United States to advocate national woman suffrage.

Elizabeth Cady Stanton, the first woman to run for a seat in the U.S. House of Representatives, runs as an independent. No woman, including herself, can vote for her. |
| 1869 | First woman suffrage amendment to the Constitution is introduced in Congress. |

Women and Political Participation

	The National Woman Suffrage Association and the American Woman Suffrage Association are founded.
1872	Congress passes a law to give female federal employees equal pay for equal work.
	Victoria Claflin Woodhull becomes the first woman presidential candidate.
	Susan B. Anthony and fourteen other women register and vote, testing whether the Fourteenth Amendment can be interpreted as protecting women's rights.
1873	In *Bradwell v. Illinois,* the Supreme Court upholds a law prohibiting women from being lawyers.
1875	In *Minor v. Happersett,* the Supreme Court rejects the argument that the Fourteenth Amendment grants women voting rights.
1876	Sarah Jane Spencer of the National Woman's Suffrage Association is allowed to speak at the National Republican Convention.
1878	The women's suffrage amendment, known as the Susan B. Anthony Amendment, is introduced in the U.S. Congress for the first time.
1879	Belva Lockwood successfully lobbies Congress to pass legislation permitting women to practice before the U.S. Supreme Court. She becomes the first women admitted to practice before the Court.
1884	Belva Lockwood, presidential candidate of the National Equal Rights Party, becomes the second woman to run in a presidential election.
1890	Wyoming becomes a state with woman suffrage.
	The National Woman Suffrage Association and the American Woman Suffrage Association merge into one organization called the National American Women Suffrage Association (NAWSA).
1892	At the Republican National Convention the first women at a convention are seated. Therese Jenkins and Cora Carleton are alternates from Wyoming.
1893	Mary Elizabeth Lease is the first female candidate for the U.S. Senate, running on the Populist Party ticket.
	Laura J. Eisenhuth becomes the first woman elected to statewide office by male and female voters when she is elected North Dakota's superintendent of public instruction.

1894	Republicans Clara Cressingham, Carrie C. Holly, and Frances Klock are elected to serve in the Colorado House of Representatives, the first women elected to serve in a state legislature.
1896	The first woman state senator in the nation, Martha Hughes, is elected to the Utah legislature.
1900	The first official women delegates (one each) attend the Democratic National Convention and the Republican National Convention.
1907	Kate Barnard is the first woman elected to statewide office by male-only voters when she becomes commissioner of charities and collections in Oklahoma.
1908	In *Muller v. Oregon*, the Supreme Court upholds a law limiting the workday to ten hours for women only.
1912	Congress creates the Children's Bureau, and as its first director, Julia C. Lathrop, is the first woman to head a major federal bureau. In *Quong Wing v. Kirkendall*, the Supreme Court upholds a law providing tax exemption to women (only) running small laundries.
1913	Alice Paul and Lucy Burns found the Congressional Union, which later (1916) becomes the National Woman's Party. More than 3,000 suffragists march in Washington, D.C., on the day of Woodrow Wilson's presidential inauguration.
1914	Annette Abbott Adams is appointed U.S. attorney for the Northern District of California, the highest judicial position held by a woman at the time.
1915	Women's Peace Party established.
1916	Republican Jeannette Rankin of Montana becomes the first woman elected to the U.S. House of Representatives.
1918	Kathryn Sellers becomes the first woman in the U.S. to hold a judgeship when she is named a judge in the juvenile court of Washington, D.C.
1919	The League of Women Voters is founded. The Women's International League for Peace and Freedom is established.
1920	Congress establishes the Women's Bureau of the U.S. Department of Labor, and Mary Anderson is it first director. The Nineteenth Amendment to the Constitution passes, giving women the right to vote.

1922	Rebecca Latimer Felton (D-GA) becomes the first woman sworn in to the U.S. Senate. This appointment only lasts two days.
	Florence Ellinwood Allen becomes the first woman to serve on a state supreme court when she is elected associate justice in Ohio.
1923	A federal equal rights amendment is first introduced in Congress.
	In *Adkins v. Children's Hospital*, the Supreme Court rules minimum-wage laws for women unconstitutional.
1924	In *Radice v. New York*, the Supreme Court upholds a law prohibiting women from working certain jobs between 10 PM and 6 AM.
1925	Democrat Nellie Tayloe Ross becomes governor of Wyoming, the first woman sworn in as a governor of Texas.
1926	Bertha Knight Landes is the first woman elected mayor of a large city, Seattle, Washington.
1927	Minnie Buckingham-Harper becomes the first African American woman to serve in a state legislature when she is appointed by the West Virginia governor to fill her deceased husband's seat.
	In *Buck v. Bell*, the Supreme Court upholds forced sterilization of "feeble-minded" women and men.
1928	Genevieve Cline of Ohio becomes the first female federal judge as a judge for the U.S. Customs Court.
	Republican Minnie Buckingham Harper becomes the first African American woman to serve in a state legislature when West Virginia's governor appoints her to the state's House of Delegates.
1931	Democrat Fedelina Lucero Gallegos and Republican Porfirria H. Saiz enter the New Mexico House of Representatives, the first Hispanic American women elected to a state legislature.
1932	Hattie Wyatt Caraway, appointed to the U.S. Senate in 1931, becomes the first woman elected to serve in the body.
	The National Recovery Act includes a provision that allows only one family member to hold a government job, which causes many women lose their jobs.
1933	Frances Perkins becomes the first woman to serve in a president's cabinet, when Franklin D. Roosevelt appoints her secretary of labor.

Republican Minnie D. Craig of North Dakota becomes the first woman speaker of a state House of Representatives.

1935   Mary McLeod Bethune becomes director of Negro Affairs in the National Youth Administration, appointed by President Franklin D. Roosevelt, making her the first African American woman to hold a major federal appointment. She also founds the National Council of Negro Women.

1936   In *Morehead v. New York ex. rel. Tipaldo,* the Supreme Court reaffirms its ruling in *Adkins v. Children's Hospital* that minimum-wage laws for women are unconstitutional.

1937   Representative Mary Teresa Norton becomes the first woman to chair a major congressional committee, the Labor Committee.

In *West Coast Hotel v. Parrish,* the Supreme Court reverses its position in *Adkins v. Children's Hospital,* holding minimum-wage laws for women constitutional.

In *Breedlove v. Suttles,* the Supreme Court holds constitutional a poll tax required of all nonblind males ages twenty-one to sixty, but only of those females in the age group who are registered to vote.

1938   Democrat Crystal Bird Fauset becomes the first African American woman elected to a state legislature, in Pennsylvania.

The National Federation of Republican Women is founded.

1940   The Republican Party includes the equal rights amendment in its platform.

1942   In *Skinner v. Oklahoma,* the Supreme Court upholds a law requiring sterilization of male and female repeat offenders of certain crimes.

1946   Eleanor Roosevelt is appointed the first female delegate to the United Nations by President Harry S. Truman.

In *Ballard v. United States,* the Supreme Court overturns the California practice of not summoning women for federal jury service when they are legally eligible for state jury service. The ruling applies only to the 60 percent of states in which the eligibility of women is deemed necessary for jury impartiality. In another case, *Faye v. New York,* the Court rules women equal and as qualified as men to serve on juries. However, women are offered an exemption and allowed to choose whether or not they want to serve.

238 ■ Women and Political Participation

1948	In *Goesaert v. Cleary*, the Supreme Court upholds a law prohibiting women from working as bartenders unless their husbands own the bar.
1949	Eugenie Moore Anderson is appointed the first female U.S. ambassador.
1952	Cora M. Brown becomes the first African American woman elected to a state senate, in Michigan.
1955	African American Rosa Parks refuses to relinquish her seat on a Montgomery, Alabama, city bus, is arrested, and launches a boycott of the city's buses.
1957	Patsy Mink enters Hawaii's territorial legislature, the first Asian American woman elected to a territorial or state legislature.
1960	Senator Margaret Chase Smith and Lucia Marie Cormier, a six-term member of the Maine House of Representatives, face each other in the first all-female race for the U.S. Senate. Republican incumbent Smith wins.
1961	President John Kennedy issues an executive order establishing the President's Commission on the Status of Women. In *Hoyt v. Florida*, the Supreme Court upholds the state's practice of systematically excluding women from juries. Women Strike for Peace is founded.
1963	The Equal Pay Act, requiring equal pay for men and women with same jobs, is enacted into law.
1964	Republican Margaret Chase Smith becomes the first woman to run for the presidential nomination of a major party. The Civil Rights Act, which includes Title VII, the equal employment opportunities section with the ban on sex discrimination, is enacted into law. Patsy Mink (D-HI) becomes the first Asian American woman elected to the U.S. Congress.
1965	In *Griswold v. Connecticut*, the Supreme Court overturns a law prohibiting the use of contraceptive devices by married couples.
1966	The National Organization for Women (NOW) is founded.
1967	Presidential Executive Order 11375 amends E. O. 11246 to prohibit sex discrimination in employment by the federal government and by contractors doing business with the government—a NOW victory!

1968	More than two hundred women from thirty-seven states and Canada convene in Chicago for the first national women's liberation conference.
	The Women's Equity Action League (WEAL) is formed as a spin-off from NOW by women who do not want to deal with the issue of abortion but do want to actively work for equal opportunity for women in education and employment.
	Women protest the Miss American Pageant as a "tyranny of beauty." They crown a live sheep Miss America and fill a "Freedom Trash Can" with various instruments of torture such as high-heeled shoes, bras, girdles, hair curlers, and false lashes.
	Representative Shirley Chisholm (D-NY) becomes the first African American woman elected to the U.S. Congress.
1969	The National Association for the Repeal of Abortion Laws (NARAL) is founded. After *Roe* passes, its name changes to the National Association for Reproductive and Abortion Rights, and in 2004 changes to NARAL Pro-Choice America.
1971	The National Women's Political Caucus is founded.
	In *Phillips v. Martin Marietta,* the Supreme Court holds in violation of Title VII, which prohibits employment discrimination on the basis of sex, the company's practice of refusing to hire women with preschool children.
	In *Reed v. Reed,* the Supreme Court overturns a state law establishing automatic preferences for males over otherwise equally qualified females as administrators of wills.
	In *Williams v. McNair,* the Supreme Court upholds a state law excluding men from certain state colleges and women from others.
1972	Representative Shirley Chisholm (D-NY) becomes the first African American woman to run for president and has her name formally placed in nomination at the Democratic National Convention.
	Jean Westwood becomes chair of the Democratic National Committee, the first woman to chair either of the two major parties.
	Republican Anne L. Armstrong is the first woman to deliver a keynote address at a major party national convention.

The ERA is passed by Congress and sent to the states for ratification.

In *Eisenstadt v. Baird*, the Supreme Court rules that an unmarried person's right to use contraceptives is encompassed within the right to privacy.

In *Stanley v. Illinois*, the Supreme Court holds unconstitutional a law automatically denying child custody to the only surviving male parent of an illegitimate child while automatically granting such custody to the only surviving female parent.

1973 In *Roe v. Wade* and *Doe v. Bolton*, the Supreme Court holds laws prohibiting abortion unconstitutional, except where such laws are restricted to last three months of pregnancy or to stage of fetal "viability."

Anne Armstrong becomes the first woman counselor to the president, appointed by President Richard M. Nixon.

Women's Equality Day, conceived by NOW and introduced in Congress by Representative Bella Abzug (D-NY), is confirmed by Congress and the president.

The National Black Feminist Organization is founded in New York.

In *Frontiero v. Richardson*, the Supreme Court overturns a law requiring married women army officers to prove "actual dependency" of spouse to qualify for spousal benefits, although spouses of married male officers automatically receive such benefits.

In *Pittsburgh Press Co. v. Pittsburgh Commission on Human Relations*, the Supreme Court bans sex-segregated "help wanted" advertisements as a violation of Title VII of the Civil Rights Act of 1964.

1974 March Fong becomes the first Asian American woman elected to a statewide position when she is elected California's secretary of state.

Lilai Smith becomes the first African American woman to be elected mayor, in Taft, Oklahoma.

Elaine Noble becomes the first open lesbian elected to a state office when she wins her race for a seat in the Massachusetts legislature.

The Women's Campaign Fund is founded.

Mary Louise Smith becomes chair of the Republican National Committee, the first woman to hold the post.

In *Cleveland Board of Education v. LaFleur*, the Supreme Court overturns a law requiring schoolteachers to leave their jobs when they become five months' pregnant.

In *Corning Glass v. Brennan*, the Supreme Court holds in violation of the 1963 Equal Pay Act a company policy of paying male night inspectors (whose jobs were historically held by women) substantially more than women.

In *Geduldig v. Aiello*, the Supreme Court upholds state denial of pregnancy disability benefits to workers.

In *Kahn v. Shevin*, the Supreme Court upholds a law granting automatic property tax exemption to the sole surviving female spouse while denying it to all males and other females.

In *Schlesinger v. Ballard*, the Supreme Court holds constitutional a law permitting women members of the armed forces more time to attain promotion as officers than is permitted to men.

1975 The U.S. Commission on the Observance of International Women's Year is established.

In *Stanton v. Stanton*, the Supreme Court holds unconstitutional a law establishing the age of female adulthood at eighteen but the age of male adulthood at twenty-one, for the purpose of determining how long to continue financial support payments from a divorced parent.

In *Taylor v. Louisiana*, the Supreme Court holds unconstitutional the state practice of systematically excluding women from state jury duty.

In *Turner v. Department of Employment Security*, the Supreme Court overturns a law denying unemployment compensation to any women in last three months of pregnancy.

In *Weinberger v. Wiesenfeld*, the Supreme Court overturns a law providing Social Security benefits to sole surviving female parents of dependent children when such parents have low or no earnings and when the deceased spouse has contributed Social Security taxes but denying such benefits to sole surviving male parents in parallel situations.

1976 Representative Barbara Jordan (D-TX) becomes the first woman and first African American to deliver a keynote speech at a Democratic National Convention.

Representative Corinne Claiborne (Lindy) Boggs (D-LA) becomes the first woman chair of a Democratic National Convention.

In *Craig v. Boren,* for the first time, the Supreme Court acknowledges that something stricter than the reasonableness test applies to sex discrimination and overturns a state law permitting eighteen-to-twenty-year-old females the right to drink "3.2" beer while denying the right to eighteen-to-twenty-year-old males.

In *General Electric v. Gilbert,* the Supreme Court upholds the right of private employers to deny medical disability benefits to workers absent for maternity-related reasons.

Planned Parenthood of Central Missouri v. Danforth combines several state cases in a Supreme Court ruling as follows: State law prohibiting abortion by saline amniocentesis is held unconstitutional. State law prohibiting abortion without written consent of husband or, for unmarried minors, without written consent of parents, is held unconstitutional. State law requiring physician to attempt to preserve life of aborted fetus is held unconstitutional. State laws establishing special record-keeping rules for abortions, requiring written consent of the pregnant woman for an abortion, and forbidding abortions of "viable" fetuses are held constitutional.

1977   Margaret (Midge) Costanza becomes the first woman assistant to the president.

National Women's Conference is held in Houston, Texas.

The Congressional Caucus for Women's Issues is founded.

In *Beal v. Doe,* the Supreme Court upholds a Pennsylvania law denying Medicaid benefits for nontherapeutic abortions.

In *Califano v. Goldfarb,* the Supreme Court overturns a federal law providing Social Security benefits to surviving female spouses of persons who paid Social Security taxes but denying such benefits to surviving male spouses unless the males could prove "actual dependency" on their wives.

In *Califano v. Webster,* the Supreme Court upholds a federal law providing women a more generous technique than that provided to men for calculating their Social Security benefits in relation to their earnings.

In *Carey v. Population Services,* the Supreme Court overturns a state law prohibiting distribution of contraceptives to persons under age sixteen.

In *Dothard v. Rawlinson,* the Supreme Court holds unconstitutional minimum height and weight requirements for the job of prison guard. However, the males-only requirement for "contact positions" within maximum-security male penitentiaries characterized by "violence and disorganization" (and in which sex offenders are mixed with other prisoners) is held constitutional.

In *Fiallo v. Bell,* the Supreme Court holds constitutional a federal law providing preferred immigrant status to children born out of wedlock to American mothers (but not children born to American fathers) and to mothers of American children born out of wedlock (but not to their fathers).

In *Maher v. Roe,* the Supreme Court upholds a Connecticut law denying Medicaid benefits for "unnecessary" abortions.

In *Nashville Gas v. Satty,* the Supreme Court holds unconstitutional the deprivation of previously accumulated seniority benefits of women returning from maternity leave (where employees returning from other kinds of disability leave do not lose benefits).

In *Poelker v. Doe,* the Supreme Court holds constitutional a local law forbidding the performance of "unnecessary" abortions in publicly funded hospitals.

In *Vorchheimer v. School Board of Philadelphia,* a local law establishing one girls-only and one boys-only high school (when coed alternatives were available) is held constitutional because a Supreme Court tie vote leaves the lower-court opinion in effect.

1978 In *Los Angeles Department of Water and Power v. Manhart,* deductions by employer of larger amounts from wages of female employees than from male employees for a pension fund are held unconstitutional by Supreme Court.

In *Quilloin v. Walcot,* the Supreme Court upholds a state law permitting divorced fathers, but not unwed fathers, to block the adoption of natural children by stepfathers. Court refuses to rule on whether statute's discrimination against unwed fathers (as opposed to unwed mothers, who also could block adoption) was unconstitutional.

1981	Sandra Day O'Connor, appointed to the U.S. Supreme Court by President Ronald Reagan, becomes the first woman appointed to the Court.
President Reagan institutes the "global gag rule," which bars U.S. family-planning assistance to any foreign health-care agency that uses funds from any source to perform abortions, provide counseling and referral for abortion, or lobby to make abortion legal or more available in their country.
In *County of Washington v. Gunther*, the Supreme Court opens the door to comparable-worth suits under Title VII.
In *Kirchberg v. Feenstra*, the Supreme Court overturns a Louisiana law that granted the husband unilateral control as "head and master" over property he owned jointly with his wife.
1984	U.S. Representative Geraldine Ferraro (D-NY) is the first woman to receive a major political party nomination for vice-president of the United States.
The National Political Congress of Black Women is founded by Shirley Chisholm.
In *Hison v. King and Spalding*, the Supreme Court rules that law firms cannot use sexual discrimination when promoting lawyers to partnership positions.
In *Roberts v. U.S. Jaycees*, the Supreme Court forbids sex discrimination by organizations in their membership policies, allowing women access to previously all-male organizations.
1985	EMILY's List is founded to elect pro-choice Democratic women candidates.
1986	In *Meritor Savings Bank v. Vinson*, the Supreme Court rules that a hostile or abusive work environment is sufficient to prove sexual discrimination.
1987	In *Johnson v. Transportation Agency of Santa Clara County*, the Supreme Court rules that an affirmative action plan for women is constitutional under Title VII guidelines.
1989	The March for Women's Equality/Women's Lives takes place in Washington, D.C.
1991	Minnesota becomes the first state to have a majority of female supreme court justices, with four out of seven justices being women.
For the first time, at least one woman serves in every state legislature in the nation.

The WISH List is formed to promote pro-choice Republican women's candidacies for public office.

In *U.A.W. v. Johnson Controls,* the Supreme Court rules that fetal protection policies violate Title VII because they classify employees on the basis of gender and child-bearing capacity rather than on individual circumstances.

1992   The March for Women's Lives takes place in Washington, D.C.

Carol Moseley Braun is the first African American woman elected to the U.S. Senate.

1993   President Bill Clinton lifts the "global gag rule."

1994   In *J. E. B. v. Alabama ex rel T.B.,* the Supreme Court rules unconstitutional the exclusion of individual jurors on the assumption that they hold particular views simply because of their gender.

In *National Organization for Women v. Scheidler,* the Supreme Court rules that abortion clinic violence can be challenged in court under a federal antiracketeering statute that carries harsh penalties.

1996   In *United States v. Virginia,* the Supreme Court rules that the Virginia Military Institute's male-only admission policy violates the Fourteenth Amendment of the U.S. Constitution, and the school must admit women.

1998   Arizona becomes the first state with an all-female executive cabinet (governor, secretary of state, attorney general, treasurer, and superintendent of public instruction).

Tammy Baldwin (D-WI) becomes the first open lesbian elected to the U.S. House of Representatives.

2000   The Million Mom March takes place in Washington, D.C., to protest the proliferation of guns.

First Lady Hillary Rodham Clinton is elected to the U.S. Senate from New York.

In *United States v. Morrison* and *Brzonkala v. Morrison,* the Supreme Court rules that when Congress gave women a federal court remedy in the Violence Against Women Act, it went far beyond its constitutional powers to regulate interstate commerce and to enforce the Fourteenth Amendment.

In *Ferguson v. City of Charleston,* the Supreme Court rules that although a pregnant woman might be coerced into a drug-treatment program, a hospital cannot justifiably conduct a drug test and give the results to law enforcement without the patient's knowledge and consent.

In *Stenberg v. Carhart,* the Supreme Court overturns a Nebraska ban on "partial-birth abortion." In violation of *Roe,* the ban failed to provide an exception that would protect the health of the woman.

2001 President George W. Bush reinstitutes the "global gag rule."

2004 The largest March for Women's Lives to date takes place in Washington, D.C., with more than 1 million people participating.

Annotated Bibliography

First-Wave Feminism

Catt, Carrie Chapman, and Nettie Rogers Shuler. 1923. *Woman Suffrage and Politics: The Inner Story of the Suffrage Movement,* New York: C. Scribner's Sons.

    Carrie Chapman Catt led the suffrage movement to its ultimate victory. She tells the story of the movement from her leadership position.

Flexner, Eleanor. 1974. *Century of Struggle: The Women's Rights Movement in the United States.* New York: Atheneum.

    Flexner's volume is the principal historical work on the first women's rights movement. It begins with a survey of women's position during the colonial and revolutionary eras and concludes with the enactment of the woman suffrage amendment in 1920.

Kraditor, Aileen. 1965. *Ideas of the Woman Suffrage Movement, 1890–1920.* New York: Columbia University Press.

    Kraditor's work presents us with an examination of the theoretical ideas that the suffragists and antisuffragists employed in the thirty years leading up to victory. She argues that there was no official ideology to the movement. Activists were strategic in their use of arguments to win their goals.

Stanton, Elizabeth Cady, Susan B. Anthony, and Matilda Joslyn Gage. 1818–1922. *History of Woman Suffrage,* Volumes 1, 2, and 3. New York: Fowler and Wells.

    Elizabeth Cady Stanton and Susan B. Anthony were the driving forces of the women's suffrage movement in the latter part of the nineteenth century. They tell the story of the movement, focusing on their involvement and political views.

248 ■ Annotated Bibliography

Wheeler, Marjorie Spruill, ed. 1995. *Votes for Women: The Woman Suffrage Movement in Tennessee, the South, and the Nation.* Knoxville: University of Tennessee Press.

    Tennessee was the pivotal state in the ratification process for the Nineteenth Amendment, which granted women the constitutional right to vote. The essays in this book help to explain how and why Tennessee came to occupy this distinctive position in the movement's history. It offers an examination into the unique culture of the South as it affected the idea of women as public citizens.

Between Suffrage and the Second Women's Rights Movement

Andersen, Kristi. 1996. *After Suffrage: Women in Partisan and Electoral Politics before the New Deal.* Chicago: University of Chicago Press.

    Andersen covers the years immediately following suffrage and challenges the idea that women had little impact on politics after gaining the vote. Women's entrance into the public sphere and their concerns transformed both the political system and the women themselves even though the male politicians resisted their efforts.

Chafe, William H. 1972. *The American Woman: Her Changing Social, Economic, and Political Roles, 1920–1970.* New York: Oxford University Press.

———. 1991. *The Paradox of Change: American Women in the 20th Century.* Oxford, UK: Oxford University Press.

    Chafe is concerned with "women's place" in society and examines the changing the roles of women in the decades following the gaining of suffrage.

Friedan, Betty. 1963. *The Feminine Mystique.* New York: W. W. Norton.

    Betty Friedan's *The Feminine Mystique* helped to launch the second women's rights movement.

Harvey, Anna. 1998. *Votes without Leverage: Women in American Electoral Politics, 1920–1970.* New York: Cambridge University Press.

    Harvey explores the puzzle of why the increasing importance of women's votes in the 1920s did not imply increasing success for the lobbying efforts of women's organizations.

Lemons, J. Stanley. 1973. *The Woman Citizen: Social Feminism in the 1920s.* Urbana: University of Illinois Press.

    Lemons presents a history of the 1920s to show that social feminism continued in that decade and did not die with the passage of the Nineteenth Amendment. Social feminists constituted an important link in the chain from the Progressive Era to the New Deal of the 1930s.

Rupp, Leila J., and Verta Taylor. 1987. *Survival in the Doldrums.* New York: Oxford University Press.

    Rupp and Taylor challenge the idea that women did not organize to influence public policy in the years following World War II and the emergence of the second women's rights movement in the late 1960s. They explore the persistence of the women's rights movement during a time in which women did not appear to exhibit any group consciousness about their role in society.

Ware, Susan. 1981. *Beyond Suffrage: Women in the New Deal.* Cambridge, MA: Harvard University Press.

Susan Ware describes the involvement of women in party politics during the New Deal. She studies twenty-eight women who achieved positions of national leadership in the United States in the 1930s.

Second-Wave Feminism

Baumgardner, Jennifer, and Amy Richards. 2000. *Manifesta.* New York: Farrar, Straus and Giroux.

Baumgardner and Richards provide an analysis of the third wave of the women's movement, which focuses on the activities of young women.

Deckard, Barbara Sinclair. 1979. *The Women's Movement: Political, Socioeconomic, and Psychological Issues.* New York: Harper and Row.

Deckard provides a broad synthesis of the social, economic, and political status of women in past and present societies. She connects the ideas of the contemporary women's movement to older ideas.

Evans, Sara. 1979. *Personal Politics: The Roots of Women's Liberation in the Civil Rights Movement and the New Left.* New York: Knopf.

Evans focuses on how the contemporary feminist movement developed out of New Left politics in the 1960s. The book is based in part on her own experience within the movement.

Ferree, Myra Marx, and Beth B. Hess. 2000. *Controversy and Coalition: The New Feminist Movement through Three Decades of Change.* 3rd ed. New York: Routledge.

Controversy and Coalition is an extensive overview of the American women's movement from the 1960s to the 1990s, including the rise of global feminism.

Ferree, Myra Marx, and Patricia Yancey Martin, eds. 1995. *Feminist Organizations: Harvest of the New Women's Movement.* Philadelphia, PA: Temple University Press.

This collection of twenty-six original essays looks at contemporary feminist organizations, how they have survived, the effects of their work, the problems they face, the strategies they develop, and where the women's movement is headed. The contributors, who are feminist scholars, examine a wide range of current and former local feminist organizations, highlighting the struggles of feminist organizers and activists have faced.

Freeman, Jo. 1975. *The Politics of Women's Liberation.* New York: David McKay Company.

Jo Freeman was one of the early leaders in the women's liberation movement. She describes the development of the liberation branch of the contemporary women's movement and what she calls "the older," more moderate branch of the movement.

Morgan, Robin, ed. 1970. *Sisterhood Is Powerful: An Anthology of Writings from the Women's Liberation Movement.* New York: Random House.

——, ed. 2003. *Sisterhood Is Forever: The Women's Anthology for a New Millennium.* New York: Washington Square Press.

Robin Morgan's edited volumes provide essays regarding the nature and significance of the movement by leaders in the women's rights movement in the early years of its resurgence and at the beginning of the twentieth-first century after its maturation.

Ryan, Barbara. 1992. *Feminism and the Women's Movement: Dynamics of Change in Social Movement Ideology and Activism.* New York: Routledge.

Relying on participation and observation of diverse groups involved in the woman's movement, interviews with long-term activists, and readings of historical and contemporary movement publications, Ryan discusses the changing nature of feminist ideology and movement organizing. Ryan portrays the successes and difficulties that women have faced in recent years in their efforts to effect social change.

Swerdlow, Amy. 1993. *Women Strike for Peace: Traditional Motherhood and Radical Politics in the 1960s.* Chicago: University of Chicago Press.

Swerdlow presents a historical account of the Women Strike for Peace. This groundbreaking movement began on November 1, 1961, when thousands of white, middle-class women walked out of their kitchens and off their jobs in a one-day protest against Soviet and American nuclear policies. The protest led to a national organization of women who fought against nuclear arms and U.S. intervention in Cuba.

Whittier, Nancy. 1995. *Feminist Generations: The Persistence of the Radical Women's Movement.* Philadelphia: Temple University Press.

Whittier examines the transformation of the radical feminist movement, focusing on its emphasis on direct action in the 1960s and 1970s and the backlash against it in later years. She uses organizational documents and interviews with both veterans of the women's movement and younger feminists in Columbus, Ohio, to trace changing definitions of feminism as the women's rights movement has evolved. She documents subtle variations in feminist identity and analyzes the striking differences, conflicts, and cooperation between longtime and recent activists.

Wilson, Marie C. 2004. *Closing the Leadership Gap: Why Women Can and Must Help Run the World.* New York: Viking.

Marie Wilson heads the White House Project. In this book she makes the case for why more women are needed in political leadership positions and what the barriers have been, and she outlines a path toward greater leadership in the public sphere for women.

Women Candidates

The authors of these works are all political scientists who have collected data to test a number of theories about the lack of women candidates for public office and what happens when women run for office compared to men's experiences. Together they provide a wealth of systematic information on women's experiences as candidates for public office and explore reasons why women are underrepresented numerically in political leadership positions.

Burrell, Barbara. 1994. *A Woman's Place Is in the House: Campaigning for Congress in the Feminist Era*. Ann Arbor: University of Michigan Press.

Burrell provides an extensive analysis of the electoral experiences of male and female candidates for the U.S. House of Representatives from 1972 through 1992 to test a number of conventional ideas about why so few women hold public office. According to the data Burrell has assembled and contrary to conventional wisdom, women candidates for the U.S. House of Representatives have competed on an equal scale with men in recent elections.

Carroll, Susan. 1994. *Women as Candidates in American Politics*. 2nd ed. Bloomington: Indiana University Press.

In this second edition, Carroll updates what was a pioneering study of women candidates and their campaigns in the 1980s. In many regards the political climate has become vastly more favorable for female candidates, but Carroll shows that opportunities are still limited by the political structure. She discusses a number of possible reforms and actual developments that may eventually contribute to larger numbers of women being elected to public office.

Dolan, Kathleen A. 2004. *Voting for Women: How the Public Evaluates Women Candidates*. Boulder, CO: Westview Press.

Dolan examines how members of the public evaluates women candidates for elective office and the conditions under which they choose to vote for them. It provides a history of women and elections in the United States and an analysis of contemporary data on public reaction to women candidates.

Fox, Richard. 1997. *Gender Dynamics in Congressional Elections*. Thousand Oaks, CA: Sage Publications.

Fox studies the California congressional races of 1992 and 1994, in which a record nineteen women were candidates for House seats. He contrasts the experiences of the male and female candidates in order to explore the ways in which gender affects campaigns for national public office. Fox asks whether women campaign differently from men and what impact their presence has on the issues in campaigns. He shows that gender still has an impact in political campaigns.

Kahn, Kim Fridkin. 1996. *The Political Consequences of Being a Woman: How Stereotypes Influence the Conduct and Consequences of Political Campaigns*. New York: Columbia University Press.

Kahn examines the impact of sex-role stereotyping on the electability of women candidates and as a central factor in the conduct and consequences of statewide campaigns. Her work is the major study of media effects on the electability of women candidates.

Seltzer, Richard A., Jody Newman, and M. Voorhees Leighton. 1997. *Sex as a Political Variable*. Boulder, CO: Lynne Rienner Publishers.

This book offers a comprehensive analysis of women as candidates and voters in U.S. politics to address questions about the underrepresentation of women in public office. Drawing on a database on women and men as congressional candidates, as well as data from the Census Bureau, exit polls, and national election surveys, *Sex as a Political Variable* examines questions about why there are so few women in office and how voters view women candidates.

Thomas, Sue, and Clyde Wilcox, eds. 1998. *Women and Elective Office: Past Present and Future.* New York: Oxford University Press.

Women and Elective Office looks at research on women as candidates up to the 1990s. The authors included in this edited volume focus on recruitment patterns, media portrayals, and voter reactions to women candidates. They address the issues of how women behave in office and the difference they make while there, including the votes they cast, the priorities they focus upon, and the impact they have on the legislative process.

Woods, Harriet. 2000. *Stepping Up to Power: The Political Journey of American Women.* Boulder, CO: Westview Press.

From the perspective of an elected public official who is an activist and aspirant for higher office, Woods presents a historical view of women's efforts to gain equality in political leadership, describes the obstacles they have had to overcome, and provides guidelines for achieving equality.

Women in Elected Office

Borrelli, MaryAnne, and Janet Martin, eds. 1997. *The Other Elites.* Boulder, CO: Lynne Rienner Publishers.

This book features original essays on women in the executive branch. The contributors have two purposes: to study the career paths of women within the executive branch of the U.S. government and to consider gender as a variable in the study of complex organizations.

Cox, Elizabeth M. 1996. *Women State and Territorial Legislators, 1895–1995.* Jefferson, NC: McFarland.

Elizabeth Cox provides a state-by-state historical chronology of women's election to their legislatures.

Foerstel, Karen, and Herbert N. Foerstel. 1996. *Climbing the Hill: Gender Conflict in Congress.* Westport, CT: Praeger.

This text explores the history and contemporary status of women members and staff on Capitol Hill. It traces the difficult history of women in Congress, their slow and painful path to political power, and their hopes and fears in the 1990s.

Margolies-Mezvinsky, Marjorie, with Barbara Feinman. 1994. *Woman's Place: The Freshmen Women Who Changed the Face of Congress.* New York: Crown Publishers.

Margolies-Mezvinsky served one term (1993–1994) in the U.S. House of Representatives. She uses her personal experience to shed light on the distinctive experiences and challenges of women serving in this high legislative institution.

Martin, Janet. 2003. *The Presidency and Women: Promise, Performance and Illusion*. College Station: Texas A&M University Press.

    Martin studies the influence of women on and in the American executive branch, exploring in detail the presidencies of Kennedy through Carter, to show both the substantive growth in women's involvement in policy making and the political showcasing of women appointees. Her analysis provides insight into the day-to-day interactions between the White House and outside groups, the outside political pressures for certain policy agendas, and the internal White House dynamics in response to those pressures.

Mikulski, Barbara, Kay Bailey Hutchison, Dianne Feinstein, Barbara Boxer, Patty Murray, Olympia Snowe, Susan Collins, Mary Landrieu, and Blanche Lincoln with Catherine Whitney. 2000. *Nine and Counting: Women in the U.S. Senate*. New York: HarperCollins Publishers.

    This book, written by all of the women serving in the U.S. Senate at the millennium, describes their rise to power, their experiences in public office, and the challenges they have faced as women with aspirations to affect public policy.

Women Leaders and Public Policy

A major question that has emerged from efforts of women to achieve equality in political leadership positions has been what difference their presence as policy makers has made. Several scholarly volumes analyze the impact on public policy of women in public office.

Carroll, Susan, ed. 2001. *The Impact of Women in Public Office*. Bloomington: Indiana University Press.

    The Impact of Women in Public Office examines the impact of women public officials serving in various offices and locales at local, state, and national levels. The essays in this volume present evidence that women public officials do have a gender-related impact on public policy and the political process, but that impact varies considerably across political environments.

Gertzog, Irwin. 2004. *Women and Power on Capitol Hill: Reconstructing the Congressional Women's Caucus*. Boulder, CO: Lynne Rienner Publishers.

    Gertzog analyzes the origin, development, and influence of the Congressional Caucus for Women's Issues and explores how the women associated with it have emerged from near-oblivion to reassert their role in the legislative process. This book is the third in Gertzog's history of the caucus and his analysis of its impact on public-policy making in Congress.

Rosenthal, Cindy Simon, ed. 2002. *Women Transforming Congress*. Norman: University of Oklahoma Press.

    This book is an edited volume of original essays by political scientists. It examines the increasing influence of women on Congress and the ways in which gender defines and shapes Congress as a political institution.

The volume follows women on the campaign trail, in committee rooms, in floor debate, and in policy deliberations, where previously the focus was on men's interests and activities.

Swers, Michelle. 2002. *The Difference Women Make: The Policy Impact of Women in Congress*. Chicago: University of Chicago Press.

Swers asks the questions of how important it is that Congress look like the country, whether we need more mothers in Congress and whether we need more women in politics in general. She evaluates whether politically significant social identities such as gender influence the legislative priorities of representatives and under what circumstance these effects occur. Swers analyzes the legislative behavior of male and female members of the U.S. House of Representatives in the 103rd (1993–1994) and the 104th (1995–1996) Congresses on women's issues legislation.

Thomas, Sue. 1994. *How Women Legislate*. New York: Oxford University Press.

How Women Legislate provides a study of the effects women have had on legislation and the lawmaking process in state legislatures, analyzing the differences between women's and men's backgrounds before entering public office and the differences in their agendas, priorities, working styles, and leadership once they are in office.

The Equal Rights Amendment (ERA)

The following five books analyze why the ERA failed to obtain the necessary votes for ratification in the states.

Berry, Mary Frances. 1986. *Why the ERA Failed: Politics, Women's Rights, and the Amending Process of the Constitution*. Bloomington: Indiana University Press.

Legal historian Mary Frances Berry argues that the ERA failed because supporters failed to make a compelling case that sex-based discrimination in the law was an urgent problem solved only by amending the Constitution. The argument for the amendment grew weaker as some states successfully implemented their own ERAs and the Supreme Court moved toward a more vigorous standard of judicial review in the area of sex discrimination.

Boles, Janet. 1979. *The Politics of the Equal Rights Amendment: Conflict and the Decision Process*. New York: Longman.

Boles places the ratification campaign in the context of conflictual politics and argues that legislators in unratifying states voted against the conflict that the ratification process had generated rather than the substance of the amendment itself.

Mansbridge, Jane. 1986. *Why We Lost the ERA*. Chicago: University of Chicago Press.

Mansbridge follows a stream of thought similar to Barry's and in addition focuses on public opinion. She believes that support for the amendment among the public was actually quite weak, contributing to its failure to be ratified.

Mathews, Donald G., and Jane Sherron De Hart. 1990. *Sex, Gender, and the Politics of ERA.* New York: Oxford University Press.

    Mathews and De Hart provide an in-depth analysis of the ratification process in the state of North Carolina.

Steiner, Gilbert Y. 1985. *Constitutional Inequality: The Political Fortunes of the Equal Rights Amendment.* Washington, DC: The Brookings Institution.

    Steiner believes that opportunity for ratification existed only between 1971 and 1973. After this period, Steiner argues, success became difficult because the amendment became associated with other political events that affected how people viewed its likely impact. It became entangled with the issue of abortion and with the draft, which became more salient an issue as a consequence of the Soviet Union's invasion of Afghanistan. Also, a staunch opponent of the ERA, Senator Sam Ervin, had his prestige enhanced following his chairmanship of the Senate committee in the Watergate hearings.

Women and the Political Parties

Freeman, Jo. 2000. *A Room at a Time: How Women Entered Party Politics.* Lanham, MD: Rowman and Littlefield.

    Jo Freeman presents a historical overview of women's entrance into party politics and emergence as party leaders before suffrage up to the emergence of the second women's rights movement.

Sanbonmatsu, Kira. 2002. *Democrats, Republicans and the Politics of Women's Place.* Ann Arbor: University of Michigan Press.

    Sanbonmatsu examines a wide variety of gender equality debates—from abortion and the equal rights amendment to child care and the role of women in the political party system from 1968 to 2000. She assesses the impact of gender issues on Democratic and Republican Party leaders and activists, their electoral strategies, and public opinion. Although reproductive rights issues have become extremely partisan, other gender issues such as women's labor-force participation and entry into politics have not. Consequently, she shows that the extent to which gender equality issues have become partisan is more limited than previous studies suggest.

Wolbrecht, Christina. 2000. *The Politics of Women's Rights: Parties, Positions, and Change.* Princeton, NJ: Princeton University Press.

    Wolbrecht studies how public debate on women's rights policy has transformed the Republican and Democratic Parties and how their positions have shifted. She explores how party leaders have reacted to developments in the area of women's rights and adopted positions in ways that would help expand their party's coalition. Changes in those coalitions—particularly the rise of social conservatism within the GOP and the affiliation of social movement groups with the Democratic party—have resulted in the polarization characterizing the parties' stances on women's rights today.

Young, Lisa. 2000. *Feminists and Party Politics*. Vancouver: University of British Columbia Press.

Young examines the effort to bring feminism into the formal political arena through established political parties in Canada and the United States. She explores how movement organizations have approached partisan and electoral politics and how the parties themselves have responded to the mobilization of feminism.

Women of Color and Political Participation

Chisholm, Shirley. 1970. *Unbought and Unbossed*. Boston: Houghton Mifflin Company.

Shirley Chisholm, the first black woman to be elected to the U.S. House of Representatives writes a biography.

Cohen, Cathy J., Kathleen B. Jones, and Joan C. Tronto, eds. 1997. *Women Transforming Politics: An Alternative Reader*. New York: New York University Press.

This set of essays displaces the experiences of white, middle- and upper-class elite women as central and brings to light the lives and actions of poor and working-class women, women of color, and others defined as marginal. It covers topics as diverse as community organizing by South Asian women in New York, the governing styles of Chicana/Latina elected officials in California, the labor struggles of working-class women in Tennessee, the participation pattern of poor African American women in Ohio, and the challenge of reproductive and sexual rights in international feminist politics, greatly broadening the way one thinks about politics.

James, Joy, and Tracery DeNean Sharpley-Whiting. 2000. *The Black Feminist Reader*. Malden, MA: Blackwell Publishers.

This volume includes ten essays on the development of black feminism. It is organized into two parts, "Literary Theory" and "Social and Political Theory," and explores issues of community, identity, justice, and the marginalization of African American and Caribbean women in literature, society, and political movements

Springer, Kimberly, ed. 1999. *Still Lifting, Still Climbing: Contemporary African American Women's Activism*. New York: New York University Press.

Contributors to this work cover grassroots and national movements exploring Black women's mobilization around such areas as the Black nationalist movements, the Million Man March, Black feminism, antirape movements, mass incarceration, the U.S. Congress, welfare rights, health care, and labor organizing. The volume includes original essays and primary source documents.

Other Works on U.S. Women and Politics

Carroll, Susan, ed. 2003. *Women and American Politics—New Questions, New Directions.* New York: Oxford University Press.

This volume brings together a set of scholarly works to provide an account of recent developments and the challenges that the future brings for women in American politics. The book examines women's participation in the electoral arena and the emerging scholarship on the relationship between the media and women in politics, the participation of women of color, and women's activism outside the electoral arena.

Ford, Lynn. 2002. *Women and Politics: The Pursuit of Equality.* Boston: Houghton Mifflin Company.

This volume brings two perspectives on equality for women to the forefront: the legal doctrine, emphasizing gender neutrality; and the fairness doctrine, recognizing the differences between men and women.

Malveaux, Julianne, and Deborah Perry. 2002 *Unfinished Business: A Democrat and a Republican Take On the Top Ten Issues Women Face.* New York: Penguin Putnam.

These two authors address ten major issues facing women in the United States today, such as equal pay, the environment, work and family, and foreign policy. Malveaux and Perry address the issues from partisan perspectives and offer solutions, ideas, and directions for women seeking to improve their lives and the lives of their family members.

Norris, Pippa, ed. 1997. *Women, Media and Politics.* New York: Oxford University Press.

The authors of the essays in this volume analyze the effect of new media frames regarding gender in U.S. politics. "Framing" refers to how issues are presented and the effects that presentation produces.

Stetson, Dorothy McBride. 1997. *Women's Rights in the U.S.A: Policy Debates and Gender Roles.* 2nd ed. New York: Garland Publishing.

This text presents a record of the changes in major policy areas affecting gender roles and the status of women such as reproduction, family law, education, work, and pay. It focuses on the development of and the changes in debates over these issues and how laws are produced, administered, and interpreted from the debates. It highlights the role of feminists in the debates and the impact of feminists on policies.

Tolleson-Rinehart, Sue, and Jyl J. Josephson, eds. 2000. *Gender and American Politics: Women, Men, and the Political Process.* Armonk, NY: M. E. Sharpe.

The essays in this volume provide an overview of contemporary empirical research on differences in men's and women's voting behavior; political leadership, beliefs, and commitments; and the role gender plays in American political institutions.

Index

AAUW. *See* American Association of University Women (AAUW)
Abolition movement, 3
Abolitionists, 90
Abortion Control Act of 1992, 22
Abortion rights, 11, 20–24, 84–85, 109–111
  and Congressional Caucus for Women's Issues, 157
  and marches, 36–41
  and National Organization for Women, 62, 84
  and public funding, 22
  and restrictive abortion laws, 21, 22
  and RU 486, 79–80
Abraham, Spencer, 114
Abzug, Bella, 67, 68, 72, 195
ACLU. *See* American Civil Liberties Union (ACLU)
Adams, Abigail, 2, 195
Adams, Brook, 116
Adams, John, 2, 195
Adams, John Quincy, 195
Addams, Jane, 52
Affirmative action, and electoral politics, 117
Afghan Women and Children Act of 2001, 195
Afghanistan, 203
AFL-CIO, 76–77
African American Women in Defense of Ourselves, 71
African Americans, 11. *See also* Black feminism
"Ain't I a Woman?" (Truth), 185–186
Alabama Solution, 218
Alabama Women's Commission, 223
Alabama Women's Initiative and the Greenbook, 218
Albright, Madeleine, 41, 159
Alcohol abuse, and pregnant women, 23
Allen, Florence Ellinwood, 161
Allen, Pam, 32
Almanac of American Politics, 153
Alvarez, Aida, 159
American Association of Law Librarians, 75
American Association of University Women (AAUW), 13, 20, 56–57
American Bar Association, 76
American Brands, 33
American Civil Liberties Union (ACLU), 39
American feminism
  and Black feminism, difference between, 10–11
  See also Feminism
American Home Economics Association, 75
American National Election Study
  and women's movement, support for, 13
American Nurses Association, 83
American Tobacco Company, 33

Index

American Woman (President's Commission on the Status of Women report), 57–58, 201
American Woman Suffrage Association, 91, 200
Anthony, Susan B., 30, 39, 84, 90, 195–196, 203
Anti-Tea Leagues, 2
Antiwar demonstrations
  and CODEPINK, 46
  and Million Mom March, 44–46
Appropriations Act of 1975, 15
Argentina, 66
Arlington Cemetery, 32
Associate National Committee on Women, 103

Barrett, Elizabeth, 34
Battered women's shelters, 56
"Battle Hymn of the Public," 41
Bayh, Birch, 34
Beers, Charlotte, 46
Beverly LaHaye Live, 78
Birth control, 11
Black feminism, 9–10, 68–69
  and American feminism, difference between, 10–11
  and suffrage movement, 7
  See also Feminism
Black freedom struggle, 55
Black liberation movement, 10, 11
Black nationalist movement, 69
Black women
  in civil rights movement, 69
  and Combahee River Collective, 70–71
  and politics, involvement in, 102
Black Women's Health Imperative, 39
Blanco, Kathleen, 137
"Bleak and lonely years," 7
B-List, 222
Bly, Nellie, 30
Boles, Janet, 75, 76
Bottini, Ivy, 33
Bound, Aida, 39
Boxer, Barbara, 38, 151
Boycotts, during revolutionary era, 1

Bradwell v. Illinois, 187–188 (document)
Brady, James S., 45
Brady, Sarah, 45
Brazil, 66
Breckinridge, Sophonisba, 131
Britt, Harry, 153
Brown, Jerry, 38, 152
"The Burial of Traditional Womanhood," 32
Burton, Phillip, 152
Burton, Sala, 152
Bush, Barbara, 120
Bush, George H. W., 37, 147
  and Thomas, Clarence, confirmation hearings, 34
Bush, George W., 159, 160–161, 198
  and abortion, 23
  and election 2000, 118–120
  and election 2004, 121–122, 123
Bush, Laura, 46, 119–120
Bush administration (George W.), 46, 105, 160
  and Title IX, 24–25

California Commission on the Status of Women, 223
California List, 218–219
California Women's Law Center, 80
California Women's Political Summit, 219
Callaghan, Catherine, 84
Campaign Corps, 149
Campaign to Stop Gender Apartheid in Afghanistan, 203
Cantwell, Maria, 114
Capital punishment, 85
Caraway, Hattie, 131
Carnahan, Jean, 121
Carswell, G. Harold, 63
Carter, Jimmy, 159, 161
Catt, Carrie Chapman, 42, 52, 102, 196
CAWP. *See* Center for American Women and Politics (CAWP)
CCWI. *See* Congressional Caucus for Women's Issues (CCWI)

Center for American Women and Politics (CAWP), 106, 151, 153, 214
Center for Women in Politics and Public Policy, 214
Center for Women Policy Studies, 83, 214
CETA. *See* Comprehensive Employment and Training Act (CETA) of 1973
Chao, Elaine, 159
Charitable work, 3
Charlton, Linda, 33–34
Cheney, Lynne, 81, 120
Cheney, Richard, 81, 120
Chicago Sun Times, 97
Chicago Tribune, 97, 136
Chicago Women's Liberation Union, 56
Chicana feminist movement, 65–67
Chicano movement, 55
Childbirth issues, 11
Chile, 41, 66
Chisholm, Shirley, 79, 132, 146, 196
Christian Right organizations, 78
Citizens' Advisory Council, 61
Civil Rights Act of 1964, 15, 16, 59, 60–62, 82, 196
  and equal rights amendment, 74
Civil Rights Act of 1990, 120
Civil rights movement, 55
  black women's participation in, 69
Civil Service Act of 1883, 159
Civil Service Commission, 57
Civil War, 90
  women's participation in, 2
Clare Boothe Luce Policy Institute, 214–215
Clarenbach, Kathryn, 61
Clarence Thomas hearings. *See* Thomas, Clarence, confirmation hearings
Classification Act of 1923, 159
Classism, 10, 11
Clinton, Bill, 45, 118, 159, 160, 162
  and abortion, 23, 38

Clinton, Hillary Rodham, 41, 44, 114, 121–122, 151
Clinton administration, 160, 161
Clymer, Adam, 97
Coalition for Women's Appointments, 68
Coalition of Labor Union Women, 83, 203
CODEPINK, 46
College, enrollment of women in, 15–16
College degrees, women earning, 16
Collins, Judy, 43
Collins, Susan, 151
Combahee River Collective (CRC), 70–71
  statement, 192 (document)
Commission on Opportunity in Athletics, 24
Commission on the Advancement of Women and Minorities in Science, Engineering, and Technology Development, 196
Commission on the Observance of International Women's Year, 72, 199
Common law, 3
Compassion issues, 106, 111
Compassionate conservatism, 118–119
Comprehensive Employment and Training Act (CETA) of 1973, 16
Comprehensive Health Manpower Training Act, 15
Concerned Women for America (CWA), 77, 78, 80, 196
Conference for a New Politics, 55–56
Congress of American Women, 43
Congressional Caucus for Women's Issues (CCWI), 155–158
Congressional Quarterly Weekly, 121
Congressional Union (CU), 30–31, 50, 200
Contemporary feminism. *See* Third-wave feminism
Contemporary liberal feminists, 4, 9
Contraception, 20, 21

Contraceptive Coverage Act of 1998, 197
Cosmopolitan magazine, 33
Cott, Nancy, 9
Coverture, 3, 197
Cox, Elizabeth, 141
CRC. *See* Combahee River Collective (CRC)
Credit discrimination, 18–19. *See also* Discrimination
Crime, and electoral politics, 116, 117
CT Permanent Commission on the Status of Women, 223
CU. *See* Congressional Union (CU)
CWA. *See* Concerned Women for America (CWA)

D'Alesandro, Thomas, Jr., 152
Daughters of Liberty, 2
DAWN. *See* Democratic Activists for Women Now (DAWN)
Daytona International Speedway, 123
Death penalty, 108
Declaration of Independence, centennial celebration of 1876, 29–30
Declaration of Rights for Women, 30
Declaration of Sentiments, 30, 203
The Declaration of Sentiments and Resolutions, 181–185 (document)
DeCrow, Karen, 64
Dees-Thomases, Donna, 44
Defense Authorization bill, 202
Defense issues, and terrorism, 107
Delaware Commission for Women, 224
DeLay, Tom, 153
Democracy in America (Tocqueville), 3
Democratic Activists for Women Now (DAWN), 219
Democratic Congressional Campaign Committee, 105
Democratic National Committee (DNC), 102–103, 105
Democratic National Committee Women's Vote Center, 207–208
Democratic National Committee's Women's Division, 103
Democratic National Convention, 103
Democratic Party, 102–103, 104–105
  and suffrage, 30
  women in, 140–143
Democratic Senatorial Campaign Committee, 105
Demonstrations, 29
  antiwar, and CODEPINK, 46
  antiwar, and Million Mom March, 44–46
"Dependency Divas: How the Feminist Big Government Agenda Betrays Women" (Independent Women's Forum report), 81
Dionne, E. J., Jr., 117–118
Discrimination. *See* Credit discrimination; Employment discrimination; Gender discrimination; Race discrimination; Sex discrimination
Displaced Homemaker Self-Sufficiency Assistance Act of 1990, 197
DNC. *See* Democratic National Committee (DNC)
"Doldrums," 7
Dole, Elizabeth, 121, 146
Dole, Robert, 97, 118
Domestic and foreign policy issues, and electoral politics, 106–109
Domestic life, and political values, 2–3
Dornan, Bob, 133–134
Douglass, Frederick, 89
Dowd, Maureen, 35
Drug abuse, and pregnant women, 23
Dunn, Jennifer, 119

Eagle Forum, 77, 80, 197, 202
Eastern Regional Conference on Black Feminism, 70
Economic Equity Act, 156
Economic issues, and electoral politics, 111–112
Economic opportunity, 10

Economic status, 18–20
Education, 3, 15–16, 111
Education Amendments, 15, 197. *See also* Title IX
EEOC. *See* Equal Employment Opportunity Commission (EEOC)
"E-Government Initiatives," 54
Eisenhower, Dwight, 94, 158
Eisenhower administration, 160
El Grito (New Mexico), 66
El Salvador, 66
Eleanor Roosevelt Legacy Committee, 221
Election campaigns, financial donations to, 101–102
Elections, presidential
　and election 1920, 91–92
　and election 1952, 94, 96
　and election 1960, 96
　and election 1964, 92–93
　and election 1980, 96–97
　and election 1996, 97, 117–118
　and election 2000, 94, 97, 101, 118–120
　and election 2002, 121
　and election 2004, 121–124
　and gender, effect of, 112–124
　and gender gap, 96–98
　and NASCAR dads, 122–123
　and soccer moms, 117–118
　and voter turnout, 92–96
　and Women's Voices, Women's Vote, 123–124
　See also Electoral politics, women's involvement in; Political parties
Electoral politics, women's involvement in, 89–124
　and economic issues, 111–112
　and feminist issues, 106–112
　and foreign and domestic policy issues, 106–109
　and gender gap, 96–98
　and scandals, 114
　and social issues, 109–111
　and suffrage, impact of, 91–96
　and Year of the Woman, 113, 114–115, 121
　and Year of the Woman governor, 121
　See also Elections, presidential; Political parties
Electoral systems
　and public office, women in, 137, 140
EMILY's List, 23, 83, 116, 123, 147–150, 208
Empire Women, 221
Employment discrimination
　and equal rights amendment, 73–74
　and gender, 16–17
　and race, 60
　and second-wave feminism, 17
　and Title VII, 60–62
　See also Discrimination; Job advertisements, and sex discrimination; Workforce, women in the
Encuentro Femenil, 66
Environmental issues, 108
Equal Credit Opportunity Act of 1974, 18–19, 197
Equal Employment Opportunity Commission (EEOC), 35, 60–61, 62, 82, 196
Equal nationality treaty, 51
Equal pay, 85
Equal Pay Act of 1963, 16, 58–59, 59–60, 197
Equal Pay Day, 59
Equal rights amendment (ERA), 8, 20, 34, 51–52, 59, 97, 188 (document), 197, 199, 202
　and antiamendment groups, 74
　and antiratification campaign, 77
　campaign for ratification of, 73–78
　groups opposed to, 77
　and military, women in the, 25
　and National Organization for Women, 62, 64–65, 75, 76, 77
　support for, 77

Equal Rights Party, 146
Equal rights treaty, 51
Equality issues, 4, 5, 109
ERAmerica, 76
Euthanasia, 85
Executive Order 10980. *See* President's Commission on the Status of Women

Fair Labor Standards Act of 1938, 53, 58–59
Families, female-headed, 19–20
Family and Medical Leave Act of 1993, 118, 120, 198
"Family Voice" newsletter, 78
Fargo, Heather, 137
Federal Elections Commission, 101, 148
Federal unemployment compensation program, 16–17
Federally Employed Women (FEW), 57
Feinstein, Dianne, 144
Felton, Rebecca, 131
The Feminine Mystique (Friedan), 198
Feminism
  and abortion, 21–22
  and Black women, 9–10, 11. *See also* Black feminism
  definition of, 4, 9
  and electoral politics, 106–112
  issues of, 11, 106–112
  See also First-wave feminism; Second-wave feminism; Third-wave feminism
Feminist bookstores, 56
Feminist groups, rise of, 82–84
Feminist health centers, 56
Feminist Majority, 39
Feminist Majority Foundation (FMF), 79–80, 202–203, 208
Feminists, types of, 4, 8
Feminists for Life of America, 23, 84–85, 208–209
Feminization of poverty, 198
Ferguson, Miriam "Ma," 135

Ferraro, Barbara, 37
Ferraro, Geraldine, 130–131, 146–147
Ferry, Thomas W., 30
FEW. *See* Federally Employed Women (FEW)
Firestone, Shulamith, 32, 55–56, 201
First National Hispanic Feminist Conference, 67
First-wave feminism, 4–9
  issues of, 4–5
  and suffrage protests, 29–32
Florida Commission on the Status of Women, 224
FMF. *See* Feminist Majority Foundation (FMF)
Ford, Gerald, 72
Foreign and domestic policy issues and electoral politics, 106–109
The Fountain of Age (Friedan), 198
Fourteenth Amendment, 90
France, 140
Franklin, Shirley, 137
Frankovic, Kathleen, 108
Freedom of Access to Clinic Entrances Act of 1993, 198
Freedom Summer '92, 12
Freeman, Jo, 55–56
Friedan, Betty, 33, 62, 63, 67, 68, 198
Fund for a Feminist Majority, 9, 79–80
Furies, 56

Gallup poll
  and military, women in the, support for, 26
  and women's movement, support for, 13, 15
Gender, and elections, presidential, 112–124. *See also* Gender gap, and electoral politics
Gender discrimination, 10
  and public office, women in, 143–144
  See also Discrimination
Gender gap, and electoral politics, 96–98, 198. *See also* Gender, and elections, presidential

Gender quotas
 and public office, women in, 140
General Federation of Women's Clubs, 52, 76–77
Georgia State Commission on Women, 224
Gephardt, Richard, 153
Gertzog, Irwin, 158
Ginsburg, Ruth Bader, 162
Girl Scouts, 76
"Girls E-Mentoring in Science, Engineering, and Technology" program, 54
Glass ceiling, 198
Goldberg, Whoopi, 41
Goldsmith, Judy, 64
Goltz, Pat, 84
Gordon, Slade, 114
Gore, Al, and election 2000, 119–120
Government services, and social issues, 111
Governors, women as, 136–137, 170 (table)
Governor's Commission on the Status of Women, 225
Governor's Office Commission for Women, 231
Graham, Robert, 122–123
Grasso, Ella, 136
Greater Kansas City Women's Political Caucus, 221
Greater Washington Health Center, 40
Greenwald, Glenda, 150
Griffiths, Martha, 60
GROW—Republican Women, 221
A Growing Crisis: Disadvantaged Women and Their Children (U.S. Civil Rights Commission report), 156
Guatemala, 66
Gun control, 108
 and Million Mom March, 44–46

Hague Conference of 1899, 41–42
Handgun Control Inc., 45
Hard-core feminists, 8
Harriet's List, 220
Harris, Patricia Roberts, 159

Hatter, Terry, Jr., 134
Hawaii State Commission on the Status of Women, 224
Hawley, General, 30
Health care, and electoral politics, 117
Health Mothers and Healthy Babies Access to Care Act, 121
Hearst Corporation, 33
Heide, Wilma Scott, 34
Hembra, 66
Henriquez, Silvia, 40
Hijas de Cuauhtemoc (Daughters of Cuauhtemoc), 66
Hill, Anita, 35–36, 71, 115
Hiring, and employment discrimination, 60–61
Hispanic women, 11
Hispanic women's movements, 65–67
Hispanics Organized for Political Equality (HOPE), 209
History of Woman Suffrage (ed. Anthony), 196
Hobby, Oveta Culp, 158
Homemaker Individual Retirement Account Act of 1996, 198–199
Homophobia, 10
Homosexuals in the military, and electoral politics, 117
HOPE. *See* Hispanics Organized for Political Equality (HOPE)
Hope Chest, 222
House Un-American Activities Committee, 42–43
How and Why Women Will Elect the Next President (Smeal), 202
Howe, Julia Ward, 41
Hughes, Karen, 160–161
Human Rights Campaign Fund, 39
Hussey, Patricia, 37
Hutchison, Kay Bailey, 151

Idaho Commission on the Women's Program, 225
Illinois Lincoln Excellence in Public Service Series, 219–220
Illinois Women's Institute for Leadership (IWIL), 220

Immigration, and electoral politics, 117
Independent Women's Forum (IWF), 80–82
Independent Women's Voice, 81
Indiana Commission for Women, 225
Institute for Women's Policy Research (IWPR), 215
Inter-Parliamentary Union (IPU), 137, 207
Intercollegiate sports, sex discrimination in, 24–25
and scholarships, 24
Interdepartmental Committee on the Status of Women, 61
International Council of Women, 196
International Telephone and Telegraph (ITT), 44
International Woman Suffrage Alliance, 196
International Women's Day, 46
International Women's Year, 71, 199
Iowa Commission on the Status of Women, 225
Iowa Women and Public Policy Group (WIPP), 220
IPU. *See* Inter-Parliamentary Union (IPU)
Iraq, 46
Iraq War of 2003, 25–26, 107
Ireland, Patricia, 12, 38, 39
It Changed My Life (Friedan), 198
ITT. *See* International Telephone and Telegraph (ITT)
IWF. *See* Independent Women's Forum (IWF)
IWIL. *See* Illinois Women's Institute for Leadership (IWIL)
IWPR. *See* Institute for Women's Policy Research (IWPR)

Jeannette Rankin Brigade, 32, 43–44
Job advertisements, and sex discrimination, 32, 60–61, 62–63, 82. *See also* Employment discrimination
Johnson, Nancy, 157
Jordan, Barbara, 199
Judiciary Committee
and Thomas, Clarence, confirmation hearings, 34–36, 115
Judiciary, women in, 161–162, 177 (table)

Keller, Helen, 31
Kennedy, Jacqueline, 42
Kennedy, John F., 42, 57, 58, 96, 200–201
Kentucky Commission on Women, 225–226
Kerry, John, and election 2004, 121–122
Khrushchev, Nikita, 42
Khrushchev, Nina, 42
Korean War, 106
Kuwait, 80

La Comadre, 66
LaHaye, Beverly, 77, 196
Lake, Celinda, 116
Lane, Ann Rice, 45
LAPD. *See* Los Angeles Police Department (LAPD)
"Late-term" abortion, 23
Latin America, 140
Lazio, Rick, 114
League of Women Voters (LWV), 7, 20, 52–53, 56, 196, 199, 209
and equal rights amendment, 75, 76, 77
Legislative leaderships positions, women in, 150–151, 171–175 (table)
Legislative Service Organization, 157
Liberal feminists, 4
Lillian's List, 222
Lockwood, Belva, 146
Longeaux y Vasquez, Enriqueta, 66
Los Angeles African American Women's Political Action Committee, 219
Los Angeles City Council, 80

Los Angeles Police Department (LAPD), 80
Louis Harris and Associations poll and women's movement, support for, 13
Louisiana Office of Women's Services, 226
Lowey, Nita, 105
Luce, Clare Booth, 151
Lugar, Richard, 143
LWV. *See* League of Women Voters (LWV)
Lynching, 10

MA Commission on the Status of Women, 226
MA Governor's Advisory Committee on Women's Issues, 226
Madsen v. Women's Health Center, 203
Mainstream Moms Oppose Bush (MMOB), 123
Majority Caucus, 63–64
Malcolm, Ellen, 148, 150
Mammography Quality Standards Act of 1992, 199
MANA, 209
Mankiller, Wilma, 199
March for Women's Equality/Women's Lives, 36–37
March for Women's Lives, 38–41, 80
Marches, 29
 and abortion rights, 36–41
 and suffrage, 30–31
Martin, Joe, 151
Martin Luther King Day, 46
Maryland Commission for Women, 226
Massachusetts Women's Political Caucus PAC, 220
McCorvey, Norma, 37
McGovern-Fraser Commission, 104
McKinley, William, 41
Medicare, 111
Mexican-American Women's Association, 65
Meyers, Jan, 151
Michelman, Kate, 84
Michigan Women's Commission, 227

Mikulski, Barbara, 35, 144, 151
Milholland, Inez, 30, 31
Military academies, admission of women to, 15
Military, women in the, 25–26
 and ground combat, 25–26
 military duties of, 25–26
 support for, 26
Million Man March, 71
Million Mom March, 44–46
Mink, Patsy, 72
Minnesota Commission on the Economic Status of Women, 227
Minor, Virginia, 90
Minor v. Happersett, 90
Miss America Pageant, 32
Mississippi Commission on the Status of Women, 227
Missouri Council on Women's Economic Development and Training, 227
Mitchell, George J., 35
MMOB. *See* Mainstream Moms Oppose Bush (MMOB)
Mondale, Walter, 64, 147
Moseley Braun, Carol, 38, 132, 146
Mothers' Peace Day, 41
Mott, Lucretia, 89
Ms. Foundation for Women, 203, 215
MS magazine, 203
Mueller v. Oregon, 74, 201
Murkowski, Frank, 142
Murkowski, Lisa, 142
Murray, Patty, 105, 115–116, 144

NAACP. *See* National Association for the Advancement of Colored People (NAACP)
NACS. *See* National Association for Chicano Studies (NACS)
NACW. *See* National Association of Commissions for Women (NACW)
NARAL Pro-Choice America, 21, 39, 84, 200
NASCAR dads, 114, 122–123

National Abortion and Reproductive Rights Action League, 84
National Abortion Rights Action League, 21, 57, 82, 84, 198
National American Woman Suffrage Association (NAWSA), 7, 29, 50, 52, 91, 196, 199, 200, 203
National Association for Chicano Studies (NACS), 67
National Association for the Advancement of Colored People (NAACP), 39
National Association for the Repeal of Abortion Laws, 84
National Association for Women Deans, Administrators and Counselors, 83
National Association of Commissions for Women (NACW), 209–210
National Black Feminist Organization (NBFO), 10, 69–70, 70–71
National Business Council for ERA, 76
National Cancer Institute, 156
National Chicano Political Conference, 67
National Clinic Access Project, 202–203
National Coalition for Women and Girls in Education, 24
National Collegiate Athletic Association (NCAA), 24
National Commission on Violence Against Women, 204
National Committee on Pay Equity (NCPE), 59–60
National Committee on the Cause and Cure of War, 196
National Conference of Puerto Rican Women, 65
National Conference of State Commissions on the Status of Women, 61
National Congress of Black Women, 78–79
National Congress of Neighborhood Women, 83
National Council of Negro Women, 56
National Council of Senior Citizens, 76
National Council of Women, 41
National Council of Women's Organizations (NCWO), 210
National Domestic Violence hotline, 204
National Economy Act of 1932, 159
National Election Studies (NES)
and women's movement, support for, 13
National Federation of Business and Professional Women's Clubs, 7, 56, 159
and equal rights amendment, 75, 76, 77
National Federation of Republican Women (NFRW), 103–104, 143, 210
National Gay and Lesbian Task Force, 39
National Institutes of Health, 157
National Institutes of Health Revitalization Act, 157
National Latina Institute for Reproductive Health, 39, 40
National Organization for Women (NOW), 9, 12, 52, 57, 62–65, 67, 68, 70, 79, 82, 97, 116, 198, 200, 202, 210–211
and abortion, 62, 84
and Bill of Rights, 62
and equal rights amendment, 62, 64–65, 75, 76, 77
and marches, 36–39
and second-wave protests, 32, 33, 34
and sex discrimination, 63
Statement of Purpose, 190–191 (document)
and Title IX, 24
and Title VII, 61, 62
and vice presidential nominee, woman as, 146–147

National Political Congress of Black Women, 78–79, 196
National Public Radio, 34
National Silent No More Awareness Campaign, 41
National Woman Abuse Prevention Center, 80
National Woman Suffrage Association (NWSA), 29–30, 91, 195–196
National Woman's Party (NWP), 30, 31, 50–52, 53, 60, 159, 197, 200
and equal rights amendment, 74
National Women's Alliance (NWA), 211
National Women's Conference, 71–73, 199
National Women's Law Center, 215–216
National Women's Political Caucus (NWPC), 36, 57, 67–68, 82, 116, 198, 203, 211–212
Native American rights movement, 199
Native Americans, 11
Natural rights movement, 5–6
Navy SEALS, 25
NAWSA. *See* National American Woman Suffrage Association (NAWSA)
NBFO. *See* National Black Feminist Organization (NBFO)
NCAA. *See* National Collegiate Athletic Association (NCAA)
NCPE. *See* National Committee on Pay Equity (NCPE)
NCWO. *See* National Council of Women's Organizations (NCWO)
Nebraska Commission on the Status of Women, 227–228
NES. *See* National Election Studies (NES)
Nevada Commission for Women, 228
New Deal, 103, 106
New Hampshire Commission on the Status of Women, 228

New Jersey Advisory Commission on the Status of Women, 228
New Mexico Commission on the Status of Women, 228–229
NEW project, 54
New York Radical Women, 32, 56
New York State Division for Women, 229
New York Stock Exchange, 82
New York Times, 32, 35, 36, 43, 62–63, 82, 97, 136
NFRW. *See* National Federation of Republican Women (NFRW)
Nieto Gomez, Anna, 66
NIH Office of Research on Women's Health, 157
Nineteenth Amendment, 7, 20, 33, 52, 91, 130
Nixon, Richard, 96, 199
North Carolina Council for Women, 229
North Dakota Governor's Commission on the Status of Women, 229
North Star, 89
Norton, Eleanor Holmes, 157
NOW. *See* National Organization for Women (NOW)
Nuclear testing, and Women Strike for Peace, 42–43
Nuclear war, 108
NWA. *See* National Women's Alliance (NWA)
NWP. *See* National Woman's Party (NWP)
NWPC. *See* National Women's Political Caucus (NWPC)
NWSA. *See* National Woman Suffrage Association (NWSA)

Occupations, high-earning, and women, 17–18
O'Connor, Karen, 154–155
O'Connor, Sandra Day, 162
Office of Women's Health Research, 156

Oklahoma Commission on the Status of Women, 229–230
Older Women's League, 39, 83
Omnibus Judgeship Act of 1978, 161
1000 Flowers, 123
Operation Witness, 40–41
Oprah Winfrey show, 120
Oregon Governor's Commission for Women, 230
Organization of Pan Asian American Women, 83
Ostberg, Kay, 39
Outrageous Acts and Everyday Rebellions (Steinem), 203

Pacifism, 106
PACs. *See* Political action committees (PACs)
Paige, Rod, 24
PAM's List (Power and Money for Choice and Change), 221
Parks, Rosa, 39, 200
"Partial birth" abortion, 23
Partial Birth Abortion Act of 2003, 84
Paul, Alice, 30, 31, 51
Pay equity. *See* Equal pay
Peace activism, 41–42
Pelosi, Nancy, 41, 105, 150, 152–153
Pelosi, Paul F., 152
Pendleton Act of 1883, 159
Pennington, Jane, 39
Pennsylvania Commission for Women, 230
Pennsylvania v. Casey, 22, 23, 39
Pennsylvania Women's Campaign Fund, 222
Perkins, Frances, 158
Persian Gulf War, 25
Peterson, Esther, 57, 201
Philippines, 41
Phyllis Schlafly Report newsletter, 202
PIPA. *See* Program on International Policy Attitudes (PIPA)
Pitcher, Molly, 2
Planned Parenthood, 21
Planned Parenthood Federation of America, 40

Planned Parenthood of Southeastern Pennsylvania v. Casey. *See Pennsylvania v. Casey*
Political action committees (PACs), 82–83
and public office, women in, 147–150
See also EMILY's List; WISH List
Political disenfranchisement, 10
Political parties
and women elected officials, 140–143
women's involvement in, 102–105
See also Elections, presidential; Electoral politics, women's involvement in
Political values, and domestic life, 2–3
Poverty, 10, 19–20
Power and Money for Choice and Change. *See* PAM's List
Pregnancy Discrimination Act of 1978, 17, 200
Pregnant women
and drug and alcohol abuse, 23
and employment, and sex discrimination, 16–17
Presidential appointments, and women, 158–159, 176–177 (table)
Presidential nominees, women as, 4, 145–146, 163
Presidential staff, and women, 160–161
President's Commission on the Status of Women (PCSW), Executive Order 10980, 57–58, 188–190 (document), 200–201
Pro-choice movement, 21–24
Procter and Gamble Manufacturing Company, 33
Program on International Policy Attitudes (PIPA), 107
Progressive Action Caucus (PAC), 64
Project "W," 219
Pro-life groups, 21
Pro-life movement, 21–23
fringe element of, 23–24

Promotions, and employment discrimination, 60–61
Proportional representation systems, 140
Protective labor laws, 201
Protests
  and first-wave feminism, 29–32
  and second-wave feminism, 32–34
  suffrage, 29–32
Pryce, Deborah, 150
Public funding, and abortion, 22
Public office, women in, 129–130, 162–163
  and Congressional Caucus for Women's Issues, 155–158
  and electoral systems, 137, 140
  and gender discrimination, 143–144
  and gender quotas, 140
  as governors, 136–137, 170 (table)
  importance of, 154–155
  in the judiciary, 161–162, 177 (table)
  in legislative leaderships positions, 150–151, 171–175 (table)
  and political action committees, 147–150
  and political parties, 140–143
  and presidential appointments, 158–159, 176–177 (table)
  as presidential nominees, 145–146, 163
  and presidential staff, 160–161
  in state legislatures, 153
  as state officials, 135–136
  in the U.S. Congress, 130–135, 152–153, 171–175 (table)
  as vice presidential nominees, 146–147
Public opinion
  and equal rights amendment, 77
  and military, women in, support for, 26
  and women's movement, support for, 12, 13–15, 68–69
Public Opinion Quarterly, 107

Puerto Rico Commission for Women's Affairs, 230

Quinn, Sally, 12

Race discrimination, 10
  and employment, 60
  See also Discrimination
Racism, 10, 11
Radical feminists, 4, 9
Rankin, Jeannette, 32, 43, 131
Rape crisis centers, 56
Rasmussen, Jeri, 148
Reagan, Ronald, 45, 96–97, 108, 147, 162, 198
Redstockings, 201
Regeneracion magazine-newsletter, 66
Regis Philbin show, 120
Rehnquist, William H., 37
Religious conservatives, and abortion, 21
Reproductive rights, 20–21
Republican Mother, 2, 3
Republican Motherhood, 201
Republican National Committee (RNC), 103, 105
Republican Party, 103–104, 104–105
  women in, 140–143
Republican Pro-Choice Coalition, 41
Republican Senatorial Campaign Committee (RSCC), 143
Republican Women's National Executive Committee, 103
Restrictive abortion laws, 21, 22
"Return to normalcy" campaign, 8
The Revolution (ed. Anthony), 195
Revolution from Within: A Book of Self-Esteem (Steinem), 203
Revolutionary era
  boycotts during, 1
  women's political role during, 1–2
Revolutionary War, women's participation in, 2
Rhode Island Commission for Women, 230
Rice, Condoleezza, 160
Rincon, Bernice, 66

RNC. *See* Republican National Committee (RNC)
Robertson, Alice, 131
Roe v. Wade, 21, 22–23, 34, 36, 37, 38, 84, 191–192 (document), 200
Roosevelt, Eleanor, 103, 201
Roosevelt, Franklin D., 43–44, 96, 106, 158, 161
Roosevelt administration (Franklin D.), 58, 103, 160, 161
Rosie the Riveter Historic Trust, 8
"Rosie the Riveter" (song), 8
Ross, Nellie Tayloe, 135
Roudy, Yvette, 37
RSCC. *See* Republican Senatorial Campaign Committee (RSCC)
RU 486, 79–80
Russia, 42

Safer, Morley, 148
SAFER. *See* Second Amendment Freedom for Everyone Rally (SAFER)
Sampson, Deborah, 2
Sanchez, Linda, 133, 134–135
Sanchez, Loretta, 133–134, 135
Sanger, Margaret, 39
Sayes, Ruby, 39
Scandals, and electoral politics, 114
Schlafly, Phyllis, 77, 197, 202
Schlozman, Kay Lehmann, 83–84
Scholarships, in intercollegiate sports, and sex discrimination, 24
Schroeder, Pat, 146
SDS. *See* Students for a Democratic Society (SDS)
Second Amendment Freedom for Everyone Rally (SAFER), 46
Second Amendment Sisters, Inc., 45–46
Second Stage (Friedan), 198
Second-wave feminism, 8, 9–11, 54–55, 104, 202
 and employment, 17
 issues of, 4–5, 9
 protests, 32–34

Security moms, 107
Senate Judiciary Committee
 and Thomas, Clarence, confirmation hearings, 34–36, 115
Seneca Falls convention of 1848, 5, 30, 89, 203
Seneca Network, 219
September 11, 2001, terrorist attack, 46, 107
Sex discrimination, 10, 15
 and employment, 16–17, 60–61
 in intercollegiate sports, 24–25
 and job advertisements, 32, 60–61, 62–63, 82
 and National Organization for Women, 63
 and workforce, women in the, 16, 17
 See also Discrimination
Sexism, 10, 11
Sexual crimes, 6
Sexual harassment, 85
 and Thomas, Clarence, 34–36
Sexual Harassment and Violence in the Military Act of 2003, 202
Shepherd, Cybill, 41
Sheppard-Towner Maternity and Infancy Act of 1921, 202
"Silent Sentinels," 31
Single-member-district system, 140
SisterSong Women of Color Reproductive Health Collective, 40
60 Minutes, 148
Slaughter, Louise, 35
Slavery, 3
Smeal, Eleanor, 9, 39–40, 64, 97, 202–203
Smith, Howard, 60
Smith, Margaret Chase, 145–146, 151
Smith, Obrellia, 45
Smolkin, Rachel, 46
Snowe, Olympia, 151
Soccer moms, 114, 117–118
Social feminists, 8

Social issues, and electoral politics, 109–111
Social Security, 111
Sojourner 21 PAC, 223
"The Solitude of Self" (Stanton), 5–6
The Source newsletter, 157
Soviet Union, 42
Spain, 41
Spillar, Katherine, 80
Stabenow, Deborah, 114, 151
Stanton, Elizabeth Cady, 5–6, 84, 89, 90, 195–196, 203
State legislatures, women in, 153
State officials, women as, 135–136
States' rights, principle of, 7
Statue of Liberty, 33
Steinem, Gloria, 41, 67, 68, 203
Sterilization abuse, 10, 11
Stevenson, Adlai, 94
"Strengthening the Family" initiative, 54
Strike Day, 33
Student protests, 55
Students for a Democratic Society (SDS), 55–56
Suffrage, 5, 50–52, 89–91
  impact of, 91–96
  protests, 29–32
  and suffragists, jailing of, 31–32
  See also Voting rights
Suffrage movement, 5–8, 203
  and Black women, 7
Suffragists, 5
  jailing of, 31–32
Susan B. Anthony Group, 23
Swing voters, 114

Taliban, 203
Taxes, and electoral politics, 117
Technology, and women, role of, 49–50
Temperance movement, 3
Tennessee Economic Council on Women, 231
Terrorism, 46, 107
Terrorist attack, September 11, 2001, 46, 107

Texas Governor's Commission for Women, 231
Third Wave Foundation, 11–12, 212
Third Wave Manifesta: A Thirteen-Point Agenda, 192–194 (document)
Third-wave feminism (contemporary feminism), 5, 11–12, 69, 203–204
  issues of, 11
Thomas, Clarence, confirmation hearings, 34–36, 71, 80, 115
Thomases, Susan, 44
Time Magazine/CNN Poll
  and women's movement, support for, 12
Times Mirror Center for the People and the Press, 12
Title IX, 15, 24–25, 57, 197
Title VII, 60–62, 82, 196. *See also* Civil Rights Act of 1964
Tocqueville, Alexis de, 3
Totenberg, Nina, 34–35
Truman administration, 161
Truth, Sojourner
  "Ain't I a Woman?" speech, 185–186
Tubman, Harriet, 71
Turner, Kathleen, 41

UFAC. *See* United Feminist Action Campaign (UFAC)
Unborn Victims of Violence Act of 2004, 23, 204
United Auto Workers, 62
United Feminist Action Campaign (UFAC), 64
United States v. Susan B. Anthony, 186–187 (document)
University of California at Berkeley, 67
University of Michigan, 81
U.S. Civil Rights Commission, 156
U.S. Congress, 105
  women in, 130–135, 152–153, 171–175 (table)
U.S. Department of Defense, 15, 25

U.S. Department of Education, 24
U.S. Department of Labor, 53, 57, 158, 204, 205
U.S. Department of War, 31
U.S. Supreme Court
  and abortion, 21, 22–23
  and Thomas, Clarence, confirmation hearings, 34–36
USA TODAY, 118
Use of force issue, 106
Utah Governor's Commission for Women and Families, 231

Vaid, Urvashi, 39
Venezuela, 41
Vermont Commission on Women, 231–232
Vice presidential nominees, women as, 146–147
Victims of Trafficking and Violence Protection Act of 2000, 204
Vietnam War, 25, 106
  and antiwar movement, 55
  and Women Strike for Peace, 42, 43–44
Violence Against Women Acts, 84–85, 204
Virginia Council on the Status of Women, 232
Virginia Slims American Women's Opinion Poll
  and women's movement, support for, 13, 68–69
"Voces de la Mujer" (Voices of Women), 67
Voting rights, 5. *See also* Suffrage

"W Stands for Women" tour, 120
WAC. *See* Women's Action Coalition (WAC)
Walker, Dian, 137
Wallace, George, 135–136
Wallace, Lurleen, 135–136
War, and peace activism, 41–42
Warner-Lambert Pharmaceutical Company, 33
Washington Post, 97, 117

Washington Surgi-Center, 40
WCS. *See* Women's Campaign School (WCS)
WEAL. *See* Women's Equity Action League (WEAL)
Webster v. Reproductive Health Services, 22
Welfare, and electoral politics, 117
Welfare reform, 85
Welfare rights, 55
West Virginia Women's Commission, 232
Western Union hotline, 80
WHEA. *See* Women's Health Equity Act (WHEA)
White House Project, 4, 154–155, 212–213
Why Women Matter (White House Project report), 154–155
Willis, Ellen, 201
Wilson, Woodrow, and suffrage, 30, 31
WIN. *See* Women in the Nineties (WIN)
Win With Women, 221
"Winning Women" campaign, 105
WIN-PAC. *See* Women Initiative PAC (WIN-PAC)
WIN-PAC. *See* Women's Investment Network (WIN-PAC)
WIPP. *See* Iowa Women and Public Policy Group (WIPP)
Wisconsin Women's Council, 232
Wisconsin Women's Network (WWN), 223
WISH List, 23, 83, 123, 149–150, 212
WITCH. *See* Women's International Terrorist Conspiracy from Hell (WITCH)
Witter, Jean, 34
WJCC. *See* Women's Joint Congressional Committee (WJCC)
WLF. *See* Women's Leadership Forum (WLF)
Women and Public Policy Program, 216

"Women and Technology" initiative, 54
Women Against Gun Violence, 45
Women Impacting Public Policy, 216
Women in Apprenticeship and Nontraditional Occupations Act of 1992, 204
Women in Politics Institute, 216–217
Women in the Nineties (WIN), 222
Women Initiative PAC (WIN-PAC), 222
Women of All Colors, 39
Women of Louisiana, 220
Women Strike for Peace (WSP)
  and nuclear testing, 42–43
  and Vietnam War, 42, 43–44
WOMEN VOTE! project, 149
WomenMatter, 217
Women's Action Coalition (WAC), 36, 204
Women's Action for Nuclear Disarmament, 83
Women's Bureau, Department of Labor, 53–54, 57, 102, 159, 201, 205
Women's Business Ownership Act of 1988, 205
Women's Campaign Fund, 82, 213, 220
Women's Campaign School (WCS), 213
Women's Congressional Caucus, 155–156
Women's Educational Equity Act of 1974, 15, 205
Women's eNews, 217–218
Women's Equity Action League (WEAL), 24, 57
Women's Health Equity Act (WHEA), 120, 156
Women's International League for Peace and Freedom, 39
Women's International Terrorist Conspiracy from Hell (WITCH), 56, 82
Women's Investment Network (WIN-PAC), 222

Women's Joint Congressional Committee (WJCC), 7, 53, 199
Women's Leadership Forum (WLF), 105
Women's movement, support for, 12, 13–15, 68–69
Women's organizations, and equal rights amendment, 20
Women's Peace Party, 42
Women's Policy, 157, 218
Women's Policy, Inc., 157
Women's Political Caucus of Broward County, 219
Women's rights convention of 1848, 5, 30, 89, 203
Women's rights movement
  branches of, 54–57
  origins of, 54–56
Women's Strike for Equality Day, 63
Women's studies programs, 82
Women's Voices, Women's Vote, 123–124
Women's Vote Center, 105
Woodhull, Victoria, 146
Woods, Harriet, 36
Workforce, women in the, 8–9, 16–18, 53–54. *See also* Employment discrimination
World War I, 205
World War II, 42, 50, 151
  and workforce, women in the, 8–9
WSP. *See* Women Strike for Peace (WSP)
WWN. *See* Wisconsin Women's Network (WWN)
Wyoming Council for Women's Issues, 232

Yard, Molly, 37, 64
Yaroslavsky, Zev, 80
Year of the Angry White Male, 114, 141
Year of the Woman, 36, 113, 114–115, 121, 141, 144
Year of the Woman Governor, 121, 136

About the Author

Barbara C. Burrell, Ph.D., is associate professor in the Political Science Department and associate director of the Public Opinion Laboratory at Northern Illinois University, DeKalb, Illinois. Her published works include *A Woman's Place Is in the House: Campaigning for Congress in the Feminist Era* and *Public Opinion, the First Ladyship and Hillary Rodham Clinton*.

NOT TO BE TAKEN FROM THE LIBRARY
THE COLLEGE OF NEW JERSEY LIBRARY
2000 PENNINGTON ROAD
EWING, NJ 08628